Teaching and Learning in College Introductory Religion Courses

To the faculty members and students who so generously contributed to this book; to Sharon Grace, whose friendship and love supported me in the writing; to my grandchildren Kristen, Bria, Lauren, and Liana, who I hope will grow up to take courses as rich and provocative as these; and in loving memory of my granddaughter Kameryn.

Teaching and Learning in College Introductory Religion Courses

Barbara E. Walvoord

BLACKWELL PUBLISHING
350 Main Street, Malden, MA 02148-5020, USA
9600 Garsington Road, Oxford OX4 2DQ, UK
550 Swanston Street, Carlton, Victoria 3053, Australia

First published 2008 by Blackwell Publishing Ltd

2 2008

Library of Congress Cataloging-in-Publication Data

Walvoord, Barbara E. Fassler, 1941–
Teaching and learning in college introductory religion courses / Barbara E. Walvoord.
p. cm.
Includes bibliographical references and index.
ISBN 978-1-4051-5841-1 (hardcover. : alk. paper)—ISBN 978-1-4051-5842-8 (pbk. : alk. paper) 1. Religion—Study and teaching. 2. Religious education. I. Title.

BL41.W35 2007
200.71′11821—dc22
2007010841

A catalogue record for this title is available from the British Library.

Set in 10.5 on 12.5 pt Dante
by SNP Best-set Typesetter Ltd., Hong Kong
Printed and bound in Singapore
by C.O.S. Printers Pte Ltd

The publisher's policy is to use permanent paper from mills that operate a sustainable forestry policy, and which has been manufactured from pulp processed using acid-free and elementary chlorine-free practices. Furthermore, the publisher ensures that the text paper and cover board used have met acceptable environmental accreditation standards.

For further information on
Blackwell Publishing, visit our website:
www.blackwellpublishing.com

Contents

Acknowledgments

This project was supported by grants from the Wabash Center for Teaching and Learning in Theology and Religion (www.wabashcenter.wabash.edu); by the University of Notre Dame, where I was a faculty member during the time of the study; and by the IDEA Center, an independent not-for-profit entity located at Kansas State University (www.theideacenter.org). The IDEA Center distributes and analyzes the national IDEA student and faculty survey used by institutions for evaluating teaching.

I am deeply indebted to the faculty members and students who participated in the study, taking time to generate and submit the syllabi, papers, reflections, and surveys that make the data so rich and productive. Faculty members persevered in data collection through, variously, a couple of tenure reviews, a heart attack, hurricane Katrina's destruction on a Louisiana campus, preparing a mother for a move into a nursing home, welcoming a new child into the family, taking an unexpected stint as department chair, meeting publication deadlines, and dealing with the daily demands of teaching, research, service, and life. Fifty-six of the faculty attended a two-day conference in summer of 2005, to review preliminary data analyses and give me additional rich and provocative ideas. Students were extraordinarily generous. Many of them wrote full and thoughtful responses about their classes. Those whom I interviewed were candid, sharing with me, a total stranger, their perceptions of the class and the stories of their development, both intellectual and spiritual.

Lucinda Huffaker, Director of the Wabash Center for Teaching and Learning in Theology and Religion through the inception and most of the execution of this project, helped to develop the idea of the project, facilitated its funding by the Wabash Center, organized and facilitated the August conference of faculty participants, answered numerous queries, and provided me with valuable advice at every stage. Members of her staff were generously supportive with time and responses: Tom Pearson, Paul Myhre, and Rita Arthur, as well as Advisory Committee chair William Placher and Director Emeritus Raymond Williams.

Bill Pallett of the IDEA Center, and members of the IDEA staff, not only provided the IDEA student evaluations and conducted statistical analyses of the data, but Bill was very helpful in interpreting the IDEA results. Mark Gunty, Assistant Director of Institutional Research at the University of Notre Dame provided essential assistance in designing the surveys for both faculty and students. Six faculty members reviewed an early draft of the faculty survey: Ken Cukrowski, Betty De Berg, Jonathan Lawrence, Patricia O'Connell Killen, Dianne Oliver, and Raymond Williams. Members of my University Seminar class of spring 2004, who were concurrently taking a theology class at Notre Dame, completed the draft student survey and gave me valuable feedback. Any infelicities in the survey questions remain my own. Brad Schantz, who had taught in a religiously-affiliated liberal arts college as well as serving as a graduate teaching-assistant at the University of Wisconsin during the semesters of my data analysis, helped me in the coding of student reflections. He devoted high energy and attention to learning the codes I had devised, applying them systematically to student handwritten reflections, and offering suggestions to me about the coding and the data. Several reviewers responded most helpfully to an early manuscript: Brian M. Kane, Patricia O'Connell Killen, John K. Simmons, Richard B. Steele, Sally Vance-Trembath, and James Wellman.

Many thanks also to those at Blackwell Publishing who brought the book into publication, especially Rebecca Harkin, Karen Wilson, Caroline Milton, Linda Auld, and Mervyn Thomas.

Introduction

> I hope to gain a greater understanding of the world around me as well as the spiritual world. (Student beginning "Exploring Religion" at a public university)

> Some of the goals I have for this class are to become more knowledgeable of the Bible, understand Christianity more, and become more spiritual . . . If the course challenges my beliefs I will listen to those challenges and then consider them and search myself to find my true beliefs. (Student beginning "Introduction to Sacred Scripture" at a Protestant college)

> I only have one goal and that's to pass with an A. Although I wouldn't mind learning about religious beliefs. No I do not think this course will challenge my beliefs for at this moment in time I have no beliefs. (Student beginning "Introduction to Sacred Scripture" at a Protestant college)

> I am willing to actually learn something and not be stubborn on the God subject! (Student beginning "Religions East and West" at a Catholic university)

> My goals are to keep my mind active and to keep my head level, to understand my place in this universe and the will of my God. (Student beginning "The Nature of Religion" at a public university)

These students are among the hundreds of thousands of US undergraduates each year, in public, religiously-affiliated, and private non-sectarian institutions, who take an introductory course in religious studies, theology, Biblical studies, and related disciplines (summarized in this study under the umbrella term, "theology and religion"). About 90 percent of religiously-affiliated institutions require such courses, and many public institutions offer religious studies as an option for fulfilling a general-education requirement, according to a survey by the American Academy of Religion (2000, p. 76, Table 46.01).

This book reports a study of students and their instructors in 533 introductory theology or religion courses at 109 colleges and universities – public, religiously-affiliated, and private non-sectarian, in every region of the US, and in Carnegie categories baccalaureate, masters, doctoral, and research. The study was supported by grants from the Wabash Center for Teaching and Learning in Theology and Religion (www.wabashcenter.wabash.edu). Survey data were collected from the 533 faculty and from 12,463 students – about 80 percent of those enrolled in the classes. The group includes 66 faculty whom their department chairs identified as "highly effective" in helping students reach course goals the faculty member had established, whatever those were. These 66 faculty and their students submitted not only surveys but also qualitative data about one introductory course taught between Fall 2004 and Fall 2005. These data included syllabi and other course materials, periodic written reflections by students about their learning in the course, a faculty journal for every class day, lengthy faculty written reflections at the beginning and end of the course, and a sample of student papers with teacher comments and grades. In six cases, I observed the classes and conducted face-to-face interviews with a sample of students. Partway through data collection, I met face-to-face with 56 of the Highly-Effective faculty to share emerging findings and to gather further information from them.

Research Questions

The research questions were:

- What were the goals for learning held by faculty and students?
- What learning and development took place?
- What were the most effective pedagogies?

Audiences and Purposes

This book has several aims:

- to provide ideas and strategies that teachers of introductory courses can adapt for their own teaching;
- to provide a fuller understanding of the introductory course for department chairs, administrators, and those who mentor faculty and graduate students;

- to contribute to a body of research about college students' intellectual, religious, and spiritual development and the factors that influence it; and
- to contribute to the public debate about the role of higher education in students' moral, religious, and spiritual development.

Methods

The study collected data from students and faculty in two sub-groups of classes. From the "Database" group of 467 courses at 47 institutions, survey data from both faculty and students were available in the database of the IDEA Center, a not-for-profit entity located at Kansas State University, that contracts with colleges and universities to administer the surveys, usually as part of the institution's evaluation of faculty (www.theideacenter.org). There were 10,279 students in this group – 82 percent of those enrolled. The Database sample included public institutions and institutions from across the country, as well as a few two-year institutions, but it was predominantly composed of religiously-affiliated (primarily Protestant) baccalaureate and masters institutions in the Midwest, Southeast, and Middle Atlantic.

The second subgroup was composed of 66 courses whose instructors were nominated by their department chairs as "highly-effective" in helping students meet the learning goals established by the faculty – whatever those were. These "Highly-Effective" classes were more widely representative than the Database group, in terms of Carnegie categories (research, doctoral, masters, and baccalaureate), geographic regions, and proportions of public, private non-sectarian, and religiously-affiliated institutions. The Highly-Effective group resembled national proportions along most parameters, except for being more heavily mid-western and, among religiously-affiliated institutions, somewhat more heavily Catholic than the national mix. The Highly-Effective faculty submitted not only surveys but also extensive qualitative data, from a class they taught in 2004–05. Data were submitted by 2,184 students (77 percent of those enrolled). Appendix A is a profile of the faculty; Appendix B is a profile of the students; Appendices C and D are the various surveys; Appendix E details how Highly-Effective faculty were chosen; Appendix F is a tally of the data collected for the Highly-Effective courses; and Appendix G is the prompt for student reflections in Highly-Effective courses).

I chose a theoretical framework for the study that emphasizes the co-creation of knowledge by observers and participants in the scenes under study. In this framework the "researcher" does not try to keep the study from being "tainted" by the viewpoints of the teacher or students, but encompasses those viewpoints in the knowledge that is being co-constructed by all participants on the scene. Both "insider" and "outsider" perspectives are valued; neither is viewed as the only truth. In fact, this research paradigm acknowledges that there are many "truths" that can emerge from a single scene. There are, however, rules and guidelines for making the research findings "trustworthy." Multiple data types from multiple sources – for example, interviews, questionnaires, and classroom documents from both faculty and students – serve to "triangulate" – that is, to bring to bear various perspectives and kinds of data that can amplify, affirm, disconfirm, or qualify one another. In this case, the data were both qualitative and quantitative, and both types were used within and across the stages of research to corroborate, complement, contradict, reframe, develop, and expand one another (Johnson & Onwuegbuzie 2004). For the survey data, I employed statistical analysis to determine predominant practices, compare groups to one another, and investigate correlations. Some of the qualitative data I coded, and these coding systems will be explained throughout the book as relevant. Other qualitative data I read and reread, looking for themes (Guba & Lincoln 1989; Lincoln & Guba 1985).

"Member checking" occurs in this research paradigm as the "researcher" returns to participants to try out her conclusions and to further incorporate their insights (Lincoln & Guba 1985). As part of co-creation and member-checking, I met during summer 2005 with 56 of the faculty participants to review my emerging findings and gather further information from them. Later, various participating faculty read emerging drafts of this book.

Definitions

"Theology" and "religious studies"

A long-standing debate has tried to define the disciplinary frames of "theology" and "religious studies" and to determine their appropriate venues within public and private higher education. Observers have pointed out that "theology" is traditionally conducted by "insiders," who use reason, logic, and evidence to shape the beliefs of their faith communities. "Religious studies" is conducted by "outsiders" who rely on some of the same tools – reason, logic, and evidence – and who draw on the methods of social science, humanities, and the arts to analyze and understand religious beliefs and practices as human phenomena. Different definitions have been proposed, however, and some observers have noted that boundaries between the two fields are blurring. Scholars argue with each other over these definitions, as I expect some readers are arguing right now with these definitions. An overview of the debate is presented in Cady and Brown (2002).

I examined the disciplinary frames that highly-effective faculty used. What I found is that most had been educated in various disciplinary frames along the way, and that, in teaching the introductory course, they often integrated and combined aspects that scholars would classify within different disciplinary frames. Above all, the faculty were characterized by attention to student needs and the desire to engage students beyond mere factual information. Thus they tried to define a disciplinary frame for the classroom that would allow all their students to participate. A "theological" frame had to accommodate the fact that not all students were "insiders" to a faith tradition. A "religious studies" frame had to accommodate the fact that many students did not want merely a dispassionate analysis of religious beliefs and practices; they wanted to develop their own. In the chapters that follow, I address the differences between "theology" and "religious studies" when they are important to the study. I asked students and faculty on a survey to indicate the importance of those terms, so that the data captured whatever the respondents meant by that language.

"Students' religious and spiritual development"

As I use the data to explore how the introductory courses affect students' "spiritual and religious" development, I want to consider aspects that most respondents would include under those terms and that will inform debate in higher education about the academy's role in fostering such development. Thus a broad definition suits my purposes.

A large national study of college student spirituality conducted by the Higher Education Research Institute (HERI 2005) defines "spirituality" very broadly: spirituality "points to our subjective life," is "reflected in the values and ideals that we hold most dear, our sense of who we are and where we come from, our beliefs about why we are here – the meaning and purpose we see in our lives – and our connectedness to each other and to the world around us. Spirituality also captures . . . inspiration, creativity, the mysterious, the sacred, and the mystical . . . spirituality is a universal impulse and reality." ("What is spirituality?" p. 1). More specific definitions are embedded within the surveys and interviews the HERI study employs.

I mean to include students' exploration of, and commitment to, religious communities and their belief systems; practices such as prayer, meditation, rituals, or mystical experiences that students may experience inside or outside any organized religion; students' quest for answers to the "big questions" such as "Who am I? Why am I here? What is the good life and how do I achieve it? What is truth? How can I know? What is my relationship to other people and to the natural world? What is the meaning of death? Is there a higher power? If so, what is it, and what does it mean for me?" What is often called "identity formation" must inevitably address many of these questions. The data suggest strongly that these questions are often intertwined for students. Tugging at one of the questions exposes a deep root system intermingled with other root systems. These questions cannot easily or neatly be divided up between church and school.

Teasing out from the data what students and faculty appear to mean, and with an eye toward the HERI definition, this is my definition: "students' spiritual and religious development" includes students' development of a relationship to an organized religion or to a religious belief system, their public or private practices/experiences of transcendence, and their quest for answers to the "big questions."

What the Study Found

Goals: The "great divide"

Faculty and students enter the theology and religion courses with different sets of goals – what I call the "great divide," discussed in Chapter 1. Faculty members' most frequently chosen goal is some form of what I call "critical thinking," which includes analyzing the historical, cultural, linguistic, literary, political, and social contexts of religious beliefs and practices; critically evaluating arguments and points of view; and constructing one's own arguments about theological and religious issues, relying on reason, evidence, and logic. These skills are emphasized in theology, religious studies, or biblical studies – all sub-disciplines with various underlying assumptions, but with a common emphasis on logic, reason, evidence, analysis, and argument. A fuller definition of "critical thinking" appears in Chapter 1.

Students much less frequently choose critical thinking. Their most frequent goals are to learn factual information, understand other religions and/or their own, and develop their own spiritual and religious lives. Faculty, even at religiously-affiliated institutions, choose the students' own religious and spiritual development as a course goal much less frequently than students do. The situation is complicated by the fact that faculty sometimes have goals they don't state formally but that guide their teaching – what I call "sub rosa" goals, where the faculty member says, "I don't state this formally, but I also want my students to . . ." and "let it happen" goals, where the faculty member says something like, "If this happened, it would be a plus, but my course is not directed toward this goal." Chapter 1 first presents general findings about faculty and student goals in the study's population as a whole. Then, drawing on students' hand-written, anonymous reflections written during the 66 "Highly-Effective" courses, the chapter discusses the different positions that students held as they entered the course, with special attention to those students – 63 percent of the total – who self-identified as Christians without expressing doubts or non-attendance. A significant portion of these "Secure Christian" students, as they entered, expected their current beliefs to be challenged in the course. Some welcomed the challenge as an opportunity to become more self-directing or to explore options; some expected to strengthen their faith through testing. Regardless of whether they welcomed the challenge or not, Secure Christian students envisioned a variety of strategies by which they planned to address any challenges. Some students planned to "keep the faith," no matter what the course presented: they planned to compartmentalize their beliefs separate from anything presented in the course; to rely on feelings to guide them; to turn to the Bible, prayer, family, or church; to maintain their beliefs in the face of alternative arguments; and/or to convert others. Some exhibited attitudes that are basic to critical thinking – openness to change, interest in hearing other points of view, or a desire to ask questions. Relatively few envisioned forms of "critical thinking" and these forms were often vague or undeveloped. Almost no students mentioned any readings or doctrines from the Christian tradition that could help them envision a relationship between faith and reason, between critical thinking and their own religious/spiritual beliefs and practices. The true dilemma of the "great divide," I think, lies not in students' desire to work on their own religious and spiritual development, but in their lack of a nuanced vision of how critical thinking can relate to belief and commitment.

Learning: Critical thinking, tolerance, spiritual development

What happens when students who want to work on their own spiritual and religious development meet their faculty members' demands for critical thinking? The broadest answer is that colliding worlds create energy. Students encounter the critical thinking their teachers value, religious beliefs and practices they never heard of, and concepts that disrupt their current notions. Students report change in their religious and spiritual development more often than their faculty have chosen those aspects as formal course goals. Students also report development in critical thinking, in tolerance and understanding of others' worlds, in self-direction, and in self-knowledge. Their most common response is a joyful sense of their own growth along multiple dimensions. But some also express struggle, anxiety, disappointment, surprise, anger, and disassociation. Some students develop in line with their entering goals – a reason why attention to goals is so critical – but other students have experiences they did not anticipate. Chapter 2 explores the student learning and development that occurred, traces the developmental paths that both Secure Christians and other types of students followed, and suggests how faculty may analyze their own students' learning and development.

Pedagogies: Care, clarity, conversation

What pedagogical strategies seem to be most effective in promoting the kinds of learning that faculty and students want? Chapter 3 takes up this issue. No "magic" pedagogical strategy appeared. But among the 66 faculty their department chairs identified as "highly effective," three principles of effective teaching emerged: first, highly-effective faculty members *care*. They care about students and about the subject matter, and they are able to communicate that care to their students. Second, highly-effective faculty are good at *clarity*: the ability to explain the subject in clear and interesting ways and to clarify goals and expectations. Third, highly-effective faculty are good at facilitating *conversation* – through interactive lecture, student discussion, response to student writing, office-hour conversations, coffee with students, email exchanges, and student peer interactions. Discussion was the aspect most frequently mentioned by students as helpful to their learning, and "more discussion" was their most frequent suggestion for improvement. Providing spaces and voices for conversation may be the most critical aspect of all.

Making space for students' religious and spiritual development

This study pays particular attention to the ways in which faculty members provide spaces and voices for students to address their own religious and spiritual lives. The survey data show clearly that many faculty, even at religiously-affiliated institutions, and certainly at public ones, are reluctant to state students' spiritual and religious development as a formal course goal, or in any way to give the appearance of pushing a particular religious view upon students. Yet the 66 Highly-Effective faculty in the study create spaces and voices by which students can integrate critical thinking with their own religious and spiritual growth.

Spaces

Faculty create *spaces* that:

1 are safe from:
   - teacher or classmate ridicule or denigration;
   - pressure to commit to a particular religious tradition; and
   - students' fear that it is wrong or dangerous to question religious beliefs.

2 provide a variety of settings for various kinds of interactions, both in and out of class:

- whole-class discussion;
- small-group discussion;
- student-led discussion;
- interaction with classroom visitors;
- email with professor and/or students;
- bulletin boards;
- papers and comments;
- office-hour conversations;
- informal "coffee": teacher with individual students;
- informal "coffee": teacher with groups of students; and
- interaction with people on field trips or site visits.

Voices

Faculty create *voices*:

1 articulating one's own beliefs:
  - *Committed critical thinker*: stating one's own beliefs as arguments, and defending them;
  - *Informant*: Stating one's own beliefs and practices as "informants" for ethnographic inquiry;
  - *Friend/colleague*: who reveals own beliefs/practices as self-revelation for purposes of mutual understanding, trust, respect, and friendship;
  - *Analyst*: analyzing one's own beliefs and practices using categories such as symbol, ritual, etc.;
  - Invited in some religiously-affiliated settings: *prayer, worship leader*;
  - NOT invited in any setting: preacher; bigot who assumes s/he is right and everyone else is wrong; evangelist who tries to convert students to a particular religious group.

2 suspending one's own beliefs:
  - *Listener*: hearing others' beliefs and arguments with an open mind;
  - *Ethnographer*: finding out about others' beliefs and practices in order to understand, respect, and study them;
  - *Devil's advocate*: critiquing one's own and others' arguments;
  - *Experimenter*: trying out other positions/beliefs/practices;
  - *Seeker*: asking questions;
  - *Teacher/facilitator*: facilitating dialogue;
  - NOT invited: the dutiful student who only complies with requirements; the student who withholds engagement and treats the class merely as an exercise to be completed.

Chapters 4 to 6 present case studies, arranged not to prove a thesis or push one mode of teaching, but to show how a variety of teachers instantiate these principles of caring, clarity, and conversation; to illustrate the multiple spaces and voices teachers can shape with their students; and to celebrate the energy, the creativity, and the engagement that these faculty bring to their teaching.

Systematic Observation and Reflection: The "Scholarship of Teaching and Learning"

I've said that the study revealed no "magic" pedagogical method. A wide variety of methods was employed by Highly-Effective faculty, including lecture, discussion, and small-group work. The key to finding one's own most appropriate pedagogy is systematic observation and reflection on one's own classroom, inquiring about goals, learning, and pedagogies. Such systematic observation, I think, is the answer to educational fads, and the filter for pedagogical strategies a faculty member observes in other teachers. This study was a type of disciplined observation in which 66 Highly-Effective faculty agreed to follow similar data-collection methods. Each had access to all his or her own classroom data and could use it for classroom changes. Individual faculty evaluating the effectiveness of their own pedagogies can follow a three-step process similar to the one employed by faculty in this study:

1 Clarify your goals for student learning and plan how to talk with your students about goals.
2 Examine your assignments and the student work you are getting, to identify strengths and weaknesses in student learning for the class as a whole. Also find out from students what they think they are learning, and what pedagogies appear to them to be most effective.
3 Plan/examine your pedagogical strategies, trying to discover how they are affecting the learning.

I suggest two additional resources for faculty wanting to undertake systematic observation of their own classrooms. One is Stephen Brookfield's *Becoming a Critically Reflective Teacher* (1995). Brookfield urges examination of the ideological and pedagogical assumptions behind one's teaching and offers practical strategies for classroom observation and reflection. The second is the movement called the "Scholarship of Teaching and Learning" (SoTL), which can be accessed through the website of the Carnegie Foundation for the Advancement of Teaching (www.carnegiefoundation.org), which has been active in promoting SoTL, and through the International Society for the Scholarship of Teaching and Learning (www.issotl.org). The movement seeks to help faculty members to employ in the classroom the scholarly habits of mind they bring to their research, using systematic observation to answer their questions about how teaching and learning are happening, and then sharing their findings with others, formally or informally, transcending the isolation of the individual classroom and bringing faculty into a "teaching commons" (Huber and Hutchings 2005).

The National Debate

I intend this study to be useful to faculty in any discipline whose subject matter raises the "big questions" about life and death, and to those who debate the role of higher education in students' spiritual and religious development. The longitudinal study of "The Spiritual Life of College Students" conducted by the Higher Education Research Institute (HERI) at UCLA, using surveys of 112,000 students at a national sample of 236 institutions, concludes:

> Today's college students have very high levels of spiritual interest and involvement. Many are actively engaged in a spiritual quest and in exploring the meaning and purpose of life. They are also very engaged and involved in religion, reporting considerable commitment to their religious beliefs and practices. As they begin college, freshmen have high expectations for the role their institutions will play in their emotional and spiritual development. They place great value on their college enhancing their self-understanding, helping them develop personal values, and encouraging their expression of spirituality. (HERI 2005, Executive summary, p. 1)

In a HERI pilot survey of college juniors, 62 percent reported that their professors never encouraged discussions of spirituality or religion, and 56 percent said their professors had never provided opportunities to discuss the meaning of life (www.spirituality.ucla.edu/reports/spirit_professoriate.pdf. See also Rainey 2006).

These revelations have energized the long-standing American debate about the role of the academy in students' search for answers to the "big questions" and their desire to explore spiritual and religious beliefs and practices. National moods are shifting, with potential consequences for the debate and for the academy. Public policy researcher Daniel Yankelovich (2005, p. B8) cites "public support for other ways of knowing" as a powerful force on higher education for the future. He observes, "While higher education has grown more scientific in its quest for knowledge, the American people at large have grown more religious, more fretful about moral 'truths,' and more polarized in their struggle to find political and existential truth." He notes that public demand to teach "intelligent design" in schools is only one manifestation of this widening conflict, and he predicts that "Unless it takes a less cocksure and more open-minded approach to the issue of multiple ways of knowing, higher education could easily become more embattled, more isolated, and more politicized" (p. B9). Higher education may want to stand by some principles that will be unpopular, so embattlement, isolation, and politicization may in part be inevitable. But the most thoughtful minds seek new ground for the discussion – ground that will protect the separation of church and state so foundational to the nation's life, and yet allow colleges to nurture in appropriate ways the full potential of their students, and to provide the nation with citizens who have deeply considered the meaning of life and death, the nature of religion, and the varieties of religious practice. One such conversation, for example, launched by W. Robert Connor as director of the Teagle Foundation, has brought together faculty members, chaplains, administrators, students, and researchers to explore whether "both religious and secular approaches [might] offer colleges a chance to help students systematically discuss the issues that seem to be on their minds and, at the same time, reinvigorate the liberal arts" (Connor 2006, p. B8).

The Highly-Effective faculty in this study have developed spaces and voices by which students can nurture their own religious and spiritual development, and can address the "big questions" of their lives, integrating the critical thinking strategies they have learned. I think faculty at all types of institutions can nurture this development without pushing any particular religious viewpoint or violating the separation of church and state. Courses that help students integrate critical thinking with their own religious and spiritual lives can make an enormous difference to students. I close with the words of two students writing anonymously at the end of their introductory theology or religion course:

> There's a big world out there. This class has opened my mind to new ideas and thoughts. (Student completing "Exploring Religion" at a public masters university)

> I have grown so much in this course! I knew I was capable of thinking critically about religion as I have about my own Christianity. (Student completing "Introduction to World Religions" at a Protestant baccalaureate college)

1

Faculty and Student Goals for Learning: The Great Divide

This chapter answers the first research question: what were faculty and student goals for learning? The chapter reveals some of the hopes and expectations students bring to their introductory theology or religion class, whether they expect the class to challenge their beliefs, and how they plan to address the challenges. It contains ideas that faculty may use for shaping their own course goals and addressing their students' goals.

The data reveal what I call the "Great Divide" in goals that faculty and students marked as "essential" or "important." Faculty, including those who taught a variety of course titles at public, private non-sectarian, and religiously-affiliated institutions, more frequently marked what I have broadly called "critical thinking" than their students did, and students more frequently marked development of their own beliefs and values than faculty did.

This chapter begins by presenting the survey data that highlight the "Great Divide." Next, the chapter presents more detail about students' goals. A section focuses on self-identified Christian students who express no doubts about their faith – 63 percent of the total students in the Highly-Effective classes. About 40 percent of these "Secure Christians" expected the course to challenge their beliefs. Some welcomed the challenge for two quite different reasons: some believed it would help them achieve self-reliance and explore alternatives, rather than blindly accepting what church or family had taught; others looked forward to strengthening their faith through testing. Whether they welcomed the challenge or not, Christian students planned to meet the challenge in a wide variety of ways, including disassociating the course from their beliefs altogether, "keeping the faith" no matter what the course presented, remaining open to new ideas, and, for a few, some form of critical thinking. Yet virtually no students, as they entered the course, mentioned doctrines, authors, or detailed concepts that might guide them in envisioning how critical thinking could help to shape their religious and spiritual beliefs and practices.

Next, the chapter offers more details about faculty goals, including what faculty mean by "critical thinking" in introductory theology and religious courses. The chapter also explores the goals that faculty sometimes voice in their journals but do not list formally on the syllabus. I call these "sub rosa" and "let it happen" goals.

I don't suggest what goals faculty *should* have; rather, I urge that faculty be thoughtful about their goals, articulate them clearly for students, find out about student goals, and conduct a robust conversation in the classroom about goals. The end of the chapter offers case studies and suggestions about how that conversation might be conducted.

The Literature on "Young Adult" Development

The literature on "young adult" development can be helpful in understanding the findings of this chapter and others, so I briefly outline it here, before turning to the data. Though the classes in the study contained some older students, 89 percent of the Highly-Effective classes contained less than 10 percent of students who were 26 or older (Appendix B). The "Database" classes, which were primarily religiously-affiliated baccalaureate and masters institutions, do not offer information on student ages, but they, too, probably contained preponderantly students under 26.

The literature variously outlines stages of development, or orders of consciousness, tied more or less securely to age, though uneven or recursive patterns of growth may cause a person simultaneously to exhibit traits of different positions. Those who have outlined these growth patterns often admit that the concept of "stages" is problematic. Rather than outline the full progression through life stages that various theorists propose, I want here to pluck from the literature some common "movements" that a faculty member may expect to find in a given class. One such movement is from "dualism" in which the world is seen in black and white, toward "relativism," in which one recognizes multiple truth claims but has no way of deciding among them, and then toward a tentative commitment that recognizes relativism but makes choices, though such choices in young adults may be hesitant or short-lived – not yet the firm "commitment in relativity" of later adulthood (Parks 2000; Perry 1998). A second, related move is from "Silence," in which one has no voice or cannot be heard toward "Received Knowing" in which one relies on external sources for truth; then toward "Subjective Knowing" in which the self asserts its opinions but resists reference to external sources or tools; then toward "Procedural Knowing," which includes mastery of academic tools that are part of analysis and critical thinking and are manipulated without the investment of the self; and finally toward "Constructed Knowing," a later adult position where the self and the tools are integrated (Belenky, Clinchy, Goldberger, and Tarule 1986). A third move is from a consciousness that can only subjectively experience the self and its needs, toward the ability to act responsibly for the welfare of others (Kegan 1994).

To those unfamiliar with the literature, I would suggest beginning with Parks, who summarizes and references her predecessors such as Perry and Fowler. Parks was the one author most cited by highly-effective teachers in the study when I asked them what they thought was the most important work on young adult development. One faculty member in the study wrote that he prefers Kegan, whose formulations are "more complex, less hierarchical, or evolutionary." Belenky and her colleagues were not often mentioned by study participants but their concepts of "voice" and of the ways in which the self can be held separate from academic work or integrated with it have been very helpful to me in illuminating how students find "voice" in the introductory classroom and how teachers create structures in which those voices can develop.

With this literature as background, the chapter first uses the survey data to outline the dimensions of the "Great Divide," and then uses the qualitative data to analyze in greater depth students' positions as they entered the course, where they wanted to go, and how they expected to meet possible "challenges" to their beliefs. Next, qualitative data further explicate what faculty wanted, especially what I include under the term "critical thinking." Finally, the chapter presents case studies and suggestions about how faculty can articulate their goals, find out about students' goals, and engage their students in productive discussion about goals.

Survey Data Reveal the "Great Divide"

Figure 1.1 shows the differences and similarities in faculty and student goals, using data from the discipline-specific surveys completed by students and faculty

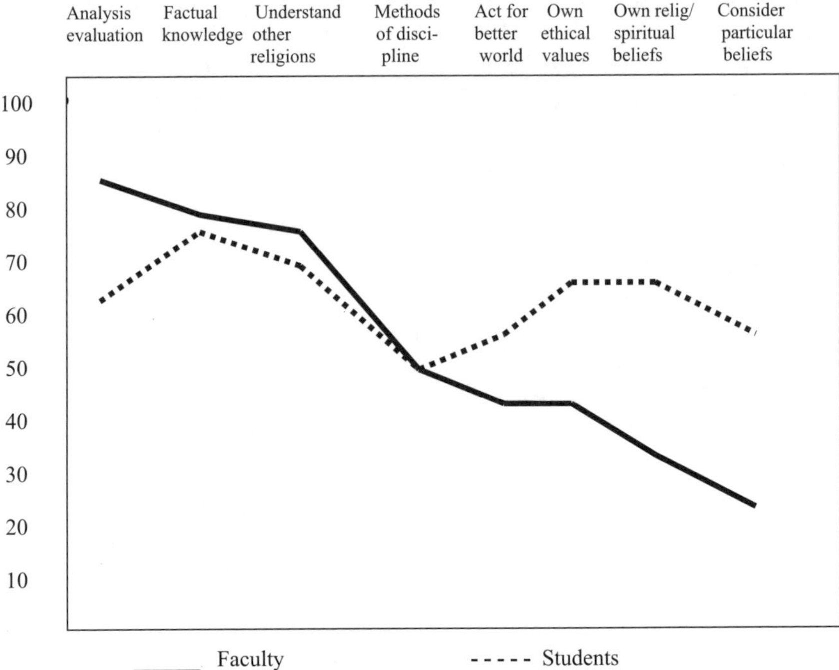

Figure 1.1 Goals marked "essential" or "important" by Highly-Effective faculty and students

in the 66 Highly-Effective classes (Appendix D). The study administered multiple surveys to faculty and students, with slightly different items and slightly different terminology for the scales, though all scales had "essential" as their first item and either "important" or "very important" as their second. A more detailed representation of faculty and student goals in the Highly-Effective classes is provided in table 1.1, which shows data from the Highly-Effective classes on two different surveys, each with somewhat different goal statements: first, the 8 discipline-specific goals I composed from a reading of the pedagogical literature in theology and religion (Appendix D), which are used for figure 1.1; and second, the 12 IDEA goals, which are used in the national IDEA system for classes across disciplines (Appendix C), and which were completed by most of the Highly-Effective faculty but not by students.

The student data show the students' goals near the end of the course, *after* they had experienced the course and had a chance to learn the faculty member's goals, but the question specifically asked them to reflect the importance of the goals *"for yourself."*

Table 1.1 Goals marked "essential" or "important" by Highly-Effective faculty and students

Goals: Survey items from disciplinary list (D) or IDEA list (I)	REL Fac (%)	REL Stud (%)	PUB/ PNS Fac (%)	PUB/ PNS Stud (%)	ALL Fac (%)	ALL Stud (%)
Critical thinking						
Develop general intellectual skills such as analyzing, evaluating, and synthesizing (D)	84	65	92	59	86	64
Learning to *analyze* and *critically evaluate* ideas, arguments, and points of view (I)	94		100		96	
Application to decisions						
Learning to *apply* course material (to improve thinking, problem solving, and decisions) (I)	76		79		77	
Factual knowledge						
Acquire a body of knowledge (e.g., about the world's religions, about the Bible) (D)	84	75	67	78	79	76
Gaining factual knowledge (terminology, classifications, methods, trends) (I)	88		71		83	
Fundamental principles						
Learning fundamental principles, generalizations, or theories (I)	91		79		88	
Understand other religions						
Understand and appreciate a variety of religious beliefs and practices (D)	71	68	92	77	77	71
Methods of discipline						
Learn the methods of the discipline (D)	55	53	42	49	51	52
Developing skills, competencies, and points of view needed by professionals in the field most closely related to this course (I)	26		21		25	
Action for better world						
Take action for a better world (D)	52	62	25	44	44	57
Values						
Develop students' moral and ethical values (D)	52	73	25	54	44	68

Table 1.1 *Continued*

Goals: Survey items from disciplinary list (D) or IDEA list (I)	REL Fac (%)	REL Stud (%)	PUB/PNS Fac (%)	PUB/PNS Stud (%)	ALL Fac (%)	ALL Stud (%)
Developing a clearer understanding of, and commitment to, personal values (I)	68		36		60	
Religious and spiritual						
Develop students' own religious beliefs and/or spiritual practices (D)	42	70	8	51	33	65
Consider or strengthen students' commitment to a particular set of beliefs (e.g., Roman Catholic, Buddhist, Calvinist, evangelical) (D)	29	63	17	43	26	57
Asking own questions						
Acquiring an interest in learning more by asking my own questions and seeking answers (I)	68		79		75	
Finding resources						
Learning how to find and use resources for answering questions or solving problems (I)	53		43		50	
Oral and written expression						
Developing skill in expressing myself orally or in writing (I)	76		79		77	

For 8 discipline-specific goals (identified on the table as "D")
N = 43 faculty, 1,294 students (77% of those enrolled) from Highly-Effective group
REL = Religiously-affiliated institutions (n = 31: 16 Protestant, of whom 5 were masters and 11 baccalaureate; 15 Catholic, of whom 1 was research, 2 doctoral, 9 masters, and 3 baccalaureate (Carnegie classifications)
PUB/PNS = Private non-sectarian college (n = 1) and public universities (n = 11: 3 research, 3 doctoral, 5 masters)
For 12 IDEA goals (identified on the table as "I")
N = 48 faculty from Highly-Effective group
REL = Religiously-affiliated institutions (n = 34: 17 Protestant, of whom 5 were masters and 12 were baccalaureate; 17 Catholic, of whom 2 were research, 2 doctoral, 10 masters, and 3 baccalaureate (Carnegie classifications)
PUB/PNS = Private non-sectarian colleges (n = 3 baccalaureate) and public universities (n = 11: 3 research, 3 doctoral, 5 masters)
Fac = Percent of the total faculty marking the goal "essential" or "important" (for IDEA) or "essential" or "very important" (for 8 discipline-specific goals)
Stud = Average of the average percentages of all classes, for students marking the goal "essential" or "very important"

A definition of "critical thinking"

I use the term "critical thinking" to refer to a particular type of intellectual activity involving analysis and argument using reason, logic, and evidence. Some faculty in the study used the actual term; others did not. A common academic understanding of critical thinking was articulated by 46 experts from fields of philosophy and education, in a consensus-shaping "Delphi" process conducted by the American Philosophical Association:

> We understand critical thinking to be a purposeful, self-regulatory judgment which results in interpretation, analysis, evaluation, and inference, as well as explanation of the evidential, conceptual, methodological, criteriological, or contextual considerations upon which that judgment is based. CT is essential as a tool of inquiry. As such, CT is a liberating force in education and a powerful resource in one's personal and civic life. While not synonymous with good thinking, CT is a pervasive and self-rectifying human phenomenon. The ideal critical thinker is habitually inquisitive, well-informed, trustful of reason, open-minded, flexible, fair-minded in evaluation, honest in facing personal biases, prudent in making judgments, willing to reconsider, clear about issues, orderly in complex matters, diligent in seeking relevant information, reasonable in the selection of criteria, focused in inquiry, and persistent in seeking results which are as precise as the subject and the circumstances of inquiry permit. Thus, educating good critical thinkers means working toward this ideal. It combines developing CT skills with nurturing those dispositions which consistently yield useful insights and which are the basis of a rational and democratic society. (Facione 1990, p. 2)

Also helpful is a critical thinking rubric developed by Facione and Facione (1994), which describes high-scoring student work:

- Accurately interprets evidence, statements, graphics, questions, etc.
- Identifies the salient arguments (reasons and claims) pro and con.
- Thoughtfully analyzes and evaluates major alternative points of view.
- Draws warranted, judicious, non-fallacious conclusions.
- Justifies key results and procedures, explains assumptions and reasons.
- Fair-mindedly follows where evidence and reasons lead.

In line with this work, I employ the umbrella term "critical thinking" to the survey items listed under "critical thinking" in table 1.1. Also relevant is the IDEA item on "learning to *apply* course material to thinking, problem-solving, and decisions." The discussion of faculty goals later in this chapter further illuminates the discipline-specific applications of critical thinking that appear among theology and religion faculty in the study.

Differences by institution, discipline, or course title

Undoubtedly, differences in goals can be found within different institutional types, course titles, disciplinary frameworks (theology or religious studies) and other factors. The sample of Highly-Effective classes that ranked the goals is quite small for generalizing about sub-groups, but because it seemed important to get some idea of what differences might exist, table 1.1 also compares religiously-affiliated institutions with the public/private non-sectarian institutions. However, my point in this study is not to compare all the permutations – how goals in religious studies classes differ from theology classes, or Bible classes from world religions classes, or religiously-conservative schools from religiously-liberal. The sample size and the disparity of goals even within those subgroups prohibit such an undertaking. Rather, my purpose here is to highlight the presence of the "Great Divide," which appears in all the classes as a group; to point to some differences between public and religiously-affiliated institutions; and above all to urge that faculty members be clear about their own goals and those of their students and conduct a robust dialogue in their classrooms about goals for learning.

Summary of findings from the survey data

These are the important findings from the survey data represented in figure 1.1 and table 1.1:

- *Faculty members' most frequent goal was critical thinking*: 96 percent of faculty rated the "Learning to *analyze* and *critically evaluate* ideas, arguments, and points of view" item from the IDEA survey as "essential" or "important" (the other choice was "not important"). Of the faculty, 86 percent rated the "Developing general intellectual skills such as analyzing, evaluating, and synthesizing" item from the discipline-specific survey as "essential" or "very important" (other choices were "somewhat important" and "not important").
- *Students less frequently chose critical thinking*: "General intellectual skills such as analyzing, evaluation, and synthesizing" is the "critical thinking" item to which both faculty and students responded. Though 86 percent of faculty chose this goal as essential or very important, only 64 percent of their students did so. Students chose critical thinking less frequently than they chose

"acquire a body of knowledge: e.g., about the world's religions, about the Bible" (76 percent), "understand a variety of religious beliefs and practices" (71 percent), and "developing your own moral and ethical values" (68 percent), and about the same as "developing your own religious beliefs and/or spiritual practices" (65 percent). A marked disparity between faculty and students' choice of "general intellectual skills such as analyzing, evaluating, and synthesizing" occurred in both religiously-affiliated and public/private non-sectarian institutions, though the disparity was slightly less pronounced in religiously-affiliated ones.

- *Students' most frequent goals were factual knowledge and understanding various religions/viewpoints*: "Acquire a body of knowledge" (76 percent) and "understand/appreciate a variety of religious beliefs and practices" (71 percent) were the goals students most frequently chose as "essential" or "very important."
- *Faculty agreed that factual knowledge and understanding various religions/viewpoints are important*: Faculty chose "acquire a body of knowledge" and "understand/appreciate a variety of religious beliefs and practices" at about the same percentages as their students. Given the disparity of other goals, however, it is likely that students and faculty had different ideas about the role of facts – whether to support knowledge of other religions or to support critical thinking.
- *Students chose values and spiritual/religious development much more frequently than faculty*: Even in *public and private non-sectarian* institutions, more than half the students ranked their own values (54 percent) and religious/spiritual development (51 percent) as "essential" or "very important" course goals. In *religiously-affiliated institutions*, that number rises to almost three-fourths: 73 percent chose values and 70 percent chose religious/spiritual development. Faculty in both types of institution were much less likely than their students to choose those items as learning goals.
- *One-third or more (32–42 percent) of faculty in religiously-affiliated institutions did* not *choose "values" or "spiritual/religious development" as a course goal*: The "personal values" item on IDEA is the only one that even remotely addresses the spiritual/religious issues, yet nearly one-third (32 percent) of the faculty in religiously-affiliated introductory theology/religion courses did *not* choose it as an essential or important course goal. On the list of 8 discipline-specific faculty goals, which adds the words "moral and ethical" to the "values" item, and includes two additional items specifically on religious/spiritual development, nearly half (48 percent) of the faculty at religiously-affiliated institutions did *not* choose "moral and ethical values" as essential or very important. In a separate calculation not shown on the table, 42 percent of the faculty at religiously-affiliated institutions did *not* choose *any* of the three items on

values and religious development that were on the list of eight discipline-specific goals (Appendix D).

- *Two-thirds to three-fourths of faculty in public and private non-sectarian institutions did NOT choose values as a course goal*: On the multi-disciplinary IDEA survey, where "personal values" was the only item addressing values / religious / spiritual development, nearly two-thirds (63 percent) of the faculty at public or private non-sectarian institutions did *not* choose "personal values" as "essential" or "important." On the list of eight discipline-specific faculty goals, which added "moral and ethical" to the "values" item and included two additional items specifically on religious / spiritual development, 75 percent of the public / private non-sectarian faculty did *not* choose the "values" item and 83–92 percent did *not* choose the two items on religious / spiritual development, as "essential" or "very important."
- *Faculty distinguished more sharply among different items on values / religion*: Faculty tended to make a sharper distinction than students did among the three items concerning values and religious / spiritual development. For faculty, students' development of *moral and ethical values* is significantly more often marked as essential or very important than consideration of a *particular set of beliefs* (44 percent to 26 percent). For students, that disparity is much smaller (68 percent to 57 percent).
- *Faculty valued oral / written expression*: More than three-fourths of the faculty (77 percent) chose this goal as essential or important on the IDEA survey. Though the qualitative data show that few students mention these goals, we do not have student survey data on this item.
- *Student goals were dispersed across a narrower range*: On the eight discipline-specific goals, where we have both faculty and student responses, the lowest goal for faculty has 25 percent of faculty rating it "essential" or "very important," and the highest goal has 86 percent. Student choices range from 52 percent to 76 percent. In other words, faculty as a group tend to express stronger preferences; student responses are spread more evenly across the range of possible goals, perhaps indicating their attempts to integrate various goals, their ambiguity about goals, the disparities among individual students about goals, their compliance to good-sounding goals that appear on a survey administered by their faculty member as part of a research project, or their sense that multiple goals are important. The qualitative data show a group of students (in the minority, but not miniscule) who determinedly do *not* want the course to address their religious and spiritual development, as well as students who strongly do – a dichotomy that may help create the smaller spread in student responses. Further, the qualitative data suggest a strong current of ambiguity among the students.

Students' Goals

What students meant by their goals becomes more clear upon examination of student reflections, written anonymously in the Highly-Effective classes. Students in the first two terms of data collection wrote *during* the course about their goals. In the third term, students wrote more extensively, to a fuller prompt, on the *very first day* of the course before they had seen the syllabus (Appendix G). This analysis relies on both types of writings. When the difference matters, it is indicated. Quotations from students or faculty throughout this volume indicate the Affiliation (public, private non-sectarian, Catholic, or Protestant) according to the AAR Census (2000), and the Carnegie classification (Research, Doctoral, Masters, Baccalaureate. I have used the old classifications. For more information on these classifications, including changes being implemented as this book went to press, see www.Carnegiefoundation.org).

Students' most prominent goal: Multi-dimensional growth

The most prominent finding from the data is that the great majority of students want to "learn," to "grow," to "expand horizons" – words they frequently used. Students writing on the first day of class often expressed multiple goals, both intellectual and spiritual:

> While taking this course I would like to challenge and be challenged spiritually and mentally. I believe it will help me to broaden my horizons, not only in the knowledge I obtain, but spiritually as well. (Protestant Masters, "Introduction to Sacred Scriptures")

> I am interested in learning not only about religious diversity but also about the underlying themes, origin of ritual and the force that is obviously compelling humans to seek out religion. Hopefully I will also gain a deeper understanding of my own faith and where I stand in the religious world. (Public Masters, "Exploring Religion")

> I am hoping for this course to help interpret the rather deeper meanings to the Bible and Christian life. I'm hoping this course can also help encourage me to become an even more Godly profound woman. I'm also expecting this course to introduce some of the other diverse religions worldwide. I'm looking forward to progress and growth as a student and a firm believer with this course. (Public Research, "Modern Christianities and World Cultures")

> The goal I have for this class is that it would deepen my understanding of Scripture. I hope that by studying the Bible in an academic context, it would improve my spiritual life as well. This course will do this by establishing more analytical habits in my daily life, so that instead of just reading the Bible, I begin studying it and deciphering its meaning and application to my life. The only way I expect to be challenged is in growth. (Protestant Masters, "Christian Scriptures")

> As a Christian, it is time to learn more about the roots and heritage of religion. A class like this is certain to religiously educate a sheltered Southern Methodist as myself. (Catholic Masters, "Introduction to Biblical Studies")

> My boyfriend told me that before I start getting stressed out about meeting all requirements and getting into all psychology classes to remember what college is all about. I realize that there are so many amazing classes that have nothing to do with my psychology major but that would be interesting to take.
>
> I am Christian. I believe in a God, and in His son Jesus. I also believe in the Holy Spirit. It's amazing though, coming to [this university] has really opened my eyes. As convinced as *I* am about there being a God, and there being a heaven and hell, other people are just as convinced as there *not* being a God or an afterlife.
>
> What intrigues me the most is how many different beliefs are out there. I would love to explore them through this class! (Public Research, "Modern Christianities and World Cultures")

This impulse for multi-dimensional growth is an important aspect of the "Great Divide." It provides a basis for the course to help students integrate both the intellectual and the spiritual, both students' own goals and the goals their professors hold for them. The multi-dimensionality also reflects movement typical of young adults – their move away from reliance on family and church, their need to explore various alternatives and broaden their horizons, and their eagerness to establish their own intellectual and spiritual directions.

One group of students for whom theology/religion classes may be especially complex is what I term "Secure Christians" who express no doubts in their faith. The next section of the chapter explores their goals.

Types of students

In the Highly-Effective group, 736 students from 25 institutions responded on the first day of their Highly-Effective classes, before they had seen the syllabus, to a prompt that asked them about their current religious/spiritual beliefs, their goals, whether they expected the course to challenge their beliefs, and how they planned to meet the challenge (Appendix G). Sixty-three percent of those students identified themselves as Christian (or Catholic, Methodist, etc.) without expressing doubts, disagreements, or non-attendance in their Christianity. I call them "Secure Christians," realizing that the term is problematic, and that these students might have had doubts about their faith which they did not express.

Another 18 percent of students self-described as Christian but expressed doubts, disagreements, or non-attendance: e.g. I am Christian, or I was raised Christian, or my family is Christian, *but* I have begun to question my faith; I don't accept all the beliefs of my church; I haven't been to church in a year. I term these "Doubting Christians." (The "Doubting Christian" category does *not* include students who explicitly named another position, e.g., I was raised a Christian but now I'm agnostic or now I have no beliefs.) Nineteen percent self-identified as atheist, agnostic, "no belief," or adherents of other religions.

This proportion of about 80 percent Christians – both secure and doubting – held basically true for both religiously-affiliated and public institutions. Though terms are somewhat different, this 80 percent is also roughly comparable to the number of students expressing some Christian denomination as a "preference" in the Higher Education Research Institute's "Spirituality in Higher Education" study, which surveyed 112,232 entering first-year students attending 236 diverse colleges and universities (HERI 2005, table 7).

The 18 percent doubters in the present study compares roughly to the 25 percent of first-year students in the HERI spirituality study who categorized themselves as "doubting" (10 percent) or "conflicted" (15 percent) (HERI 2005, figure 1).

In other words, one could cautiously say that the proportion of students in the Highly-Effective classes is not radically different from the proportions one would likely find across the nation, though any individual class or school might present a different balance. One implication for teachers is that a class in some public institutions may contain as many Christian students as a class in a religiously-affiliated institution.

Secure Christians expecting challenge to their beliefs

The prompt for the first day asked students whether they thought the course would "challenge your beliefs." Students seemed to interpret this to mean that the course would present ideas that called their beliefs into question, and/or that they, themselves, would be vulnerable to having their beliefs changed.

A little over 40 percent of the "secure Christian" students in both public and religiously-affiliated institutions said yes, they expected a challenge. They expressed a variety of attitudes and strategies to deal with the challenge. This next section focuses on the 40 percent of Secure Christians who expected a challenge.

Welcoming a challenge

Some Secure Christians welcome a challenge. They give two reasons: some stress they want to establish independence from the authority of church or parents and to explore new options – a common move for "young adults" as they seek autonomy, the literature suggests.

> I have been attending church since I was born. Because of that, religion is in my house, instilled in my personality, and a *routine*. As you get to a certain point in your life you have to do something called making your faith your own. That's where this class fits in. To know why you believe what you do and why that is the "right" thing to believe, you must first know what other faiths put their beliefs in. I hope by gaining insight into other religions I can see both sides of an argument so I can have the choice of which side is right for me. (Public Masters, "Exploring Religion")

Though these students are moving away from authority-bound positions, they still reflect "dualistic" notions that there is a "right side" to an argument. That same assumption is reflected in students who believe they will become stronger in the faith through meeting challenges. They reflect a notion that an academic course can "test" one's faith and make it stronger, either because one resists the temptation to change, and/or because one uses knowledge to build a stronger basis for one's faith and to eliminate doubt. These statements lack a realization that theorists connect to later-life development – accepting that one must make choices in the face of multiple defensible truth claims and in the face of doubt.

> I really hope that this does challenge my beliefs, because faith needs to be tested. (Protestant Baccalaureate, "Introduction to the Bible")

> I do expect this course to challenge my beliefs since I am limited in my knowledge. But I plan to deal with these obstacles without fear and overcome them. I believe doubts in one's beliefs can be good because it allows one to study and research in order for the doubt to be eliminated,

> thus making the individual [word omitted: stronger?] in his/her beliefs. (Public Research, "Modern Christianities and World Cultures")

Wanting challenge yet guidance

Though students often express a desire to come independently to their own ideas and beliefs, they also express the desire for community, connection, and mentoring – aspects that Parks (2000) highlights as typical of young adult development.

> I want the chance to explore, to be challenged with what I know to be true. I don't want someone just to give me a book and say, "here, read this and interpret it for yourself." I also don't want someone to give me a book and say, "read this and it means . . ." I want a middle between the two, I want to interpret for myself but be able to ask questions and hear what others have to say. (Protestant Masters, "Christian Scriptures")

Many Secure Christians, then, say they welcome challenge, but for somewhat different reasons – seeking independence and choice, or believing that testing can strengthen their faith. Either position may still carry "dualistic" elements. Students may seek both challenge and guidance. The ambiguity of their positions is typical of "young adult" development.

Secure Christians' strategies for meeting challenges

Whether they welcome challenge or only expect it to happen, Secure Christians exhibit a number of strategies by which they plan to meet the challenges. The first strategies discussed below are primarily intended to ward off change and help the student "keep the faith." Next are strategies that leave open the possibility of change and even begin to envision the use of "critical thinking" in relationship to faith.

Secure Christians' strategies: Keep the faith

The first group of Secure Christian students' strategies focuses on helping students resist change by compartmentalizing the course or the intellect from any relationship to belief; by relying on authorities such as God, the Bible and family; by relying on strength of feeling; by using evidence to back up feelings; by heroic affirmation of one's faith against all challenges; and by engaging in dialogue but sticking to one's own beliefs and/or trying to convert others. The voice here is that of the Believer, sometimes cast almost as Ulysses and the Sirens, facing a world tempting but dangerous:

- *Compartmentalize*: I expect this course to be a basic study of the different types of religion throughout the world. I plan to learn what is needed to get a good grade. I am a Baptist and grew up in a land where the Baptist ways were taught. I do believe that if I do as God has planned for me and obey his words then Heaven is where I will go after death here on earth. I am sure this course will challenge my beliefs because not all religions believe the way the Baptists do. I will plan to learn the way the teacher wants to put on paper, although nothing will ever change my beliefs of God. (Public Masters, "The Nature of Religion")
- *Rely on feelings*: I do not expect this course to challenge my beliefs, but to only strengthen them. I base my personal beliefs on faith and how it feels in my heart, not by what I can prove with evidence. (Protestant Masters, "Christian Scriptures")
- *Rely on Bible, prayer*: My current spiritual beliefs: I am part of a non-denominational Christian Church, we have Bible study every Wednesday night and meet together Sunday mornings. I believe in living for God each day and strive to be more Christ like each day. God is very important to me. I think this course will help me to understand other religions better, what they believe, and why they believe those things, so I can look to the Bible and understand better and relate to other people. I think the course may challenge my beliefs, help me to think in a deeper way, see things in a different light. The way I would deal with that is to look to the Bible and see if it is Biblical and to definitely pray about it. (Public Masters, "Religions of the World")
- *Rely on family, church*: I do not think this course will challenge my beliefs, but if it does I plan to talk with my family or church about any questions I will have. (Catholic Masters, "Theology 200: Ultimate Questions")

Some students plan simply to stick with their own beliefs and keep the faith, despite anything that might appear in the teaching or dialogue of the course:

- *Stick with my beliefs*: I think my beliefs might be challenged, and I hope to stick with my beliefs. They were instilled in me as a child, so I hope they'll hold up as an adult. (Public Masters, "Religions of the World")
- *Keep the faith*: I think that every religion course will challenge your beliefs not challenge but pressure your beliefs. I plan to keep the faith that's how I'm going to deal with it. (Protestant Baccalaureate, "Introduction to World Religions: The West [Judaism and Islam]")

The words "open mind" are very common in students' reflections, but may mean different things, including listening to others but holding fast to their own beliefs anyway: "I do expect to have this course challenge my beliefs and to deal with this I plan on being open minded, but stick up and follow what I believe in" (Protestant Masters, "Introduction to Sacred Scriptures").

Several students intend a one-sided dialogue in which they try to "convert" others:

> In this course I want to learn the differences in all the cultures and compare the differences to mine. I want to be able to learn the differences in Christianity. I am a Christian and my goal here on this Earth is to serve God and make disciples of all nations. I think there will be some challenges because other beliefs will be introduced to me. Although I won't change my religion, I will have to learn how to argue that Christianity is true and that Jesus Christ died for us on the cross. Later in the future I would like to debate with my non-Christian friends to hopefully convert them to Christianity. (Public Research, "Modern Christianities and World Cultures")

Secure Christians' strategies: Limited kinds of "critical thinking"

So far, the various strategies Secure Christians use for meeting challenges to their beliefs have focused on protecting the student's beliefs from change. The next group of strategies I broadly collect under the umbrella term "critical thinking." In their anonymous in-class writings (as opposed to survey answers), only 8 percent of the students spontaneously mention any form of "critical thinking" in any context. Almost no students display a well-articulated, detailed concept of how analysis, argument, evidence, and logic might *shape* their faith or how critical thinking would interact with prayer, reading the Bible, listening to authority figures, or other ways of knowing. This section explores the limited ways in which students do express the intention to use "critical thinking."

First, some students exhibit one or more of four attitudes that form a basis for critical thinking: 1) being open to change; 2) wanting to understand the opposing view; 3) wanting to "study it for myself;" and 4) wanting to ask questions. These categories emerge from the data, but are consistent with the dispositions associated with "critical thinking" (Facione 1990).

Attitudes: A basis for critical thinking

- *Open to change*: My religion is Lutheran. I am very active in my church and I am greatly influenced by it. I rely on God very much and consider it to be

an important part of my life. I hope that in this course, it will challenge my current beliefs and open my mind to other ideas and beliefs. I don't want to be afraid of the challenges. I want to see them as ways I can grow in my religion and beliefs. (Public Masters, "Exploring Religion")
- *Understand others*: I hope to be able to train my eyes and ears to be sensitive to my surroundings. To be able to put myself into the viewpoints of others and to try to see life from their point of view. To be able to understand the forces that influence their history, culture, and also economic and political aspects of life. (Public Masters, "The Nature of Religion")
- *Study for myself*: I expect this course to confirm my beliefs [Christian] and teach me new things that I have not yet discovered for myself in the Bible. If something comes up that challenges my beliefs, I will study it for myself and decide if things will change. (Protestant Masters, "Christian Scriptures")
- *Ask questions*: My own religion of Catholicism has always intrigued me. I have always asked many questions about the faith and how things began and why. Through this class I hope to discover some of the origins behind different religions and in doing so find some answers to my questions. (Public Masters, "Exploring Religion")

Vague references to "thinking academically"

In addition to these four foundational attitudes – openness to change, understanding others' viewpoints, thinking for oneself, and asking questions – some students envision how critical thinking strategies might change, confirm, or nourish their own religious and spiritual lives. Within the 8 percent of students who mention critical thinking processes in some way, many only hint broadly at academic processes such as "think it through," "take an educated view," "think academically about God," or they may refer to "knowledge," "analysis," "evidence," "reason," and "logic," without explaining how these intellectual activities will work.

> I am a Christian and understand how Christians view God but would like to understand how others do. I have never really academically thought about God and thus it will be very interesting to experience a different angle of God. (Private Non-Sectarian Baccalaureate, "The Experience of God")

> I am unsure in what ways this course will challenge me, but I do expect it to. When it does I will need to stay calm and work through with reason and logic as best as I can. (Protestant Masters, "Christian Scriptures")

Limited uses of critical thinking

Beyond vague references, some students express more specific ways in which critical thinking might relate to their religious beliefs or help to form them. These include providing a concrete basis for belief, using evidence to back up feelings, separating fact from fiction, and using new information to expand on old. All these strategies are limited or naïve in some ways. The following student looks for a "concrete basis," again reflecting the hope expressed by an earlier student that doubt can be eliminated and faith can be cemented in place: "I would hope this course does challenge my beliefs and that I will be able to work through those challenges. When the course is finished I think I will have a more concrete background of my belief than before" (Protestant Masters, "Introduction to Sacred Scripture").

The next student, similarly, looks for evidence, not to *shape* a considered position but to *back up feelings*. The feelings seem to come first: "I am sure that this course will challenge my beliefs, but through this challenge I hope to become an even stronger Christian. The challenge this course will provide will force me to realize and use evidence to back up my points and feelings" (Protestant Baccalaureate College, "History of Christian Thought").

The next student operates with two very limited and insufficient categories – fact or fiction: "I would like to understand religion more and help differ from fact and fiction" (Public Masters, "Religions of the World").

A final student faces "relativism" (everyone has their own opinions), and plans not to reason about other views, but to "fall back on what I know," though the statement then goes on to suggest using new information to expand. The student ends with the belief cited earlier, that challenge makes faith stronger, but this time the words are "learn" and "grow" – a more open view:

> I hope that this course will challenge my beliefs. I know that everyone has their own opinions about religion and the Bible. To deal with the challenge I plan to fall back on what I know and use the new information to expand on that. I think everyone's beliefs should be challenged. That is how you learn more about them and grow spiritually. (Protestant Masters, "Introduction to Sacred Scripture")

The positions outlined so far – exhibiting the four attitudes basic to critical thinking, and envisioning limited modes of critical thinking – are predominant among the small proportion of students who mention critical thinking at all. Primarily, this is what a faculty member can expect to see in a classroom. There do appear in the data, however, a few students who exhibit more robust notions of critical thinking and its relation to religious and spiritual development. The data do not allow identification of the age of each responding student, but several of these students reveal biographical facts that indicate they are older than the usual 18-year-old college entrant.

More robust uses of critical thinking

These few students mention strategies for critical thinking that are closer to the definitions and goals of the faculty. The first student articulates a classic view of theology as "faith seeking understanding." Operating within a faith which is "the defining feature of my life," the student intends to "think critically" to understand the Bible better, define terms, and find "biblically-based" answers to replace "opinions":

> I am entering this class in a different context than most of the other students, so my goals may (or may not) look different from the other students. I entered this institution as a Freshman, but took a few years off to get married and have a baby, so one of the main goals is to re-introduce my mind to the world of academic thinking, of thinking critically, as opposed to the instructive thought of motherhood. I believe that there is nothing more important than the ability to think critically, backed by knowledge, about one's faith, and even after two decades of being a Christian, I hope to come away from this class with a better understanding of the Bible and to more richly define words we Christians so often throw around and a clear biblically-based answer to some of my stronger opinions – which really are then just opinions – regarding issues with the church.
>
> I am looking forward to the class and expecting a challenge, both spiritually and practically. But since my faith is, as it should be, the defining feature of my life, I'm ready. (Protestant Masters, "Christian Scriptures")

One of the most interesting statements comes from this student who begins to envision a complex way of using critical thinking, hoping the course will provide "tools/options with which to negotiate my personal beliefs."

> My religion is Catholicism. I'm constantly on the search for answers to unanswerable questions and often times run into personal beliefs that seemingly contradict my religion. I enjoy and hope to continue reconciling the two. This course will help me think about much of what I've been taught about religion in a new way and give me more tools/options with which to negotiate my personal beliefs. I most definitely

expect the course to challenge my beliefs. I plan to deal with it open-mindedly and enthusiastically. (Private Non-Sectarian Baccalaureate, "The Experience of God")

Conclusions about students

What can the faculty member expect to find as learning goals for students in his or her classroom? I've not treated here those few students who *only* say they just want to get a good grade or fulfill a requirement. The data suggest that that's *part* of the motivation for many students, but most students in the sample said, or also said, that they expected to grow and learn. Students may appear silent, even withdrawn, or they may focus on grades, but the data reveal that students are thinking and learning: "there's a lot going on beneath the surface," as one faculty member said. Students' desire to learn and grow is the most important fact for the faculty member to keep in mind.

One type of student for whom the class might be problematic was Secure Christian students who expected the course to challenge their beliefs. This discussion has devoted special attention to that group. Secure Christians, whether they welcomed challenge or not, had strategies to meet the challenge, including strategies to allow them to "keep the faith," strategies that indicated readiness for critical thinking, strategies that envisioned limited types of critical thinking, and, for a very few students, more robust notions of how critical thinking might help to shape their religious and spiritual development. One can speculate about the influences that lie behind these limited understandings of critical thinking and students' failure, for the most part, to even mention critical thinking in their open-ended in-class writings. Influences surely include contemporary US culture's emphasis on religion as an individual, emotional experience; the culture's anti-intellectualism and its suspicion of the academy; in some cases, students' religious communities' emphasis on faith as contrary to intellect, and their fear that questioning is wrong; the fact-focused emphasis of their previous schooling; and their own developmental need to let the self learn to speak without reference to external tools or frames.

In addition to Secure Christians in all their diversity, most classrooms, even at religiously-affiliated institutions, also had Doubting Christians, students who said they had "no beliefs," Muslims, atheists, agnostics, and more, all going in *their* various directions. The presence in a single classroom of all these students coming from different worlds, traveling in different directions, and speaking with many voices, challenges the faculty member to be thoughtful and purposive about articulating goals for student development. The next section will examine the learning goals formulated by Highly-Effective faculty in the study.

Faculty Goals

Table 1.1 presented the survey data on goals for faculty in both the Date Base and Highly Effective groups. This section draws on the qualitative data for the Highly-Effective faculty, who reflected in more detail upon their goals. Though goals were affected by the faculty member's own background, by disciplinary frame (e.g., theology, religious studies), by course title, and by institutional type, some common themes emerged.

Common themes

Highly-Effective faculty were characterized by:

1 careful articulation of goals;
2 attempts to understand student goals and to discuss goals with students;
3 a concern for students, keen observation about students' situations and needs;
4 a commitment to nurture students' development beyond mere acquisition of factual knowledge, though faculty took different degrees of responsibility and different approaches for nurturing students' spiritual and religious journeys;
5 a commitment not to force students into any particular belief or practice, but to invite questions and provide tools to explore the questions;
6 a view of themselves, their students, and religious practices as developing and evolving, not static;
7 a desire for students to engage actively with the course material, their peers, and the faculty member (when faculty were asked an open-ended question about what traits of their students they liked least [Appendix D], they nearly always mentioned students who were disengaged, not students who failed to learn X or Y); and
8 an emphasis on what this study broadly calls "critical thinking."

"Critical thinking"

This chapter earlier defined "critical thinking," referencing statements of national consensus and using the survey items from this study. Qualitative data reveal more detail about how teachers of introductory theology and religion describe the collection of intellectual tasks I term "critical thinking." These intellectual tasks include:

- analysis of the cultural, historical, economic, sociological, political, ideological, linguistic, literary, symbolic, and other aspects of religious beliefs, texts, and practices;
- use of evidence and reason to reach conclusions and to formulate and critique arguments;
- use of multiple perspectives to understand an issue; and
- the achievement of interpretive distance from their own autobiographies and communities.

Attitudes, dispositions, and habits of mind that accompany these activities are:

- the belief that it is desirable, not disloyal or dangerous, to question, critique, and change one's own former beliefs and assumptions, whether religious and/or intellectual;
- a respectful recognition that positions other than one's own may contain truth, and that "truth" itself is highly complex;
- abandonment of simplistic, stereotypical views of those different from oneself;
- a view of religions, societies, and their own spiritual/intellectual lives as not static but developing and changing; and
- reliance on one's self, in addition to authorities such as parents, church, and others, to determine one's beliefs and commitments.

"Sub rosa" goals and "let it happen" goals

Sometimes, course goals that concerned changes in students' attitudes were not stated formally, but revealed by the faculty in their journals or conversations. Here is part of the journal of a faculty member teaching "Introduction to Biblical Literature" at a public research university:

> While I have specific academic goals in mind for my students . . . of greater importance to me is a goal I don't explicitly state but underlies my pedagogy: I want students to gain a sense of the Bible as the product of specific cultures and eras – ones far different from ours – so that . . . they will be less inclined to use the Bible as an absolute standard to hold over another person or as a tool to bend their will to their own agenda.

On the survey of eight discipline-specific goals, this faculty member marked "Take or be inclined to take action for a better world" as "very important," and wrote in the margin "Not an explicitly-stated goal, but is an aim in my teaching via ideological critique of biblical texts."

Such "sub rosa" goals appear in both public and religiously-affiliated institutions. They typically express the hope that students will:

- not merely use critical thinking in an academic way, but act on what they learn;
- not necessarily adopt, but at least consider, a particular world-view (this might be the Enlightenment world-view of the critical thinker, and/or, at religiously-affiliated institutions, a particular set of religious beliefs and practices);
- recognize the complexity of all "truth" claims;
- transcend what faculty call "bias," "stereotypes," or "prejudice" – uni-dimensional, simplistic, often negative views of cultures or religions;
- acknowledge the situatedness of religious beliefs, practices, and texts; and
- respect and consider points of view with which they may disagree.

"Let it happen" goals are similar to "sub rosa" goals in that they are not stated formally in the syllabus. They are actually not even goals. They are outcomes the faculty members are content, even happy, to see realized, but from which they deliberately keep hands off. One faculty member who teaches "The Nature of Religion" at a public masters institution circles the survey goal statements that address religious beliefs, values, and taking action for a better world (items e, f, g, and h on survey, Appendix D). To explain, the faculty member writes:

> May all happen and would be a plus – e.g., understanding and appreciation of a variety of religions probably would increase one's own appreciation for one's own religion. [These goals] would all probably happen from any well taught course in literature, history, sociology, etc. But I am not a pastor and I do not have the spiritual growth of my students directly in mind as I prepare and teach a course. A course in religious studies may increase "faith and commitment" in a particular student and/or it may decrease or destroy faith and commitment. Either outcome would be valid and perhaps desirable for that given student.

The existence of "sub rosa" and "let it happen" goals suggests that the "Great Divide" between students who want to work on their religious and spiritual lives, and faculty who do not choose that aspect as a goal, is complex. It's not so much that there are clearly defined camps, but that, for faculty, goals related to students' spiritual and religious development are complex, multi-layered, not well-defined, and perhaps uncomfortable to formally articulate. Yet, as Chapter

3 will show, faculty often arrange their pedagogical practices to create spaces for these goals to be addressed and for students to achieve their own goals for spiritual and religious development. It's a complicated picture.

Allowing some goals to operate at the "sub rosa" and "let it happen" levels serves several purposes for faculty: it manages a faculty member's concern about where the line is between inviting students to explore new worlds and unduly pressuring them. It keeps possibly controversial goals out of the line of anyone's fire. It provides a private space where developing goals and thoughts can be worked out. It brings otherwise unarticulated assumptions and motives into consciousness. It keeps the stated, formal course goals relatively simple, concentrating on critical thinking tools and attitudes that are widely accepted in the academy.

However, some faculty in the study recognize the situated nature of those widely accepted critical-thinking goals, too.

Critical thinking as a situated goal

Here are two faculty musing about the situatedness of all classroom goals, including the principles of "critical thinking," which the faculty member identifies with the Enlightenment:

> Why are we so sure or secure in Enlightenment principles? Shouldn't our prejudices be critically looked at? This seems to be the elephant in the room. It is so big and so prevalent, it must be right. I'm not sure. Particularly because it is hard to define (sign of ideological muddling); it is taken for granted (sign of political power); it assumes a professional class that is taken care of (sign of acute privilege); it also tends to question group allegiances (sign of indifference to political affiliations, sign of a leisured class). Trust me, I like all the privileges of my class, but shouldn't these be questioned, and why are we trying to reproduce our prejudices with such equanimity and pride!! (Public Research, "Introduction to World Religions")

> Of course, ironically for a person who tries really hard to check his own biases at the classroom door, all of these goals are my own biases coming home to roost. The goals are ultimately about what is important, what is "real" for me. So I, like my students, have to do quite a lot of meta-thinking in order to *nosce meipsum*, and constantly check that my goals for them are in their best interest (as best I am able to surmise what is best for them). It is a daunting and exceedingly rewarding responsibility. (Public Doctoral, "Introduction to World Religions")

I don't think it's necessarily bad to have several levels of goals, at both formal and informal levels. I don't think it's bad that different faculty have diverse goals. I don't think critical thinking is a bad goal – just situated and complicated like all goals. I think that the religion/theology faculty in this study are doing an admirable job of trying to articulate learning goals in an academy deeply conflicted about how to address students' religious and spiritual development. The answer to this complexity, I believe, is "quite a lot of meta-thinking" about one's goals – their underlying assumptions and values, and one's reasons for choosing them – as well as conversation with one's students about learning goals. Those who educate future faculty, who hold workshops for faculty, who mentor faculty, or who organize conversations about higher education's role in students' religious and spiritual development can help faculty members to articulate all their goals, to analyze the assumptions and agendas behind those goals, to share them with other faculty, and to plan effective classroom conversations about goals. A resource especially helpful in examining assumptions behind goals and pedagogy is Brookfield (1995).

Cases: Constructing Goals, Discussing them with Students

This section uses three case studies to explore with greater specificity the issues of faculty goals: their rhetorical framing, their content, and faculty members' ways of conducting conversations with student about goals. These cases are useful for several purposes:

- providing concrete examples and illustrations of the general findings about goals that emerged from the other data; and
- modeling how faculty members can subject their own goals to careful analysis and can plan conversations with students about goals.

To highlight differences in goals among faculty even in similar disciplinary frames, I have chosen three faculty who teach "Bible" courses – one in a public research university, one in a Catholic masters-level university, and one in a Protestant baccalaureate college. The cases demonstrate how each teacher shapes goals and engages students in dialogue about goals.

The issue of "voice" is an ongoing theme in this study. In the following cases, and in the chapters on pedagogy, frequent questions will be: What 'voice' does the student bring to the classroom – the voice of the dutiful memorizer, the believer, the seeker? What voices does the faculty member encourage – the critical thinker? The believer who uses critical thinking? What voices are present in the classroom? Which voices are privileged? How does the faculty member create structures and spaces for these various voices and for the integration of critical thinking with students' own values and their religious and spiritual development?

Case 1: Prof. Sorrell: "Biblical Literature" in a Public Research university

Prof. Sorrell [a pseudonym] teaches "Biblical Literature" focusing on the "Hebrew Bible" in a public research university. He has received high honors in his department and university-wide for the quality of his teaching in the introductory course.

Goals

In a written reflection, he reveals how his thinking about the course has grown and changed over time, as he wrestles with how to help his students relate to these ancient texts.

> After graduating from seminary in 1977, I harbored a desire to deepen my understanding of how the Bible came into existence, the cultures in which it is rooted, and the languages in which it is written. Even as a pastor I was concerned with helping my congregation(s) understand the Bible within those contexts, and thereby help delineate in what ways its writings could be utilized by people of faith today . . . When I began teaching "Introduction to Biblical Literature" in the fall semester of 1991, I saw my role as helping students gain exposure to conclusions biblical scholars draw about the origins of the literature of the Hebrew Bible and its cultural-historical environment. While that remains central to my work in this class, I have also seen the need to help students understand the literary shape of the Bible. By that I mean, not simply to help them understand how a piece of biblical literature evolved over time, but also to what effect. What is gained for the reader by knowing, for instance, that P expanded J's narrative in Genesis? How is the reader affected by realizing that v. 7 in Amos 3 was supplied by an editor/redactor?
>
> Since first teaching the course, I have also become convinced of the need to acknowledge critical differences in perspective between our day and that of the author(s) and first recipients of this literature. For instance, how does our reading of the patriarchal narratives from the concerns of feminism highlight concerns that would not have been uppermost to the author(s)? How do our convictions about abuse of children affect our reading of the sacrifice of Isaac?

Prof. Sorrell's description of how the course has developed reveals that, over the years, he has made more room in his course for modern meaning-making, including that of his students – for questions about what it means to the reader to know that P expanded J in Genesis and how a modern feminist views the patriarchy reflected in the biblical text. Both the "reader" voice and the voices of modern feminists and other critics have entered the classroom.

For the semester of data collection for this study, his formal, syllabus goals were that students would:

- become acquainted with the Hebrew Bible, how scholars have studied it, and what they have discovered;
- explore the Bible's diverse responses to life, quests for meaning, and expressions of religious experience; and
- develop skills for reading the Bible.

Prof. Sorrell's goal about Biblical scholarship will include teaching about the controversies in the field and the approaches (for example feminist) that different scholars have brought. But his stated goal for this area is simply for students to "become acquainted" with these findings and points of view. Uses of this knowledge are left to the student. The second goal is "explore . . . expressions of religious experience." The verb implies stronger involvement, but still leaves the student to decide what is to be concluded from the exploration. A third goal is to "develop skills for reading the Bible." Prof. Sorrell teaches a strategy for reading that he describes this way: "I require students to learn a method of 'close reading' that involves coloring texts with markers that serve to highlight and distinguish themes and motifs that appear throughout a passage. By seeing where such themes and motifs congregate, students have a tangible means to describe how meaning arises for them from the passage. Students write papers that reflect their facility in this method." Students acquire the reading skill and use it in papers for which they are held accountable, but they "describe" how the method leads to meaning-making "for them." The meaning the student achieves must be text-based, but is their own meaning. These goal statements are complex, subtly defining where students will be required to exhibit particular knowledge and skills, and where they will be left on their own to draw conclusions and apply what they are learning to their own lives.

Prof. Sorrell also has a "sub rosa" goal that amplifies his formal syllabus goals. He is the one described earlier who wants students to be "less inclined to use the Bible as an absolute standard," and who, on the survey question about goals, marks "Take or be inclined to take action for a better world" as "very important," and writes in the margin, that this goal, though not officially stated, is "addressed through ideological critique of Biblical texts."

In sum, these goals imply the following two elements that are common to faculty in the Highly-Effective group:

1 *An open door for student meaning-making*: the language of the syllabus is couched as the critical and disinterested study of the biblical texts, but it also increasingly has left room for modern meaning-making, including that of his students, who are required to conduct critical analysis of the text and invited to make meaning "for them," and whose voices in the classroom describe this meaning-making; and
2 *Goals for student engagement and action*: there is no pressure on students to act in any particular direction, and certainly no pressure to adopt a certain religious belief system, but the "sub rosa" goal expresses the hope that students will engage and act in their world, not just learn a critical thinking tool for textual analysis.

Conversation with students about goals

Prof. Sorrell, like many of the highly-effective faculty, takes time at the beginning of the course to address the goals that students bring with them, and to engage his students in dialogue about goals. He does so with two strategies: one is a classroom exercise in which he elicits students' responses to questions about their own views of the Bible and their hopes/apprehensions about the class. The other, which he does in another class, is a voluntary hour outside of class in which he talks honestly with his students about his own life and theirs. He describes these strategies in his journal:

> Classroom sharing exercise
>
> One of the frequent obstacles to achieving the aims of my course is the pre-understanding of the Bible students bring with them. Typically it is reading the Bible through a theological lens of what the Bible must "teach" on every page, whether from a particular theological perspective or a conception of biblical ethics. Another problem is preconceptions of the Bible's character, either as an infallible divine utterance or as a book of myth (in the popular sense). In view of these issues, in the first class session I utilize an exercise requiring that students answer briefly without signing their names, two questions on a half sheet of paper: 1) What, in your view, is the most satisfactory description of the Bible? (using "I think," "I believe," or "I feel" language); 2) What hopes or apprehensions do you bring to this class? After giving students a few minutes to write responses, my TA and I collect the papers and

> redistribute them so that each person has someone else's paper. [Note from BW: if there is no TA, to help distribute, or if you want to get a little laughter and lively action going, you can have students crumple their papers into balls and, when you give the signal, each closes his/her eyes and throws the paper across the room. Students then scramble to retrieve the balls nearest them.]
>
> Each student reads the response on their paper as if it were their own statement. Doing so allows students to perceive the diversity of views of the Bible their classmates bring to the course so that they are not shocked when they hear others raising questions exposing assumptions about the Bible different from their own. Responses to the first question run the gamut from "The Bible is the inerrant word of God," to "The Bible is a compilation of stories about ancient Israel," to "The Bible is a repository of ethical standards by which we can live." I affirm each of these as valid understandings in their peculiar settings, but indicate that we will be following a different approach: understanding the Bible as the product of particular times, societies and individuals. I stress that what we do is different from the approach taken in faith communities and promise to adumbrate those differences in the next class period.
>
> Responses to the second question circled around what students wanted to get out of the course: content of the Bible, a non-religious perspective on the Bible, familiarity with biblical scholarship, etc. This exchange allows me to comment on issues important to students, such as whether this course will be taught as a religion course or a religious studies course; whether I am out to show the Bible as "merely" a human product, devoid of divine influence; whether they will be able to comprehend what's going on if they haven't grown up with the Bible.

Two spaces are involved in Sorrell's strategies: the world of the university and the world of "faith communities." The opening exercise allows students to enter classroom dialogue in voices that employ "I feel" and "I believe" and to express their personal goals, wherever those come from. The professor affirms the value of those voices in their appropriate settings, but makes clear that the classroom requires a different voice.

Out-of-class meeting with students

> In the other course I'm teaching this semester, "Early Christian Literature," a student revealed he had learned I once was a pastor and he wondered how I integrate the sorts of conclusions about this literature

> I present in class with my sense of faith. I have scheduled a meeting outside of class time (and outside the structure of the class) to address that question for any students interested, and more than half the class indicated they would like to attend. I wish I could offer something similar for students in this class, but feel awkward initiating it.

Prof. Sorrell wants his students to understand the differences between the university and faith communities, and to locate the class firmly in the university. However, his students inhabit both spaces, and so does he. He wishes he could create a meeting ground – out-of-class space for himself and his students to meet – in which they could talk about how to bring these two worlds together, but he feels that students should initiate such a meeting. Another faculty member at a public research university, Prof. Veldman, actually schedules such a meeting. His case is described in chapter 4. This volume will continue to examine the spaces and structures that faculty create for students to figure out how to bring together the world of the classroom and the worlds of their religious and spiritual lives.

The second case examines a faculty member who also teaches the Bible, this time in a Catholic institution. Her goals, and her way of talking with students about goals, are similar yet different from Prof. Sorrell's.

Case 2: Prof. Tilden: "The Gospels" in a Catholic University

Prof. Tilden [a pseudonym] teaches "The Gospels," a course located in the "Theology" department, to 35 students at a Catholic masters university. During the year of this study, despite being a junior faculty member, she received the college's teaching award. More information on her class can be found in her full case study in Chapter 6. Here I show only her goal statement.

Goals

Her stated course objectives in the syllabus are:

1. Students will demonstrate an ability to engage in a critical study of primary, foundational religious expressions, such as sacred texts.
2. Students will become conversant with the gospel texts, and be able to comment critically on their historical, literary and theological significance.
3. Students will demonstrate an ability to engage in debates about what can be known historically about Jesus in the context of first century Judaism.
4. Students will demonstrate an engagement with the Christian belief of God's self-revelation in Jesus Christ and so develop an understanding of the faith(s) expressed by the gospel writers and the community of the early Church.

Critical thinking skills dominate the first three items: critical study, and debate about historical issues. Like Sorrell, Tilden wants to develop skills for study of sacred texts. Like Sorrell, she wants students to become acquainted with scholarship on the biblical texts and to consider the text in light of historical information. The student's voice is that of the scholar, critically studying and debating.

Yet several factors are unique to the religiously-affiliated institution. First, the biblical texts are to be studied for their "theological" significance. "Theology" historically has been the use of reason and logic by "insiders" to shape the beliefs of their own community. No public institution in the study had a department of "Theology." Second, students will "develop an understanding" of the faith expressed by gospel writing and the early church. Many religion courses in both secular and religiously-affiliated settings ask students to develop an empathic understanding of the religious beliefs under study. But Tilden's statement then goes farther: students will "demonstrate an engagement" with the Christian belief. The word "engagement" is often used, by faculty in both non-sectarian and religiously-affiliated institutions, to mean that the student actively considers a point of view, and/or invests energy and interest in the course material. But a non-sectarian classroom would not ask students to "engage" Christian belief; that phrasing is unique to religiously-affiliated institutions. Yet there is also room in Prof. Tilden's statement for the students to make whatever decisions they wish. "Engagement" is being requested, but not necessarily commitment or belief.

The differences and similarities between Sorrell's and Tilden's goals are quite typical of those between non-sectarian and religiously-affiliated institutions in the Highly-Effective group as a whole. In both types of institution, the faculty goals are different from those of many of the students. Some "Secure Christian" students are likely to find the course material disturbing, and to struggle with ways to integrate what they are studying in the classroom with their own religious and spiritual development. Among the relatively few angry and disaffected students in the study, a number are students at conservative religious institutions for whom the course contradicts deeply-held beliefs.

Conversations with students about course goals

Like Sorrell, Tilden takes pains to find out about her students' goals and to engage students in dialogue.

Goals as part of learning names

On the very first day in class, Prof. Tilden begins with the "name game." She describes it in her journal:

> My strategy is to give the students a couple of minutes to meet the person next to them, find out who they are and why they're taking this course. I know for most of them this is a required class so I tell them I won't be offended if they say "required" and then use this as an opportunity to encourage them to allow themselves to think beyond "required." They might surprise themselves. After the students have met their "new friends," I have them introduce them to the class. We start with two and I repeat the two names. Then, we go on to the next two; I repeat the two names and then recall all four names. Then the next two; I repeat the two names and then recall all six names, and so on, until I can run off all the names. Then I challenge the students to do the same – someone usually takes the bait.

Many Highly Effective faculty members stress the importance of learning names. Some ask students to turn in notecards on the first day, with one fact about themselves. Faculty study these to get to know the students. Some download photos of the students if their institution makes that available, or they take a class photo, or photos of small groups of students, labeled with names, to study outside of class. Some ask each student to come to their office for a few minutes during the first week or two, just to say "Hi," reinforce the name, and chat long enough to know something about the student.

Prof. Tilden's name exercise asks students to share their course goals (why you are taking the course – go beyond "it's a requirement") with their neighbors. Contrast this with Sorrell's practice of letting the writings be anonymous. Sorrell's method is perhaps likely to elicit more candid information because anonymous, but at the cost of enhancing students' connection with their neighbors.

A variation on this game is to have each student, as they introduce their neighbor, say the names of everyone who has already been introduced (this lets the professor off the hook!). If the class is too large, the student or professor can say only the names of the most recent four or six people who have been introduced. In a really large class, this exercise can be done by students in small groups, so each student learns only the names of the group. The group can write a short, informal report for the professor and/or the class on the goals that were mentioned there.

Offer models

Next, Prof. Tilden urges her students not to be fearful about questioning. She offers models from their own tradition: Job and Aquinas, who found ways to integrate the intellect and faith.

> After this exercise, I give the students a motto for the course from Immanuel Kant: *Sapere Aude!* Dare to know, have the courage to use your reason. Model to them that it's okay (and good!) to question, for example Job's refusal to accept the thinking of his day on suffering as retributive justice and his courage to question that view of suffering; challenge them to question everything – including the teacher!
>
> I also tried to show an awareness that some will find the notion of asking challenging questions in relation to personal faith threatening. Tell them about theologian Thomas Aquinas' model in the *Summa* – he considers a question (such as whether there is a God) and then thinks about every possible objection to the questions. Is he trying to destroy faith? No. He's seeing if it can be defended rationally: is it reasonable to believe this?

The examples bring other voices into the classroom, and they suggest models for student voices: Job's voice questioning received religious tenets; Aquinas' voice applying reason to faith; Kant's voice saying, "Dare to use your reason."

The first class day ends with a discussion of the nuts and bolts of the syllabus and a discussion of rules about plagiarism.

Invite "concerns"

The second class day begins this way:

> At the start of the class I asked for students to fill out a blank sheet of paper with their name, email, and any concerns that they had at this stage. One girl wrote "Please help me forgive God for taking my mother." Wow. I will email her in a couple of days.

Prof. Tilden has made clear in class that she meant for students to express academic concerns connected to the syllabus. The student has replied as a distressed person to her therapist or pastor. The student misreads the assignment or is unable to form her concerns in a more academic way. Prof. Tilden does email her, inviting a meeting. When the student comes to the office, she talks briefly about her loss, which is very recent. Prof. Tilden suggests she talk with the university chaplain – someone qualified for this kind of spiritual guidance. Prof. Tilden then tries to help the student frame her concern in an academic way. The "please help me forgive God," from a distressed student to a therapist, becomes the academic goal, "I want to find a way to forgive God" or "I want to explore the issues of death and loss" – a different voice. By asking for "concerns" written in class and then reading them at home, Prof. Tilden gains information she welcomes, concerning students' own experiences and questions that will impact their work in the course. She also gives herself time to respond in a thoughtful way.

Case 3: Prof. Cosby, "Introduction to Biblical Studies," in a Protestant College

Prof. Michael R. Cosby [his real name] teaches at Messiah College, whose mission statement calls it a "Christian college of the liberal and applied arts and sciences," whose mission is "to educate men and women toward maturity of intellect, character and Christian faith in preparation for lives of service, leadership and reconciliation in church and society" (www.messiah.edu). An award-winning teacher, Prof. Cosby has published widely on teaching and learning (1999, 2005, 2006, forthcoming 2008).

Goals

His syllabus for "Introduction to Biblical Studies" states these goals:

1 Gain a fundamental knowledge of ancient Mediterranean cultural norms, and understand the significance of reading the Bible in the light of these.
2 Be aware of the development of the canon of Scripture and some of the historical processes involved in the transmission of biblical books.
3 Interact with various theories on the inspiration of Scripture.
4 Become proficient in using the inductive Bible study method.
5 Know how to employ the basic research methods and tools used in biblical exegesis.
6 Learn to identify and responsibly interpret the various literary genres contained in the Bible.
7 Be able to reflect on contemporary issues in light of biblical teaching, applying them to daily living.

Prof. Cosby, in a reflection, explains how he developed his pedagogy:

> I got interested in teaching while a staff member for Inter Varsity Christian Fellowship, working in the Northwest. I discovered during that time that I have gifts in teaching. One of the largest influences on my pedagogy was the small group, inductive Bible study method promoted by InterVarsity. I thrived on the open discussion much more than simply listening to lectures. Down through the years as I have taught many college classes, I still hearken back to the dialogical method

> of instruction – asking questions that push students to see for themselves what the biblical text actually says rather than simply telling them what it says.

On his website, he explains the "inductive" Bible study method:

> Carefully examining the details of a particular text in an attempt to understand what its author means to communicate. This usually involves three steps: a) Observation. Who, What, When, Where, How? b) Interpretation. Why? c) Application. How does it apply today?

He differentiates "Inductive" study from two other types:

1 "Deductive," [which is] reading the Bible using a set of beliefs as a guide for interpreting what you read. Problem: Denominational belief systems typically predetermine what you see in particular passages. Deductive study is often used as a means of proving what you already believe (find what you look for); and
2 "Topical," [which is] looking up a number of verses to see what they say about a chosen topic. Problem: verses are often read without considering their context.

This course emphasizes aspects of what I broadly call "critical thinking:" analytic tools, historical and cultural contexts of the Bible, literary genres in the Bible, and interaction with "various theories." Yet there are important differences between this course and the public university Biblical Literature course of Prof. Sorrell. Critical thinking tools are used, and students are asked to stretch beyond their "deductive" and "topical" modes, but they are still believers, using critical thinking methods to better apply biblical teaching to their daily lives. A key is the terms that would sound out of place in a public university: reference to the Bible as "Scripture," for example, invokes a community that considers the book sacred. The phrase "biblical teaching" implies learning from the Bible, despite its situatedness in human history. In the Christian context, the faculty member's goal is to move students from a semi-magical to a more nuanced view of the Bible based on evidence of its cultural and linguistic history, and to present various theories about its "inspiration," but not entirely to dethrone it as "Scripture," capable of "teaching" modern students.

Conversations with students about course goals

Prof. Cosby is keenly aware of how students' goals for spiritual growth as they understand it may cause difficulties in the class. In a reflection, he writes:

> My class will stretch students tremendously with respect to their view of Scripture. They will be troubled at what a human document it is, because most will have a semi-magical view of Scripture. So I need to be very sensitive to their struggles with their faith – not just their difficulties with the academic content.

Prof. Cosby illustrates three different methods of addressing students' goals.

Whole-class discussion

The first method is class discussion after the course has begun, opening with a simple question. During the fourth class meeting, after students have read about the "canonization process," he asks his students "how well they had coped with the new material" on the canon. He writes, "There was no doubt that many of them were rattled. Many participated, expressing how they responded to the material. Most were taking it in stride by arriving at some very half-baked ideas of how God was at work in the process." Students, in their writings, express appreciation of "discussion" generally in the class, and particularly of this discussion of the canon. One student writes, "I like how we can discuss openly our beliefs on the subject. I also like how you challenge us on our beliefs. I really like when we discussed the canonization process because it made [me] realize some of the truths about Christianity that I was not aware of before. I really enjoy some of the small group discussion on the more difficult and challenging questions about our own personal beliefs. I really enjoy this class, it is *so* much fun!"

Student's written reflections

A second method Prof. Cosby uses to spur conversation about goals is the reflection written by students for this research project. On Oct. 12, about 6 weeks into the course, students wrote in class for about 10 minutes: "What are your goals for learning in this course? What actions of the teacher so far are most effective in helping you learn (please focus on specific actions)? What actions by the teacher, by you, and by other students might make the course more effective for your learning, and why (please focus on specific actions)?" The research project left it to the faculty member to decide how to use these in-class writings. Prof. Cosby produced a written summary of the students' responses, in a neutral tone, and handed it to all his students. For the "goals" section, he reported, "most class members emphasized that you want to learn more about the historical/cultural background of the Bible so that you can do a better job of interpreting and applying biblical passages." Distributing such a summary can help students see where they stand in the spectrum of class responses; it can also serve as the basis for further class discussion.

Textbook organization

A third way of addressing student goals is embodied in Prof. Cosby's own hermeneutic textbook, *A New Introduction to Biblical Studies* (forthcoming). Intended for students at both public and religiously-affiliated institutions, his text deliberately tries in several ways to meet students' goals. I summarize here not to sell his textbook but to explore how textbooks can help teachers address students' goals and to show one teacher's ways of doing so. First, each chapter of the text contains "so what" reflection questions for students to ponder or discuss. Regardless of whether the faculty member chooses to focus on such issues in class, these questions can help students meet their goals of personal religious and spiritual development that grows organically from what they are studying in class. Second, the text emphasizes hands-on analysis of texts, by the students, using provocative questions for analysis – questions by which students take ownership of textual interpretation. After their own analysis, students can more readily confront scholarly interpretations. Third, the text follows a sequence derived from students' developmental process, rather than chronology or canon. For example, students first study Biblical "short stories" to analyze plot and character. Then they study wisdom literature, with its rather obvious origins as collections of textual and oral traditions from a variety of sources. Then they read *Job*, with its obvious inter-textual dialogue representing different points of view. These experiences help students acquire textual, cultural, and historical understanding of Biblical texts, to prepare them to read, for example, the two creation stories in Genesis.

These case studies have illustrated a variety of types of goals and ways of framing goal statements and structuring discussion with students about goals. The main point here is that, because goals are such a complex issue in these classrooms, and because of the "Great Divide," it is important for faculty members to construct their goal statements carefully including consideration of the "voices" their students will use in the classroom, and to engage their students in discussion about goals.

Suggesting the Relationship between Students' Beliefs and Course Material

The three cases above illustrate multiple aspects of goals and are intended as an overview of the issues of constructing goals and sharing goals with students. In each case, the faculty member suggests how students might integrate the course material with their own beliefs. Prof. Sorrell emphasizes the differences between the course's intellectual enterprise and the basis of personal faith. Prof. Tilden asks for "engagement" of the student with Christian belief. Prof. Cosby wants students to apply biblical teaching to daily living. Because this issue of how students will integrate the course material with their religious and spiritual lives is so complex, this section presents additional faculty statements about how this integration may be accomplished.

Prof. Carr: "Exploring Religion," Public Masters university

Prof. Amy Carr [her real name], at Western Illinois University, states more explicitly than some other public university faculty that one of her course goals is to use both "insider" and "outsider" perspectives, and to "clarify ongoingly your own ultimate values and convictions."

> *Purpose of the Course*: This course has two main objectives: First, it introduces three religious traditions (Judaism, Christianity, and Islam) through a comparative approach that highlights the scriptures, doctrines of God, and worship/ritual styles of each religion. We will also engage questions of inter-religious conflict and dialogue. As we will see, Judaism, Christianity, and Islam share a common heritage; scholars of religion sometimes call them the "monotheistic" religions, for each takes as its starting point a belief in one God who creates, sustains, judges, and redeems the universe.
>
> The course does not assume that you practice a particular religion; nor is it a course which will ask you to memorize lots of facts about different religions. But the course does assume: 1) that religion reflects abiding human concerns; and 2) that as citizens and as societies, we are more likely to make informed decisions in a religiously-pluralistic world if we cultivate an awareness of the complexity, internal conflicts, and wisdom within every religion, and learn how to analyze the phenomena of religion using both insiders' and outsiders' perspectives. In studying religion with these assumptions in an academic context, you can strengthen your own ability to do the following:
>
> - Develop a capacity to perceive religious texts, beliefs, and practices with both empathy and criticism.
> - Become familiar with the many ways of interpreting sacred texts and the internal diversity within every religious tradition.

- Compare ideas of God and forms of worship and ritual within Judaism, Christianity, and Islam.
- Recognize and investigate religious sorts of questions.
- Identify some of the diverse cultural, social, political, and personal roles played by religion.
- Clarify ongoingly your own ultimate values and convictions.

Prof. Vance-Trembath: "The Christian Village," in a Catholic university

Prof. Sally Vance-Trembath [her real name], who was teaching at the University of San Francisco at the time of this study, addresses the relationship between students' own religious/spiritual life and the theological reflection that is the aim of her course. While some professors hold "let it happen" goals that remain unstated, Vance-Trembath articulates such a goal in her syllabus, noting that, while the course may enhance your own faith, it's not *about* that:

> Theology is critical reflection upon faith. Because this class is a university class, the critical reflection will be even farther away from catechesis than any adult education or more advanced high school classes you may have attended. One of the hallmarks of Catholicism is how it has embraced and encouraged the intellectual life. At the same time, this critical reflection has as its object the most personal and meaningful aspects of human life. It reflects upon our experience of the Living God and that God's personal presence in each person's inner life and in the corporate life of the community. Therefore, a constitutive part of the critical reflection is the respect for and attention to the various experiences of God that all of us will bring to this study. While this course may indeed enhance and develop your own faith life, it is not materially about your faith life; it is materially concerned with critical reflection upon the meaning of human existence and God's existence. Wherever you as an individual person find yourself with regard to these questions of meaning, will in no way effect the grade you earn in this course. The grade you earn corresponds to how well you engage these questions at the university level.

Prof. Starkey: "Questions of Faith" at a Protestant Masters university

Prof. John Starkey [his real name] teaches at Oklahoma City University, which "embraces the United Methodist tradition of scholarship and service and welcomes all faiths in a culturally rich community that . . . focuses on students' intellectual, moral, and spiritual development to prepare them to become effective leaders in service to their communities" (www.okcu.edu). Prof. Starkey teaches a course titled "Questions of Faith," which he describes as addressing "spirituality" as well as "theology." He envisions that students will "combine" an affirmative confession with critical questioning. In his syllabus, he makes explicit an attitude shared by many faculty in the study – that their students (and they, themselves) are not frozen in the beliefs of the moment but will develop and change over their lifetimes.

Prof. Starkey introduces the course thus:

> *Description and nature of the course*
>
> On the one side, the course is an introduction to *spirituality*, to our felt response to the depths and riches of the Reality that surrounds us and yet lies deep within us as well – the Reality that Christians and many others often call by the name "God." On the other side, this course is also an introduction to *theology* (Greek theos [God] + logos [word]), to the intellectual questions and responses that tend to arise when people try to understand their religious faith in a reflective, sometimes even critical, way.
>
> *Overall vision of the course*
>
> This course is intended to help you clarify your personal approach to combining an affirmative confession of faith with a critical questioning about faith to find a lived spirituality integrated with communal religion in a way that can mature over a lifetime.

Prof. Wall: "Christian Scriptures" at a Protestant Masters university

Prof. Robert W. Wall [his real name] teaches at Seattle Pacific University, whose mission statement calls it "a premier Christian university fully committed to engaging the culture and changing the world by graduating people of competence and character, becoming people of wisdom, and modeling grace-filled community." His syllabus explicitly sets the academic material of the class within the context of prayer, the work of the Holy Spirit, and a student's relationship with God:

> The college experience, if it is all that it should be, seeks after truth with integrity in a place that values trust over power. At a Christian college, where the Bible is treasured and studied as the word of God, understanding what the Bible teaches is a necessary path leading to the truth about God. In this class, students often encounter ideas about

> God that are new and different. Perhaps students will hear or read material assigned for this course that they have previously been taught is "wrong," "liberal" or "dangerous" by trusted friends and faith traditions. The aim of these challenges fostered within a Christian college classroom is deeper theological understanding and an invigorated relationship with God. For this reason, Seattle Pacific University considers learning Scripture sacred business – a holy practice that requires buckets of patience and loads of time the student sets aside for study and prayer as s/he joins the Holy Spirit for a life-changing season of Christian nurture.

These last four short cases illustrate different ways in which faculty members have tried to spell out more clearly the relationship between intellect and spirit, without crossing the boundaries they want to maintain, and while giving students freedom to make their own choices. Given the limited concepts about critical thinking and its relationship to faith with which students enter the course, faculty members' care in crafting goal statements can be the first step toward appropriate structures by which students can address, expand, or revise their goals.

Conclusion

This chapter has explored the "Great Divide" between students, who often focus on development of their own religious and spiritual lives, and faculty, who almost universally prioritize "critical thinking." The chapter has outlined the various positions from which students begin the course, and how they expect to address challenges to their faith, either by protecting their faith from change, or by being open to (usually limited) forms of "critical thinking." The chapter has also illustrated with examples and short case studies the various ways in which faculty members have shaped their goals and have structured conversations with their students about goals. A theme throughout has been the ways in which goals establish a basis for various student "voices."

Introductory theology and religion courses are on the front line of the national debate about the relationship between intellectual and religious/spiritual development and about the role that institutions of higher education, whether secular or religiously-affiliated, should play in students' development. Findings from the present study affirm the research by the Higher Education Research Institute (HERI) and others, which points to students' widespread desires to develop their religious and spiritual lives in their college years. The findings from this study suggest the great complexity of goals that may exist in a single classroom. The findings also suggest the need for faculty, administrators, and institutions to be clear about how they believe their institutions and their classrooms can help students develop as whole persons, bringing together their intellectual and spiritual worlds.

Specifically, faculty members in their own classes can ask themselves, or share in discussion with their colleagues, questions such as:

1 What are my goals for student learning?
2 Do I have "sub rosa" and/or "let it happen" goals? What are they? Am I content to leave them in that state, or would it be better to state them more formally?
3 How will students understand the goals I state on my syllabus? Will they get the meanings I intend?
4 What are the ideological and political implications of the goals I have adopted?
5 What does "critical thinking" mean to me, and how do I believe students can use critical thinking to shape their own religious and spiritual practices and beliefs?
6 How do I want to structure the conversation with the students about my goals and their goals? In what forum should their goals be elicited? Anonymous or not? As goals, concerns, hopes/apprehensions, or some other frame? How will I handle student goals the course cannot address?
7 What voices for students do my goals imply?

Appendix H presents suggestions for those planning workshops, study groups, or teaching seminars in which present or future faculty work on their own courses.

2

Were the Goals Met? Students' Academic and Spiritual Development

This chapter addresses two related issues:

1 What can we say in general about students' learning and development in their introductory theology/religion courses, in both the Database courses and the Highly-Effective courses?
2 How can faculty members evaluate the quality of learning and development in their own classrooms?

The primary finding for the national sample – both the Database group and the Highly-Effective group – is that students and faculty perceived that significant learning took place along many dimensions: critical thinking skills, facts and principles, and understanding other religions or points of view. Students also reported development in their spiritual and religious lives, even when their faculty members had not stated those aspects formally as course goals.

These conclusions rely on two types of data: faculty members' survey responses (Appendix D) about whether their students had achieved the course goals "better than I expected," "about as well as I expected," or "not as well as I expected;" and, second, what students perceived they learned, as reflected in the IDEA evaluations administered to all the Database classes and to most of the Highly-Effective classes (Appendix C). This chapter first reviews the survey data about what faculty and students thought students learned. Then it uses the qualitative data to examine various kinds of development for various kinds of students. Going back to Secure Christians whose goals were examined in Chapter 1, the study outlines their paths of development, as well as the development of Doubting Christians, Agnostics, Atheists, and Adherents of Other Religions. Finally, the chapter suggests how faculty members may analyze the learning in their own classrooms.

What Faculty Thought Students Learned

On the survey about how well students achieved the goals (Appendix D), faculty generally reported that students achieved course learning goals as well as, or better than, the faculty had expected. Faculty member's beliefs about student learning were reflected in students' grades. In the 47 classes that reported students' grades, the average grade on a 4-point scale was 3.2 – a good, solid "B." Forty percent of the students received A, 37 percent B, 14 percent C, 4 percent D, and 3 percent F.

A sense of the tone of faculty reports about student learning can be gained from the following two comments:

> I must say that I did accomplish my goal of helping students to improve their critical thinking and their writing abilities. I saw improvement across the board in student writing and in their abilities to think and talk about the topic of religion critically. (Protestant Masters, "Introduction to Religious Studies")

> I was pleasantly surprised by some of [the students'] responses to how this course affected them intellectually and personally, which is one of the fundamental goals of a General Education course. Our goal in Comparative Religion is to nurture a critical mind and sometimes this is hard to gauge because it is hard to climb into a student's heart and mind. Much is going on beneath the surface and while we may see glimpses of it in a well-wrought paper or an apt comment during class – much more is going on beneath the surface in these intro classes. Several students commented on a new-found appreciation for the power of religion in our world. Many also mentioned how they felt they were given the tools to think more critically and objectively about religion. When asked how this course changed their thinking about religion in particular, they again reported an increased critical appreciation. One student even reflected that she had gained a better sense of what had influenced her own thinking about religion – a nuanced response. Several also commented on the idea that they felt they looked at religion more in-depth. This surprised me because I always feel that we gloss over so many things in an intro class. Finally, many mentioned they gained a new appreciation for religions that were previously foreign to them. This was gratifying to learn, for these points are fundamental in our field. (Jeanette Reedy Solano, California State University Fullerton, "Religion and the Quest for Meaning")

Faculty members' analysis of student learning relies on their evaluation of student work in exams, papers, and class contributions. Because the quality and types of student work were so varied, I made no independent analysis of the quality of student work. Brief examples within the case studies in the final chapters give some sense of the variety that occurred. This chapter turns next to student perceptions of their own learning.

What Students Thought They Learned

One-half to three-fourths of the students, in both the Database Group and the Highly-Effective Group, reported "substantial" or "exceptional" progress, on the IDEA survey (Appendix C), for goals that the instructors chose as essential or very important (Table 2.1).

About three-fourths of the students reported progress on the three goals of factual knowledge, principles, and values. About two-thirds reported progress on "analyzing and critically evaluating ideas." These percentages were roughly

Table 2.1 Students' self-reported "substantial" or "exceptional" progress on learning goals chosen by their instructor as "essential" or "important" on IDEA survey

Learning goals	Database group students (%)	Highly-effective group students (%)
Gaining factual knowledge (terminology, classification, methods, trends)	78	75
Learning fundamental principles, generalizations, or theories	74	74
Developing a clearer understanding of, and commitment to, personal values	74	83
Learning to *apply* course material (to improve thinking, problem solving, and decisions)	68	64
Learning to *analyze* and *critically evaluate ideas*, arguments, and points of view	68	66
Acquiring an interest in learning more by asking my own questions and seeking answers	64	65
Gaining a broader understanding and appreciation of intellectual/cultural activity (music, science, literature, etc.)	64	62
Developing skill in expressing myself orally or in writing	57	51

n = 467 Database classes; 53 Highly-Effective classes
The full IDEA survey is in Appendix C

the same for the Database Group and the Highly-Effective Group. The goal least well achieved according to students was oral and written expression.

Differences by institutional type

The Highly-Effective group's more extensive data reveal differences according to institutional type. Sample size makes comparisons among institutional types tenuous, but I undertake them here, with the same caveats as in chapter 1: other differences such as course title or disciplinary framework (theology or religious studies) undoubtedly also create differences in learning outcomes, but the purpose of this study is to present the general trends for all the classes as a group, to suggest those differences that follow lines of institutional type, and, above all, to urge faculty members to examine the learning outcomes for their own classes.

Table 2.2 shows the Highly-Effective group's student reports of their learning by institutional type. For reference, the table repeats earlier material on the

Table 2.2 Students in Highly-Effective courses reporting "substantial" or "exceptional" progress on IDEA learning objectives chosen as "essential" or "important" by their instructors

Learning goal	Religiously-affiliated courses(1) (%)	Public courses(2) (%)	Private non-sectarian courses(3) (%)
Gaining factual knowledge (terminology, classifications, methods, trends)			
Percent faculty choosing this goal as "essential" or "important"	87	91	75
Percent responding students reporting achieving "substantial" or "exceptional" progress on this goal	76	73	86
Learning fundamental principles, generalizations, or theories			
Percent faculty choosing this goal as "essential" or "important"	92	91	75
Percent responding students reporting achieving "substantial" or "exceptional" progress on this goal	81	63	78
Learning to apply course material (to improve thinking, problem solving, and decisions)			
Percent faculty choosing this goal as "essential" or "important"	76	73	100

Table 2.2 *Continued*

Learning goal	Religiously-affiliated courses(1) (%)	Public courses(2) (%)	Private non-sectarian courses(3) (%)
Percent responding students reporting achieving "substantial" or "exceptional" progress on this goal *Gaining a broader understanding and appreciation of intellectual/cultural activity (music, science, literature, etc.)*	65	56	71
Percent faculty choosing this goal as "essential" or "important"	50	91	75
Percent responding students reporting achieving "substantial" or "exceptional" progress on this goal *Developing skill in expressing myself orally or in writing*	61	63	62
Percent faculty choosing this goal as "essential" or "important"	76	73	100
Percent responding students reporting achieving "substantial" or "exceptional" progress on this goal *Developing a clearer understanding of, and commitment to, personal values*	55	32	58
Percent faculty choosing this goal as "essential" or "important"	74	18	50
Percent responding students reporting achieving "substantial" or "exceptional" progress on this goal *Learning to analyze and critically evaluate ideas, arguments, and points of view*	87	60	46
Percent faculty choosing this goal as "essential" or "important"	92	100	75
Percent responding students reporting achieving "substantial" or "exceptional" progress on this goal *Acquiring an interest in learning more by asking my own questions and seeking answers*	70	52	75
Percent faculty choosing this goal as "essential" or "important"	71	91	100
Percent responding students reporting achieving "substantial" or "exceptional" progress on this goal	69	49	72

[1]n = 38; [2]n = 11; [3]n = 4

proportions of faculty who chose the various goals as "essential" or "important" (see table 1.1), so the reader can gauge any disparities between the percentages of faculty who marked the goal important or essential, and the percentages of students who reported substantial or exceptional progress on it.

Table 2.2 suggests the following conclusions about the Highly-Effective classes where the IDEA survey was administered (because the number of private non-sectarian institutions in this sample is so small, these conclusions concern only religiously-affiliated and public institutions):

- *Students in religiously-affiliated institutions more frequently reported progress than students at public institutions.* This was true not only for values, but also for understanding principles, for oral/writing skills, and for every area I characterize under "critical thinking."
- *Nearly three-fourths of those at religiously-affiliated institutions and over half of those at public ones reported making substantial or exceptional progress in areas I term "critical thinking".*
- *In both public and religiously-affiliated institutions, students reported achieving substantial or exceptional progress on development of their own values more frequently than faculty chose it as a course goal.* This suggests that development of values takes place whether faculty list it as a formal course goal or not.
- *The goal that students most frequently reported achieving in religiously-affiliated institutions was development of personal values, followed by principles, facts, and critical analysis.*
- *Despite students' reports of learning critical thinking, they reported developing their values at an even higher rate.* Thus once again, the "great divide" appears. In chapter 1, the divide appeared between faculty goals and student *goals*. Now it appears between faculty goals and student reports of the *achievement* of goals. In both cases, faculty emphasize critical thinking, while students emphasize values and religious/spiritual development.

To show this disparity in starker relief, Table 2.3 shows the ranking of faculty *choices* of goals and students' report of their *achievement* of the goals. Table 2.3 uses the percentages in Table 2.2, but arranges the items in rank order, with "1" being the most frequent. The table illustrates that developing values was fourth most frequent in *faculty choice*, in both public and religiously affiliated institutions, but developing values was first in *student report of learning* at religiously-affiliated institutions and third in public universities. Learning to analyze and critically evaluate was first as a goal for faculty at both religiously-affiliated and public institutions, but it was fourth or fifth for student achievement.

The chapter turns next to the qualitative data to explore in more detail the students' developmental patterns throughout the course. This section focuses

Table 2.3 Frequency of faculty choices of goals as "essential/important" and student report of "substantial/exceptional" progress on goals

Learning objective	Religious		Public		Private non-sectarian:	
	Faculty choice	Student progress	Faculty choice	Student progress	Faculty choice	Student progress
Gaining factual knowledge (terminology, classification, methods, trends)	2nd	3rd	2nd	1st	2nd	1st
Learning fundamental principles, generalizations, or theories	1st	2nd	2nd	2nd	2nd	2nd
Developing a clearer understanding of, and commitment to, personal values	4th	1st	4th	3rd	3rd	8th
Learning to *apply* course material (to improve thinking, problem solving, and decisions)	3rd	6th	3rd	4th	1st	5th
Learning to *analyze* and *critically evaluate ideas*, arguments, and points of view.	1st	4th	1st	5th	2nd	3rd
Acquiring an interest in learning more by asking my own questions and seeking answers	5th	5th	2nd	6th	1st	4th
Gaining a broader understanding and appreciation of intellectual/cultural activity (music, science, literature, etc.)	6th	7th	2nd	2nd	2nd	6th
Developing skill in expressing myself orally or in writing	3rd	8th	3rd	7th	1st	7th

first on the Secure Christian students, who comprised 63 percent of the total students in the Highly-Effective classes; then students who self-identified as atheist, agnostic, or what I termed Doubting Christian; and finally self-professed adherents of other religions such as Buddhism, Judaism, or Islam.

Developmental Patterns of Secure Christian Students

Chapter 1 outlined the goals of Secure Christians in the Highly-Effective classes, and the ways in which they expected to meet potential challenges to their beliefs. Some planned to "keep the faith" through various strategies, and some expected to use critical thinking, though often in limited ways. Did these students meet their goals? Did they achieve other goals they did not expect? The question can be addressed through students' in-class anonymous written reflections (Appendix G). The reflections written on the very first day and then again by the same student toward the end of the course are especially helpful. These data exist for 25 classes at 24 institutions of all types. Beginning reflections were completed by 742 students (83 percent of those enrolled), and final reflections by 692 students (77 percent of those enrolled). Slightly over half of the reflections (467 reflections, 52 percent of those enrolled) were matched by the student with her or his first-day reflection. Thus they allow analysis of the changes that took place in the same student across time. Also useful for this purpose are those of the non-matched final reflections in which the student refers to his or her incoming goals.

I did code the matched reflections, but I did not calculate quantitative correlations between beginning goals and final results because the sample is fairly small for such correlations, and because each student typically reported multiple goals and multiple outcomes. In general, however, the data suggest that students' incoming goals did influence outcomes, but that some students developed in ways they did not expect. Some students who entered with the intention of "keeping the faith," not allowing the course to influence their beliefs, succeeded in doing so. Other students, however, opened the door to change. Students whose entering goals were for growth and exploration generally achieved those goals, though some of them were surprised or disappointed when they discovered what the course actually would do. All this variety and complexity suggest strongly that faculty are wise to pay close attention to students' goals and to conversation about goals early in the course.

Student development followed four patterns: keep the faith, struggle, surprise, and growth/critical thinking. The growth/critical thinking pattern was the most common. Many students reported development along multiple fronts. Though some students specifically mentioned developing critical thinking skills, so their remarks were coded in that category, it was clear to me from the data that all kinds of student development were influenced by students' encounter with faculty members' almost universal emphasis on what I have broadly called "critical thinking."

Growth/critical thinking

Contrary to some stereotypes, the introductory theology and religion course did not throw great numbers of its Secure Christian students into struggle and doubt about their faith. Nor did it leave them untouched. By far the most common response to the course, as the survey data summarized earlier also indicate, was a wide-ranging, often joyful exploration and change across multiple dimensions, including elements of critical thinking.

Attitudes: A basis for critical thinking

Students reported acquiring the attitudes mentioned in Chapter 1, which lead to critical thinking: 1) being open to change; 2) wanting to understand the opposing view; 3) wanting to "study it for myself;" and 4) wanting to ask questions.

Be more open-minded; understand other views

> This course has not affected my spiritual journey, but has made me more open-minded. This course has taught me to see other countries practicing Christianity and the differences and similarities portrayed in these countries to the US. This course has broadened some of my view with Christianity. I have always related Christianity with faith, I did not see Christianity in a political viewpoint like El Salvador, Rwanda, or South Africa did. (Public Masters, "Exploring Religion")

Becoming more "open-minded" was a common phrase among all students, no matter what their initial position. For some Christians, it meant becoming more tolerant, less judgmental of other points of view. Sometimes it meant also a wider recognition of the validity of other religions. These findings affirm the HERI Spirituality study results, that the first-year students they tested generally exhibited "a high level of religious tolerance and acceptance." For example, two-thirds of the HERI sample disagreed with the proposition that "people who don't believe in God will be punished" (2005, p. 4). A student from one of this study's religion courses reports achieving a non-judgmental stance.

> This course has helped me to be more open and understanding of other religions. It helped me to not judge religions until I have learned more

> about what they do and what they believe in. (Public Masters, "Exploring Religion")

Study for myself

Some students exhibited the typical movement of young adults from authority-bound positions, in which they depend on others to define their beliefs, toward claiming their own beliefs, and making their own decisions (Parks 2000).

> This course has challenged my beliefs. It has opened my mind to views I never even thought of or knew about. I know now that there is a great deal to learn and know about in order to develop my own views about theology. I cannot rely solely on what I learn at church and hear from other people. I need to develop my own thoughts and views through study. (Protestant Baccalaureate, "Christian Theology")

Ask questions

Some Christian students focused on the role of the course in raising questions about their beliefs, and seemed relatively comfortable about that process.

> The biggest thing this class has done for me is to challenge what I believe in and why. This class has put me on a mad quest to ask questions about Christian theology, questions I would have never asked if I did not take this class. This course has challenged my religious beliefs and the way I am dealing with it is by doing research on my own. (Protestant Baccalaureate, "Christian Theology")

> In the beginning of the course I wanted to strengthen my religious beliefs [Catholic]. I really don't know if that has happened. I think this class has raised more questions for my faith, but hopefully in the end it will strengthen my beliefs. (Public Masters, "Exploring Religion")

These attitudes are often found in the literature as characteristic of young adults as they reach beyond their childhood experiences. The attitudes are not by themselves critical thinking, but are important dispositions that set the stage for critical thinking.

Forms of critical thinking

In addition to these attitudinal changes important to critical thinking, some students mentioned specific critical thinking skills or activities, including the ability to read more deeply, to think critically about religion, to critically analyze, and to look for evidence. Chapter 1 noted that, at the beginning of the course, only a very few students mentioned any thinker or theological work that could help them integrate critical thinking with their own spiritual/religious journeys. Their papers, exams, and in-class reflections at the end of the course show a very different story, as students reflect on the works they have read.

Clarify my own beliefs

> As far as what has been most helpful about the class, writing my reactions to the various theologians helped clarify my beliefs, as did having those ideas exposed in front of the class and to the professor. (Private Non-sectarian Baccalaureate, "The Experience of God")

Read more deeply

> The skills I've gained are priceless – the most valuable one for me was learning to read objectively, and attempting to read without bias. (Protestant Baccalaureate, "Christianity and Religious Diversity")

> This class helped me to change my old way of thinking about scripture which was the simple idea of 1 + 2 = 3, just taking what was read literally, but now I look deeper into the scripture and look for a more meaningful and accurate understanding of the point being made in the scriptures. (Catholic Masters, "Introduction to Biblical Studies")

Think critically

> I have grown so much in this course! I knew I was capable of thinking critically about religion, as I have in my own Christianity.
>
> Through this course I have acquired the knowledge I need to think critically about the religious traditions of Judaism and Islam. Through this, though, I have gained better understanding of what my own beliefs are and where they overlap or contradict with Judaism and Islam. I did not expect at all to appreciate Islam as much as I now do because of this course. The principles that it was founded on, peace and social justice, fall in line almost exactly with my own life approach and have encouraged me to act to bring back and emulate the principles of social justice for all in Christianity, based on the example set by Christ.
>
> On my own, I was driven to look more closely at the person of Christ and what he did to help the poor and needy. I now hold dearly

> the messages of peace brought by Muhammad and Jesus Christ, but since I am Christian want to re-ignite those messages in Christianity and the world.
>
> My understanding of Islam was extremely limited [before] this course. I knew that I had relatives that were Muslim in Croatia a few generations back and remembered my mother crying at the news in 1995 when Croats and other ethnic groups of the former Yugoslavia were massacred. The course encouraged me to talk with my mother and grandmother about who in our family had been Muslim and I learned that my grandmother's grandparents were a Muslim and a Catholic and that Muslims in our family suffered long before they came to America. My study of Islam brought me closer to the story of my Muslim ancestors. (Protestant Baccalaureate, "Introduction to World Religions: The West [Judaism and Islam]")

Critically analyze, look for evidence

The "critical thinking" emphasis of the course often led students to report that they critically analyzed their beliefs, looking for evidence.

> I've learned from this class critical thinking skills and problem analysis and solving skills. Nothing was concluded in this class without strict thinking, evidence, and analysis. I can apply this in all other areas of my life, which helps my habits of mind. (Protestant Baccalaureate, "Introduction to the Bible")

The question whether, and in what ways, students progressed in their critical thinking, and in their ability to integrate critical thinking with their spiritual and religious development is complex. However, these data suggest that the majority of students in the Highly-Effective classes did make progress in these directions. A minority of students, however, followed paths that were more ambiguous.

Keep the faith

Chapter 1 noted that some Secure Christians expected to meet any challenge to their beliefs by "keeping the faith," through strategies such as compartmentalizing, relying on feelings, relying on the Bible and prayer, relying on family and church, sticking with their beliefs despite any ideas presented in dialogue, or trying to convert others. Some of these Secure Christians, at the end of the course, reported having carried out these strategies:

> No, this class has not affected my religious beliefs because I am not going to change my religion from a class. (Protestant Baccalaureate, "Introduction to World Religions: The West [Judaism and Islam]")

> I don't think the course has challenged my religious beliefs. I think after taking a few religious studies courses, I have conditioned myself to slightly separate what is discussed in these classes from my own religious life. It's not to say, however, that these courses are useless. I think they have raised difficult questions that cause me to think upon once in awhile, yet there are also questions I think that no person may be able to answer. (Public Masters, "Exploring Religion")

Struggle

Some Secure Christian students found that the course did influence them – it threw them into a state of anxiety or struggle. Some resolved the struggle by re-affirming their faith, using some of the same "keep the faith" strategies as those students who had never let the course influence their beliefs. Others took a position that "it's all a mystery we can never understand." Still others remained in struggle at the end of the course.

Reaffirm my faith

Some students reported struggle, but announced that they had worked their way through it. From the vantage-point of the literature on young adult development (e.g., Parks 2000), their answers and solutions may be temporary or tentative, as they move and change across their lifetimes. However, this group of students rarely acknowledged that their positions might be provisional. The need for certainty seems strong. In response to their struggle, they return to a re-affirmation of faith through several different mechanisms.

This first student has moved through a recognition of why atheists and agnostics think as they do, then through what Parks and others would term "radical relativism," accompanied by a sense of hopelessness, and then to a reaffirmation that "Christianity is the truth." The student does NOT claim that, *despite* the reasonableness of counter arguments, he/she chooses Christianity – a position that might move toward Perry's "Commitment in Relativism" (1998). Rather, the student seems only able to argue from the failure of the opposition's arguments. Christianity provides answers where others say answers cannot be found. Nonetheless, the student does not merely affirm his/her beliefs in the face of evidence; there is a reasoning process here, an attempt to deal with the opposing arguments.

> There was a time during the course of this semester where I was forced to question everything I had ever believed. I was unsure if Christianity was anything more than a manmade story. Dr.[professor's name] allowed me to see how many of the philosophers in history questioned in the same way. I began questioning everything I heard at church and analyzing it in the human perspective. At times I was overcome by a feeling of hopelessness and felt life was without meaning. This is what this class did. It made me see how atheists and agnostics could think how they do. Even further it made me see that every religion has as much reason to think they have it right as does any other religion. In the past 2 weeks, however, this class has reenergized my faith. Through continued learning about the thought of atheists I have seen where they have no answers. Their argument is incomplete, as much so, if not more so, than the Christian argument. Religion provides answers where agnostics say answers can't be found. This class has been hard on me emotionally. However, I am grateful I took it as I am confident I can stand before an atheist and proclaim my faith without feeling threatened. Christianity is the truth where other ones seem to want to ignore what they can't answer. I am a strong Christian today because of the knowledge I gained. (Protestant Baccalaureate, "History of Christian Thought")

Some students respond to information about the flaws in the church by affirming some overarching principle. This student uses a principle about "change" to accommodate new information about how much Christianity has changed over the years:

> This course did challenge my beliefs somewhat in that just how much Christianity has changed over the years. One likes to believe in the solidarity and steadfastness of their religion, but with Christianity that's just not so. At first, I thought that it was a reflection of flaws in the religion, but now I see that not only has Christianity changed, but society and culture have changed as well. Change is not necessarily a bad thing, it's just how we as people respond to change that can be bad. (Protestant Baccalaureate, "The History of Christian Thought")

Another student, faced with historical evidence of the church's flaws, fits that information into an overarching belief that humankind gives God a bad name, but God is not affected.

> This thing that I did when I stepped into this classroom on the first day, was to remember that this, although we will talk about God and his

> people, is not anything like a church or Bible Study. My beliefs have remained with me and are now strengthened, as they should be every day. This course has not challenged my religious beliefs in a way that I would consider threatening. I always knew that man had given God a bad name over and over again throughout history (crusades, etc.); but never thought that what man did, God's sinful creation, reflected on God and His holiness. (Public Masters, "Exploring Religion")

So far, students have based their reaffirmation of their faith on some kind of reasoning that deals with the opposing facts and arguments, even though their reasoning may be incomplete or unsophisticated. A more shaky ground is assumed by this student, who moves out of disillusionment with the church by arguing that the church has improved. The student's position is vulnerable to evidence that the church still does have significant flaws, but the student chooses not to consider that option.

> It was hard for me to accept that the Catholic Church did some pretty horrible things in the past. At first it made me skeptic to be such a devoted Catholic. I just could not believe that the church I was told to follow no matter what, could of done such horrible things and be just so utterly wrong. I am beginning to restore faith however and realizing that is not how the church is run anymore. (Catholic Masters, "The Christian Tradition")

Many reaffirming students do not achieve even the type of reasoning illustrated above, based on flaws in the opposition's arguments, on an overarching concept, on distinctions between the good nature of Christianity and the imperfection of human actions, or on a belief that the church has improved. Instead, they rely on a relationship with God; they simply assert their own beliefs and feelings despite any evidence or arguments they have encountered; or they stick to a position because it is too painful to give it up.

Rely on God

> In learning about how Christianity evolved, I have a greater understanding of the concepts of religion and find myself more critical of the established church. I find a lot of the history and decisions illogical and unfounded yet understand it in the time frame it occurred.
>
> It greatly increased my knowledge of the church's history, martyrs and theologians. I've accepted that I need to find my own personal relationship with God and pray to him to help enlighten me in His

ways. (Catholic Baccalaureate, "Introduction to Theology" [self-identified as wife, mother and nurse])

Believe despite evidence

[Day 1] I believe that the Bible is God's word to man. I believe that I can learn much from it, and to live my life by it is the only way to live. I believe in God. I believe that he is three persons in one – Father, Son, and Holy Spirit. I believe he has a purpose and a plan for each person on this earth. I believe that I was made to glorify him. My only goal, right now, is to become closer to God, to know Him more, and to become completely and totally dependent upon Him. I think that this course will help me to see God and the Bible in a new way and that will help me accomplish my goal. I think that this course may challenge my beliefs. I hope that I continue to trust in God, and believe that the struggle and the challenge are all a part of his plan to make me a better disciple of Christ.

[End] This course has helped me gain a plethora of knowledge about the Bible including its origins, history, reproduction, social and political context, authors. With this new knowledge my view of the Bible, at first, changed a lot. As I learned how it was written, who made it, and how it was put together, I began to have a conflict within my own mind about its authority. Because of the way it was made (orally then written) and the contested authorship and authority of the books, I began to doubt that it was still divine, God-breathed, and error-free. I did not know how I could know the facts of the Bible, such as these, and still take it at its word. As the semester progressed I still have no evidence that it is an authoritative book, but I believe that it is, because if the Bible is not true and real I have lived something that is not true for 18 years. Right now, I cannot accept that. The processes of thinking that our professor taught us were very helpful to my learning and development. Instead of giving us an answer when we asked a question, which frustrated many students, he helped us think about it on our own. I found that this helped me make connections within the text of the Bible and my own beliefs. [The professor] also helped me solidify my own thoughts by having us write various reflection papers. (Protestant Baccalaureate, "Introduction to the Bible")

I have learned a lot about religion in general. This course has reinforced to me the vast difference between religion and spirituality. However, this course seems to take the approach that religion is merely a

> construction of mankind. That may be true. But that being said, spirituality is different. At the core, there is still a God, who is at the center of my beliefs. This I know to be true, even if science attempts to explain him away. (Public Masters, "The Nature of Religion")

No answers; affirm mystery

Some students moved from a search for certainty to a greater realization of the complexity of issues and of life, realizing that perhaps "there aren't necessarily any answers," emphasizing the "mystery" of God, or discounting theologians.

> I still don't feel like I have grown spiritually to be able to more strongly defend my ideas. At the same time, I realize with this class that there aren't necessarily answers, and not knowing doesn't make my beliefs any less valid. (Private non-Sectarian Baccalaureate, "The Experience of God")

> I also have come to my own conclusion that most theologians are forever studying the Word trying to justify everything by relating various literature with present day objects. It's as if they think that they're on the same level as God. There are some things that will always be a mystery, and stupid Earthly interpretations will never come out correct. (Catholic Masters, "Introduction to the Christian Tradition")

> This class has turned my spiritual journey upside down. I came in thinking I was strong in my beliefs but after awhile I realized I didn't know what I believed in anymore. I had to start over, almost, and I went through a time of really questioning God, myself and the people who have taught me about God, including my Professor. I have grown closer to God through my questioning and praying about issues and if anything I have learned to accept that some things about Him will always be a mystery – and that's part of the beauty of Him. (Protestant Baccalaureate, "Christian Theology")

Frustrated with lack of answers

This student expresses frustration with being asked to move away from what the young adult development literature would call dualism and reliance on authority, toward greater independence.

> This course taught me the history of the Bible. I was supposed to learn a thought process that would help me look deeper than my questions; however, all this process did was frustrate me. There are times when I just need to know the answer, or an affirmation that my answer is right. At those times, I don't want to be asked another questions, have a discussion, and then leave the class still not knowing anything more than I did at the beginning. (Protestant Baccalaureate, "Introduction to the Bible")

Remain in struggle

Some Christian students at the end of the course continued to feel a sense of struggle, anxiety, or discomfort, a sense of disillusionment with their religion, the loss of old certainties, and/or a sense of alienation from their religious communities.

> My religious journey has just taken a sharp turn down a different path. I thought I knew where I was going but I was wrong. This class has caused me to ask more questions than I thought it would. I can also see how in the Bible it says to have fear in God – yeah, well I can now see that. I'm a little out of my comfort zone now. I'll need to look further into this now. (Protestant Baccalaureate, "Christianity and Religious Diversity")

> I hoped to have grown stronger and more faithful in my beliefs, but instead I feel as though I struggle with my religion. The purpose of the writings is to teach people how to live a righteous life, however the teachings convey a different side of Christianity or its previous ideas such as the acceptance of slavery and persecution of women or acceptance of more than one wife. That all these ideas once were taught as being OK scares me and makes me question more. (Catholic Masters, "Introduction to Biblical Studies")

Surprise

In addition to the two main positions described above – keep the faith and struggle – some Secure Christian students focused on their own surprise about the course content or approaches. Some embraced what they took to be the unexpected course goals and worked hard to accomplish those goals. Others remained disappointed or even angry.

Embrace new goals

[Day 1] I hope that this class increases my knowledge of other religions and also the one I have grown up with, Christianity. Learning about the ideas of God that others hold will help me develop my own ideas better. Hopefully, I will respect other ideas as much as others will respect mine. I have an open idea of what God is and the role of religion in my life. This class could help narrow down the exact ideas that I find true for myself. I don't like to know a little about a lot of religions and this class could give me a chance to know a lot more. Knowing more and deepening my beliefs and understandings of the world around me is very important to my "spiritual journey."

[Nov. 2] Now that I've spent considerable amounts of time in this class, I realize that it is not about the spiritual side of religion. I could spend years studying a religion and still not know why those members have faith, how they feel or how their feelings or emotions compare to mine. I have gained academic knowledge of other religions. Ethnography is a great skill to analyze that knowledge to understand part of the habits of those religious people. However, it is more important to me to know, understand how the deeper connections to the unseen, unstudyable work and happen. This type of knowledge, I now am sure, can never be learned or studied in a classroom. I've grown up with Christianity, but that is so vague that it doesn't really describe my feelings or practices. I wouldn't know how to describe my current religion/spiritual beliefs and I doubt anyone can very accurately. The goal of my journey is the same, to know more. This class has helped me, like any new experience would. The class has not challenged any beliefs that I have held, only because those deeper, immediate responses to new things are so trained and entrenched within me. This class has helped to shed light on some of my beliefs that I have never questioned – which is a bonus because I may have never known that I just took things for granted without knowing why. Maybe I'll never nail down my beliefs and maybe I will. The reason I took this class was to help understand myself through the understanding of how others operate. This has been successful. I hope all this rambling on helps. Why didn't the egg cross the road? Because it was a little chicken. (Public Masters, "The Nature of Religion")

I went into this course expecting to deepen my faith in my belief. However, that is not the way to look at it. As I have learned it is that what is said in the Bible is a template for our beliefs. The stories told

> are done so for some audience. You have to examine the world behind the text and the world of the text when interpreting the Bible. (Catholic Masters, "Introduction to Biblical Studies")

It is impossible to judge whether those students who modified their own original course goals to embrace those of the professor were taking a path that was good for them. They may simply be exhibiting a reliance on authority that is itself inimical to critical thinking. Or they may be "trying on" new modes in a fashion typical of young adults. Or the move to new goals may be a real opening for them into modes of thinking they have not before considered. Whether students adopt the faculty member's goals, or whether they resist and cling to their own, both deserve careful consideration by the faculty member, including issues of authority, power, and young adult development.

Disappointment with the course

A small number of students expressed disappointment that the course was not what they had wanted.

> [Day 1] I am a pastor's kid and have gone to the same Baptist church my whole life. My parents are very good at explaining the Bible and Christianity to me. I also want to know exactly what the Bible says about issues that society thinks nothing about, i.e., gay marriage, abortion, teen pregnancy, etc. I want to be able to decide for myself what I believe and really start developing my own faith instead of just believing something because my parents do. I hope this course does challenge what I believe because I need to be able to handle being challenged. I'm not very good at making decisions by myself, and I need to do that more often so I get used to it. I am excited about this class! [smile sign]
>
> [End]: The course has affected my development of knowledge, skills, and habits of mind. It has helped me learn more information, develop my critical thinking skills better, and shape my habits of mind. The course has not affected my religious beliefs or practices; I still believe the same as I did before taking the class – Jesus is the Son of God and the Savior of the world. This course didn't challenge my beliefs as much as I thought it might. I dealt with the small challenge by rereading the information. Talking about the study guide and taking quizzes helped me develop academically. Class discussions helped me broaden my views about certain aspects. I don't necessarily believe what someone else said, but I can see where they are coming from. I did not get as much out of this class as I had hoped I would. Maybe this is because

> I had the wrong expectations for this course. (Protestant Baccalaureate, "Introduction to the Bible")

> [Day 1] My hopes for this class include a desire to better understand the beliefs and attitudes of those around me. I want to have a greater world view, but my intent in this class is not academic, rather it is spiritual. I am a member of the United Pentecostal Church International (UPCI) and I hope to be better able to describe myself and my beliefs through a greater knowledge of those around me. I do not expect to have beliefs challenged at all, because I *know* what I believe to be *truth*.
>
> [End] This class has not challenged my beliefs at all. In truth, I have been quite disappointed by the class. I learned only basic facts about major religions. I really don't believe I learned a whole lot this semester. (Public Masters, "Religions of the World")

> The class really hasn't helped me with my own spiritual or religious journey. Even when we talked about Christianity, we didn't go into, I feel, the core principle and values of it. The small group discussions helped me learn the most because it was easier to portray my own personal feelings about the topic. (Catholic Masters, "Religions East and West")

These disaffected students are a minority, but their disappointment highlights tensions that most students reflect – how to integrate the academic content of the course and their teacher's emphasis on critical thinking with the goals they have for their own spiritual journey. The final student's statement that group discussions were most helpful because "it was easier to portray my own personal feelings" may indicate that, in fact, the small group discussions served mixed purposes, and may in some cases have been a protected space where students could return to modes of conversation about faith that were unaffected by the course material or by the critical thinking the faculty member was trying to teach.

In sum, most Secure Christian students reported joyful expansion and change. They did not appear anguished about challenges to their beliefs. They found new independence in their own religious choices, new open-mindedness about other beliefs and practices, new knowledge about themselves and their world, and new ability to think critically. Some students who had expected their beliefs to be challenged found that the course did not do so; instead, it taught them to think in new ways. However, some of the Secure Christians experienced struggle, which might persist throughout the course, or might be resolved by reaffirmation of faith. For this reaffirmation, they employed strategies such as compartmentalizing the course separate from belief; relying on prayer, the

Bible, church, or family; maintaining their faith through argument and reasoning against opposing viewpoints they met in the course; or simply reaffirming their faith despite any evidence. Some students were surprised by the course's content or approach; they either embraced the new goals or remained disappointed with the course.

Developmental Patterns of Agnostics/Atheists/Doubting Christians

Students who, at the beginning of the course, had self-described as agnostic, atheistic, or what I termed "doubting Christians" (see chapter 1 for definition) exhibited three different kinds of movement during the course: 1) growth; 2) skepticism; and 3) remaining unsure of what to believe.

Growth

As with other groups of students, the most common response of agnostics, atheists, and doubting Christians was a sense of growth and change, including joyful exploration and change, clarification of their beliefs, incorporation of aspects from other religions, or a new view of Christianity or religion in general:

Joyful exploration and change

> To begin with, it must be said that *all* of my expectations for this class were not only met, but also expanded . . . Because I am a mixture of Agnostic/vaguely Christian, this course didn't really challenge many of my beliefs. Rather, it helped me develop a better sense of myself and my spiritual standing. I identified with many of the aspects of both Islam and Judaism, and since I didn't have any rigid set of religious beliefs, it was easy for me to incorporate them into my own personal beliefs. As corny as it sounds, this class made me feel like a more intellectual and spiritual, if not just a better, person. (Protestant Baccalaureate, "Introduction to World Religions: The West [Judaism and Islam]")

Clarify my own beliefs

> [Student self-describes as "not anything in particular" and has lived and studied in Japan] I thought I don't have any religions on my own but I realized my thinking or the way I act are definitely influenced by Shinto and Japanese Buddhism. (Protestant Baccalaureate, "Religions of Asia")

Incorporate other religions

> I have my own religious beliefs based on what I have taken from many religions. A little agnostic in some areas, a little self as in Buddhism (breathe), a little nature as in Wiccan/Pagan. Even a little Christian from time to time. I was raised Catholic so I understand the Catholic ways too. I'm really interested in Buddhism/Hinduism and am hoping to include the deeper findings in my everyday life. (Catholic Masters, "Religions East and West")

New views of Christianity or religion

A number of agnostics, atheists, and doubting Christians gained a new respect for, or knowledge of, Christianity, or they learned to temper their earlier broadside criticisms.

> As an agnostic and a long-time questioner of the religion in which I was raised, my beliefs were challenged in this course. Although, when all is said and done, I'm still an agnostic, and I still feel deeply drawn toward spirituality without the clothing of organized religion. But, with the breadth of work we've read on understanding of God, particularly Buber, Niebuhr, McFague, and Keller, my conceptions of how God could interact in the world and how we might conceive of God have expanded greatly. Particularly, with the two female/feminist theologians we've read, I've found new ideas, metaphors, that help me clarify my thinking. I really appreciate that we've read McFague and Keller because in so much of the country right now, religion and paternalism/patriarchy/nationalism seem to be becoming ever more enmeshed. (Private Non-Sectarian Baccalaureate, "The Experience of God")

> I have reconsidered my religious beliefs immensely. I didn't really have a faith before this course, but now I understand what the Bible means and what is important to me in life. (Protestant Baccalaureate, "Introduction to Sacred Scripture")

Skepticism

Some students reported that their skepticism and relativism were affirmed by the course.

> Wow! This course has affected my spiritual and religious journey in a good way. Growing up in a Christian, Methodist household, I was

> always skeptical of the overall – sin and you go to hell – because we all sin. I didn't understand Jesus' role because there was life thousands of years before him, and how our "year" system started with Jesus. Anyway, this course was a validation for my skepticism of Jesus as the savior and how hypocritical many Christians are. This course has helped me to understand humans' capability of evil in light of their profound religious beliefs. I don't doubt Jesus, the premise behind Christianity or its intention, but I do doubt people, their words and how that contradicts their actions . . . This course has challenged me to face the reality of human violence toward people and their environment. Regardless to what religion they identify with. I absolutely love this teacher, this course, coming to class every day and being enlightened! (Public Masters, "Exploring Religion")

> It did not really challenge my beliefs but instead kind of supported my idea of there is no one religion that is right. (Protestant Baccalaureate, "Religions of Asia")

Still unsure

Some students who entered the course unsure of their beliefs left it still unsure, though most of them appreciated the new knowledge they had gained as well as recognizing that their journey is likely to be long and complex, and a single course is not going to solve everything.

> [Day 1] I am actually in an unsure state right now when it comes to religion and my beliefs. I attend a Methodist church on a weekly basis and it has become more habit than anything else. I believe in a supreme being but my beliefs stop there. I do hope this course will help me on my spiritual journey. While I do attend church, I even feel that I'm not Christian. Maybe deep down I may be. Guess we will see. As I said I hope this class will help me.
>
> [October 31] Currently I feel that I have learned a lot about religion in general from this course. The course has allowed [me] to look at it from an outside perspective. I have also dubbed this my "think outside of the box" class. Not much history has been covered but I think the class has focused more on the details and specifics of a religion more so than the history – even though some history has been covered.
>
> I do think my views of religion have changed while being in the class so far. I am still in my unsure state of what to believe but I do think this class has helped me there. Even if a little bit. I do in fact find the

class very interesting and look forward to the discussions. (Public Masters, "The Nature of Religion")

Developmental Patterns of Muslims, Buddhists, Jews, Others

Students who stated they were adherents of Islam, Buddhism, Judaism, Wiccan, or other traditions followed many of the same patterns as the group of Doubting Christians, Atheists, and Agnostics: most reported joyful exploration and change. Some clarified their own beliefs or came to understand other beliefs, including Christianity, in new ways. Some moved toward skepticism, relativism, or greater uncertainty about where they stood.

> I was truly fascinated by some other religious thoughts, such as Jainism, and Confucianism. Also, I could reflect on myself as a Buddhist through this course. (Protestant Baccalaureate, "Religions of Asia")

> I learned something about God as a possibility of his character that made me feel closer to him than any visit to church (mosque for me) ever could have. (Public Research, "Modern Christianities and World Cultures")

Conclusions: Student Learning

The classrooms in the study were energetic sites of movement and change, as students' desire to work on their own spiritual and religious development met faculty insistence on critical thinking. Patterns of student learning were enormously varied, including various strategies for "keeping the faith" apart from anything presented in the course, and including students' experiences of struggle and disappointment. Yet the strongest pattern was joyful growth, including growth in critical thinking. I think we can reasonably say that students, on the whole, emerge from the introductory theology / religion course as better critical thinkers and as more thoughtful, informed, and tolerant spiritual and religious persons than they were at the beginning.

This chapter's intent is not only to present the findings of the study, but also to suggest how faculty can evaluate the learning in their own classrooms, in order to choose the pedagogies that will be most effective. This process of analyzing a whole class's work is certainly based on the grading process, but it differs in two major ways:

1 Its purpose is to identify strengths and weaknesses in the learning of the class as a whole, not merely to determine what grade John or Juanita should get.

2 It seeks detailed modes of assessing student learning in various areas, not just overall grades. In other words, it seeks to say, not merely "students in this class received an average grade point of 3.2," but rather, "students in this class, as a whole, were strong in A and B, but weak in X and Y." The latter statement gives the teacher something specific to work on.

The faculty member can gather information about student learning in two ways:

1 Ask students what they thought they learned, and what pedagogical strategies helped them (Examples are the prompt used for this research [Appendix G] and Prof. Bateson's mid-term student self-evaluation in chapter 6). You need not ask students about their spiritual/religious development if you are uncomfortable doing so. It's enough to pose three questions:
   - List your course goals and ask students to indicate how well they believe they are reaching them.
   - Ask them to identify the pedagogical strategies that are most effective for their learning.
   - Ask them what strategies they believe would better help their learning.
2 Aggregate results from student work to identify class-wide strengths and weaknesses. One way to do this is through rubrics, about which I and Virginia Anderson have written elsewhere (Walvoord and Anderson 1998). Prof. Bhattacharyya's rubric in chapter 5 (Figure 5.1) is an example of one teacher's attempt to use the "rubric" format for systematic analysis of student work. Prof. Bateson's grading sheet in chapter 6 uses a somewhat different format.

Once the faculty member has a systematic, detailed understanding of strengths and weaknesses in student work, and of what students thought they learned and what they found most helpful, the faculty member is ready to think about the pedagogies that would result in highest learning in his/her particular classroom, given his/her own personal style. Pedagogies are discussed in the next chapter.

3

Pedagogies: What Influenced Student Learning?

Chapters so far have examined the learning goals of both teachers and students, as well as the kinds of student learning and development, both intellectual and spiritual/religious, that took place. The overall conclusion is that significant learning took place in the classrooms. The next question is, what pedagogical strategies appeared to influence these changes? This is the third step of the course planning/reviewing process this book models: 1) construct/evaluate faculty and student goals for learning; 2) construct/evaluate assignments and exams that will both teach and demonstrate achievement of the goals, and examine student work and student reflection to determine how well goals are being met; and 3) construct/evaluate the learning experiences that will most effectively nurture student achievement of the goals.

This chapter first summarizes existing literature on the pedagogical practices that best enhance student learning. Then it describes what each type of data revealed about the effectiveness of various pedagogies. Finally, the chapter boils all these different insights down into three principles of best practice for faculty teaching introductory theology and religion courses: caring, clarity, and conversation. The chapter ends by exploring how faculty constructed spaces and voices for students to integrate critical thinking with their own spiritual/religious development. This is a short chapter because it serves as a summary and overview; lengthy examples of its findings are provided by the case studies in the final three chapters.

Before beginning the analysis, however, it is important to acknowledge that the pedagogical practices, while important, are only part of the picture: learning is a creative interaction between teacher and student. As one faculty member in the study puts it: "When a class of mine works it works because I have taken the time to get to know the quality of my students' minds, and they were at a time in their life when it mattered to them to have someone take notice."

It is also important to acknowledge that "best practices" don't quite account for the ineffables of teaching. Another faculty member writes:

> In the end, I'm certain the researchers can find some "best practices" that, when applied, will impact classrooms positively. Even just by being able to articulate "creative pedagogies," "concern for students," and "commitment to relevancy," I am motivated to do my utmost to make it work, every time. My hunch remains, though, that there is something mysterious that pervades the classroom. The mystery remains out of our control, blessing when it blesses, and looking away when it looks away. When it blesses the classroom, I know magic can occur. I adored it when I experienced it as a student. And I cherish it when it happens as a teacher.

Review of the Literature

A number of researchers have identified pedagogical "best practices" in higher education. This section of the chapter summarizes the research, as a framework for the next section, which presents the findings of the present study.

A foundational, highly-regarded work on college outcomes and the factors that affect them is Pascarella and Terenzini's (2005) comprehensive review of research. Several findings are important:

- Student engagement – the time, effort, and attention students invest in the learning process – is the key to learning (pp. 602, 613). Thus pedagogies that promote engagement are most effective.
- Students change holistically. Their in-class and out-of-class lives are interconnected in complex ways (p. 603).
- Clarity, expressiveness, and organization/preparation are important teacher skills that can influence student learning (p. 646).
- Interaction with faculty and peers is an important factor for student development (p. 614).

- The dominant instructional paradigm, of which the lecture is the centerpiece, is effective in promoting knowledge acquisition and cognitive skill development. However, the most effective teaching and learning require active student involvement and participation. The best approach is to use a variety of approaches, "from teachers teaching students to students teaching and learning from other students, and students 'constructing' rather than receiving knowledge, with information technology and service experiences added to the mix . . . The evidence implies neither an instructional hierarchy [between lecture and other models] nor a need to replace one paradigm with another. Rather, researchers have turned the spotlight on ways to make the dominant model even more effective than it already is and have pointed out *additional approaches* to effective teaching and learning" (pp. 646–7).

An earlier research summary by Chickering and Gamson (1987, 1991), both well-known researchers, expressed many of the same themes in "Seven Principles of Good Practice in Undergraduate Education." Good practice:

1 encourages student–faculty contact;
2 encourages cooperation among students;
3 encourages active learning;
4 gives prompt feedback;
5 emphasizes time on task;
6 communicates high expectations; and
7 respects diverse talents and ways of learning.

Feldman (1996), in a review of the literature, compared the teacher qualities (as listed on student surveys) that correlated most strongly with: 1) student learning as measured externally; and 2) students' overall ratings of their teachers. The two lists contained 18 common dimensions of good teaching, which, on the basis of the correlations, Feldman (1996, p. 44) ranks as high, moderate, and low importance to both learning and student overall ratings. Those qualities with highest importance are:

- Teacher's preparation;
- Course organization;
- Teacher clarity and understandableness;
- Teacher's stimulation of students' interest; and
- Student-perceived outcome or impact.

Of moderate importance are:

- Teacher's elocutionary skill;
- Clarity of course objectives and requirements;
- Teacher's knowledge of subject; and
- Teacher's enthusiasm.

Working from different types of qualitative data, including systematic assessment of student memories, observation of exemplary professors, nomination letters for teaching awards, and students' ratings of the "best" and "worst" teachers they ever had, Joseph Lowman (1996, p. 38) proposes a two-dimensional model of effective teaching:

> Exemplary college teachers, then, appear to be those who are highly proficient in either one of two fundamental sets of skills: the ability to offer presentations in clearly organized and interesting ways or to relate to students in ways that communicate positive regard and motivate them to work hard to meet academic challenges. All [exemplary teachers] are probably at least completely competent in both sets of skills but outstanding in one, or, occasionally, even both of them.

Ken Bain (2004) used classroom videotaping and observation, interviews, review of course material, student work, and teacher reflections to study about 70 exemplary faculty in a variety of disciplines. He arranges his findings as answers to six questions:

1 *What do the best teachers know and understand?* Know their subjects, continue to learn, take a strong interest in the broader issues of their disciplines, and have at least an intuitive understanding of human learning. They "assume that learning has little meaning unless it produces a sustained and substantial influence on the way people think, act, and feel."
2 *How do they prepare to teach?* Begin with questions about student learning objectives rather than about what the teacher will do.
3 *What do they expect of their students?* "More." Also, "they avoid objectives that are arbitrarily tied to the course and favor those that embody the kind of thinking and acting expected for life."
4 *What do they do when they teach?* Methods vary, but teachers try to create a "natural critical learning environment" in which "people learn by confronting intriguing . . . authentic tasks that will challenge them to grapple with ideas, rethink their assumptions, and examine their mental models of reality. These are challenging yet supportive conditions in which learners feel a sense of control over their education; work collaboratively with others; believe that their work will be considered fairly and honestly; and try, fail, and receive

feedback . . . in advance of and separate from any summative judgment of their effort."

5 *How do they treat students?* Reflect a strong trust in students. Believe students want to learn. Often display "openness with students and may, from time to time, talk about their own intellectual journey . . . They often discuss openly and enthusiastically their own sense of awe and curiosity about life."
6 *How do they check their progress and evaluate their efforts?* They employ "some systematic program – some more elaborate than others – to assess their own efforts and to make appropriate changes."

General points:

- Faculty do not blame their students for any of the difficulties they face.
- Faculty "generally have a strong sense of commitment to the academic community . . . seeing their own efforts as part of a larger educational enterprise." (pp. 15–20)

The findings from the present study affirm the general trends in the teaching literature, but they make those findings specific to introductory religion and theology. Particularly useful is Lowman's point that effective teachers must be competent both in clarity and in relating to students, but may excel in one or the other; Pascarella and Terenzini's point that faculty may use a variety of methods including the lecture; and Bain's point that effective teachers use a variety of methods, but they all create a "natural critical learning environment." Those points help to explain why the group of 66 Highly-Effective faculty in this study use a wide variety of different methods, from lecture to small-group interaction, and why their classrooms are dynamic and compelling to their students.

The next section of this chapter outlines the findings from each of the various types of data that helped to elucidate effective teaching practices. The end of the chapter draws it all together into a set of principles and guidelines for teachers of introductory theology/religion.

Findings from Data

Five types of data were used in the present study to identify best pedagogical practices:

1 reflections by faculty about what they thought accounted for their effectiveness;
2 students' evaluations;

3 student survey item asking students to identify the most important quality of a teacher of introductory theology / religion;
4 students' anonymous in-class written reflections, several times during the course, on what actions by the teacher, classmates, or the student him/ herself most helped them learn, and what suggestions they would have for changes in the course; and
5 comparison of the pedagogical strategies of teachers with low IDEA scores and those with high IDEA scores.

None of these measures is perfect or complete, but together they suggest what might be the most effective pedagogical strategies for introductory theology / religion.

Faculty reflections

The first of the five data types is end-of-course prose reflections from the Highly-Effective faculty, who were asked, "What aspects of your philosophy, strategies, preparation, or style seem most fully to have accounted for your effectiveness as a teacher? What would you answer if someone said to you, 'You're respected as a highly effective teacher – what's the secret of your success?'" (See Appendix D). Faculty prose responses were coded. Care for students was by far the most frequent aspect, followed by organization / preparation and excitement about the material:

- care for students (80 percent);
- being excited / enthusiastic about the subject matter (29 percent); and
- being clear and well-organized (27 percent).

This overwhelming emphasis on care for students reveals, I think, what good teaching feels like from the faculty end – that their care for students informs everything else. The next four types of data all reflect student points of view, and focus on the behaviors of teachers that students can observe.

Correlations of IDEA student survey items

For students in both the Database and the Highly-Effective classes, the study correlated:

- IDEA survey question 41, which asks for level of agreement with the statement "Overall I rate this instructor an excellent teacher;" *with*

Table 3.1 Correlations between student ratings of teacher excellence and student-reported pedagogical practices in Database classrooms

Item	Correlation	*p* value
Explained course material clearly and concisely	0.892	<.0001
Introduced stimulating ideas about the subject	0.857	<.0001
Found ways to help the students answer their own questions	0.847	<.0001
Displayed a personal interest in students and their learning	0.845	<.0001
Made it clear how each topic fit into the course	0.841	<.0001
Demonstrated the importance and significance of the subject matter	0.808	<.0001
Explained the reasons for criticisms of students' academic performance	0.732	<.0001
Stimulated students to intellectual effort beyond that required by most courses	0.726	<.0001
Inspired students to set and achieve goals which really challenged them	0.715	<.0001
Gave tests, projects, etc. that covered the most important points of the course	0.695	<.0001

- students' reports of various pedagogies employed in the course (IDEA questions 1–20, 33–35 and 44–47 [Appendix C]).

Table 3.1 shows the most significant of these correlations, with the strongest at the top. The table gives the correlations for Database faculty; the correlations for Highly Effective faculty did not substantially differ.

The strongest correlations occurred for the teachers':

- explaining course material clearly;
- introducing stimulating ideas;
- helping students answer their own questions;
- displaying a personal interest in the students; and
- making clear how each topic fit into the course.

These findings correspond closely to the research literature summarized earlier. Notice that the items could fall into two groups, similar to Lowman's two points: 1) presenting material clearly and in an interesting way; and 2) communicating regard and care for students.

Student survey: Most important quality of teacher

Another type of data used to identify effective pedagogies was an end-of-course survey for students in Highly-Effective classes. The survey asked, "Which is the most important quality for a teacher of introductory theology or religion: 1) communicating enthusiasm for the subject matter and methods of the discipline; 2) being available to students for help; 3) being clear and well-organized in presenting the material and explaining expectations; 4) being nonjudgmental about students' beliefs and opinions" (Appendix D). Table 3.2 presents students' responses.

Clarity takes first place, followed by enthusiasm and being non-judgmental. Revealing one's own beliefs and being available for help are significantly lower. This finding is interesting because being nonjudgmental is higher than "being available to the students for help." Many students enter theology/religion courses with strong goals for their own spiritual and religious development. In some ways, they need the teacher to stay out of the way and let them wrestle. Some of the strongest student comments of disapprobation came from those few students in the Highly-Effective sample who believed (rightly or wrongly) that the teacher was imposing his/her own beliefs on them, and that students would be penalized for differing.

Student reflections: "What helped learning"

Another type of data is the anonymous prose reflections from 1,328 students in 48 Highly-Effective classes toward the end of the term. Students were asked

Table 3.2 Students' choice of "Most important quality for teacher of introductory theology/religion"

Item	Percent of total responses
Being clear and well-organized in presenting the material and explaining expectations	35
Communicating enthusiasm for the subject matter and the methods of the discipline	27
Being nonjudgmental about students' beliefs and opinions	26
Being willing to reveal his/her own religious and spiritual beliefs or struggles	8
Being available to students for help	4

n = 1,397 students in 51 Highly-Effective classes

Table 3.3 Pedagogical Strategies mentioned as enhancing learning, in student written reflections

Strategy	Percentage of students mentioning this item
Clarity	
Use of audio-visual/board	15
Powerpoint	12
Handouts, online material	12
Stories, examples relating material to the everyday, current events, teacher's own life	10
Presentations, lectures	9
Being clear	7
Total clarity	*65*
Conversation, discussion, interaction	
Discussion	30
Small-group work	9
Assignments, tests	9
Daily writing/quizzes	6
Study or review sessions	5
Openness and care by teacher	2
Total conversation	*61*
Other items	
Course readings	12
The topic of study	9

n = 1,328 students in 48 Highly-Effective classes. A single student reflection may be coded in several categories

what specific actions by the teacher, the student, or student peers had helped their learning and development and what actions might make the course more effective for their learning (Appendix G). Responses were coded. Table 3.3 shows a balance: 65 percent mentioned actions that enhanced clarity, and 61 percent mentioned actions that enhanced what I call "conversation" – interaction between student and teacher that forces the student to articulate what is being learned – including class discussion, small-group work, and assignments.

Again, the two-part model suggested by Lowman appears: ability to present material clearly and in an interesting way; and, second, communicating regard and caring to students, and engaging them in conversation with the teacher and peers, through classroom discussion and through assignments.

It is particularly important to notice that "discussion" is the single most frequent item mentioned by students as helpful to their learning. In their anonymous prose writings, students expressed over and over again that they wanted to talk, they wanted to hear other peoples' ideas, and they wanted a chance to express their own. Discussion was also cited by some students for helping them be clearer about the course material or about their own thoughts.

Yet not all highly-rated classes had discussion. There were four Highly-Effective classes in which no student mentioned discussion as an action that helped learning, and 6 classes in which less than 10 percent of the coded responses mentioned discussion. On the other hand, in one class, 80 percent of the students mentioned discussion as helping their learning. The next most frequent were 76 percent, 71 percent, and 62 percent. This wide range reinforces Lowman's notion that exemplary faculty may excel in different areas, and Bain's observation that exemplary teachers use a variety of methods but all create a natural critical learning environment.

A range of student responses also existed for teachers' Powerpoint presentations (also termed "slides" by students, and often made available online as well as in the classroom). In one class, 80 percent of the students praised the Powerpoints. The next-highest were 53 percent and 34 percent. The class whose students most highly praised the Powerpoint had only 20 student enrolled, though other high-Powerpoint classes had 45 and 58 respectively. Use of Powerpoint varied widely among the classes; in 33 classes, no student mentioned Powerpoint.

"Group activities" also varied widely. The three highest-scoring classes, where students most often mentioned group activities as helping their learning, had 71 percent, 50 percent, and 36 percent. These were all small classes of around 20 students, though some large classes also used group work that students found helpful. On the other hand, in 20 classes, no students mentioned group activities, and in an additional 14 classes, less than 10 percent did so.

Students reflections: "Suggestions for change"

In another type of data, the students from the first two terms of the study were asked what suggestions they had for what the teacher, the student him/herself, or fellow students could do to help the responding student learn more effectively. Many students left this question blank or wrote "no suggestions" or "the course is fine as it is." In every class, however, there was at least one student who made suggestions for change. When students did make suggestions, there was some difficulty interpreting them because some students appear to have misread the question to mean what DID the teacher do to improve learning,

Table 3.4 Students' most frequent suggestions for change

Item	Number of students suggesting this item	% of total suggestions*
More discussion	10	15
More/better student preparation for class	7	11
More student contribution to discussion	7	11
More clarity in lectures	5	8
Different topics; discuss other viewpoints, other religions; more hermeneutics; we run out of time to cover everything; we are a very liberal class, students and professors alike – at times I wish we were a bit more balanced. I think it would help us find a greater richness in the texts as well as helping to see their shortcomings.	4	6
Readings are too hard, we should go through them more in class; course moves too fast	4	5
More group assignments, group work	3	5

*Some students made more than one suggestion; n = 1,773 students, who made a total of 1,191 suggestions (some students made more than one suggestion, some made no suggestions)

rather than what COULD the teacher do. Also, some students responded in present tense rather than subjunctive, e.g. "Discussion is really helpful," making it difficult to determine whether the student was expressing appreciation or making a suggestion for more discussion. Nonetheless, I did code these responses to see what topics were most frequent, either as affirmation of what the teacher was doing or suggestions about what the teacher, the student, or fellow students could do. Results strongly affirm the importance that students place on discussion and on clarity (table 3.4).

Note the high emphasis on discussion, and on students' own preparation for discussion. A typical student comment:

> This course was very interesting because I thought that I would be really looking at other religions, but what I found was that I looked very critically at my own throughout the process. Learning about the other religions allowed me to look at what I believe and practice. I came to some realizations about both and I think that is what I will take most from the course. I think that the group discussions really

helped me, but it would help more if people had actually read the book and knew what we were discussing. (Catholic Masters, "Religions East and West")

Comparison of less-effective and more-effective teachers

The Database group was composed of teachers across a spectrum of teaching excellence; the Highly-Effective teachers were selected by their chairs and, for the most part, their excellence was affirmed by their IDEA scores, though there were a number of variables that made the comparison difficult. To find a single measure of "effectiveness" on which to rate all the teachers, the IDEA Center took all the faculty members who completed the IDEA survey, including all the Database faculty and 54 of the Highly-Effective faculty, and divided them by IDEA scores into top third, middle third, and bottom third, using a score that combined students' reported progress on objectives the instructor had marked "essential" (50 percent), plus the average of the teacher excellence and the course excellence scores (questions 41 and 42. See Appendix C). Among these three groups – top, middle, and bottom – there were no significant differences in the learning objectives teachers chose as "essential," or in student perceptions of the difficulty of the course or the amount of work assigned. So it's not being easy that accounts for student ratings of excellence.

A difference that seems important, however, is that, with one exception, for each of the 20 teaching methods students reported, instructors in the top third employed the method more frequently than the middle third, and the middle third more frequently than the bottom third. With one exception, the differences were always statistically significant between the top and bottom groups. A reasonable conclusion might be that teaching effectiveness has something to do with variety. It may be that the variety of teaching methods in the highly-effective group is a sign of faculty members' flexibility and their ability to choose among teaching methods depending on their goals and their students' needs. It's back to Bain's observation, again, that exemplary teachers use various methods to achieve a natural critical learning environment.

The one exception is students' report that the instructor "formed 'teams' or 'discussion groups' to facilitate learning." The middle third used the method most, with the top third and bottom third not significantly different from each other. The anomaly of the "group discussion" question is puzzling because "discussion" is so highly-praised and desired by students. It may be that the ambiguity on this one item in the IDEA results reflects the difficulty of doing discussion groups well, while maintaining students' perception of the "clarity" and "organization" that they also highly value.

Principles: Care, Clarity, Conversation

Taking together the insights offered by previous research and by this project, three principles emerge for enhancing learning and development in introductory theology and religion classes.

1 *Care* for oneself, for one's students, and for the subject matter;
2 *Clarity* in presenting the material and in communicating expectations; and
3 *Conversation*: opportunities for students to interact and be heard, whether it be through in-class discussion, writing, or out-of-class conversation.

The case studies in the chapters that follow will illustrate how the principles of caring, clarity, and conversation were instantiated by faculty with very different personal styles, backgrounds, course titles, teaching environments, and levels of student preparation and motivation.

This study has focused special attention on a particular aspect of the class "conversation" – the ways in which faculty create spaces and voices for students to integrate academic with spiritual/religious development. The next section of this chapter summarizes those findings from the data. The cases in the following chapters provide illustrations.

Integrating Critical Thinking and Spiritual Development

A significant theme in the qualitative data was the way in which faculty addressed the "Great Divide" – how they structured spaces and voices by which students could integrate critical thinking and their own spiritual development. The strong student emphasis on "discussion" was, I believe, an indication of their desire for these spaces and voices. The cases in the final three chapters will illustrate a variety of ways faculty structured these spaces and voices, but here I want to summarize.

Part of what faculty do is described by John K. Simmons (2006) in an article on "neutral enthusiasm." His starting point is that the spiritual concepts being studied "inherently inspire personal transformation." Thus students' identity formation and spiritual/religious development take place as a result of the *material itself*. Simmons advises letting the "content do the work." He writes, "Any boundary crossing between teaching about religion and spiritual guidance occurs in the minds of students as they align course content with their own quest for wholeness, meaning, and purpose in life" (p. 41).

However, the teacher's ways of structuring and using the material are also very important. Teaching at a public university, Simmons draws on principles of religious studies, including phenomenology, to suggest what he calls "neutral enthusiasm" on the part of the teacher, who does not advocate any given religion, but shows enthusiasm about the religions under study and about the religious explorations of the students. Simmons outlines six strategies that "have proven useful in allowing religious studies content to move freely across the supposed boundary between teaching about religion and spiritual guidance in the classroom" (p. 42):

1 "Power over Truth: concentrate on the impact of religious claims upon individuals and communities rather than on truth claims."
2 "Behavior before Belief: focus on what adherents do."
3 "Go Anthropological: . . . take a video camera . . . or take the students to visit religious sites."
4 "Welcome Opposing Viewpoints: via video or guest presentations, present opposing views and be 'enthusiastic' about student concerns and comments."
5 "Compare and Contrast Religious Phenomena: apply this classic religious studies technique."
6 "Remember, We Are the 'Liberal Arts': The way around the dilemmas of 'teaching spirituality' is to recognize the natural connection between religious studies and classic liberal arts themes. The liberal arts offer paradigms for human possibility. Religion embodies archetypal patterns of human personal and cultural self-maintenance and transformation. The liberal arts tell us about the interconnection of all human creative activity, be it art, philosophy, literature, or music. Religious Studies offers some of the most striking examples: religion providing patterns of cultural self-maintenance; spirituality engendering patterns of self-transformation. Asking a student to be cognizant of a spiritual dimension and its capacity to spark whole person identity formation is not the same as promoting a particular religious perspective, if the pedagogical effort is firmly grounded in *neutral enthusiasm*."

The qualitative data from the present study affirm the transforming power of the content of courses in theology and religious studies, and the role of the six strategies in helping to cross boundaries between teaching about religion and spiritual guidance. However, the data from this study *expand* Simmons' list of strategies in two ways. First, data from the present study emphasize the power of critical thinking. Students are not just learning "about religions," although they hold such knowledge as a frequent goal and find it useful; students are being taught *critical thinking strategies* that can serve as tools for religious and spiritual development. Thus critical thinking is itself a boundary-crossing device. Second, the application of course material and critical thinking to students' own lives need not take place solely in the student's own mind, and is not limited to the six strategies Simmons mentions. Much can be learned by using the framework of "spaces and voices" to understand how faculty support students' integration of intellectual and spiritual/religious growth.

Faculty in both religiously-affiliated and public or private non-sectarian institutions manage spaces and voices in various ways and in various combinations. What is common to them all is that the "pulpit," the "preacher," and the "evangelist" are not invited, nor is the "therapist." In some religiously-affiliated institutions, students are *invited* to consider adopting a particular stance as their own, but faculty express strong feelings that they should not *pressure* students to adopt a particular religious tradition or viewpoint. Thus faculty in all types of institutions felt able to use their own mix of the strategies listed below without crossing boundaries of church-state separation, or boundaries between inviting and pushing. The following is a summary of their strategies; the cases in the next chapters will provide examples.

Faculty follow these practices to create *spaces* and *voices*:

Spaces

The spaces should be safe:

- from teacher or classmate ridicule or denigration;
- from pressure to commit to a particular religious tradition; and
- from students' fear that it is wrong or dangerous to question religious beliefs.

They should provide a variety of settings for various kinds of interactions, both in and out of class:

- In class:
  - whole-class discussion;
  - small-group discussion;
  - student-led discussion; and
  - interaction with classroom visitors.
- Out of class:
  - email with professor and/or students;
  - bulletin board;
  - papers and comments;
  - office hour;
  - informal "coffee": teacher with individual students;
  - informal "coffee": teacher with groups of students; and
  - interaction with people on field trips or site visits.

Voices

The voices of students may articulate beliefs or suspend them:

- articulate one's own beliefs as:
  - *committed critical thinker*: stating one's own beliefs as arguments, and defending them;
  - *informant*: Stating one's own beliefs and practices as "informants" for ethnographic inquiry;
  - *friend/colleague*: revealing one's own beliefs/practices as self-revelation for purposes of mutual understanding, trust, respect, and friendship;
  - *analyst*: analyzing one's own beliefs and practices using categories such as symbol, ritual, etc.;
  - invited in some religiously-affiliated settings: *prayer, worship leader*; but
  - *not* invited in any setting: preacher; bigot who assumes s/he is right and everyone else is wrong; evangelist who tries to convert other students to a particular religious group.
- suspend one's own beliefs:
  - *listener*: hearing others' beliefs and arguments with an open mind;
  - *ethnographer*: finding out about others' beliefs and practices in order to understand, respect, and study them;
  - *devil's advocate*: critiquing one's own and others' arguments;
  - *experimenter*: trying out other positions/beliefs/practices;
  - *seeker:* asking questions;
  - *teacher/facilitator*: facilitating dialogue; but
  - *not* invited: the dutiful student who only complies with requirements; the student who withholds engagement and treats the class merely as an exercise to be completed.

Not all faculty will use all spaces and voices in the same way, and there is no "magic" method, but thoughtful attention to spaces and voices can result in a combination that maximizes the kinds of learning and development that both faculty and students desire. Case studies in the next three chapters will illustrate.

How to Use the Case Studies

The final chapters present case studies from a variety of class sizes and course titles. Each case is arranged in the same sequence: goals, assignments, evidence of what was learned, pedagogical strategies, and then student evaluations. This sequence illustrates a model that any faculty member can use to systematically observe and reflect on his/her classroom.

I have not organized the cases to support a single thesis, but have tried to leave the cases open for various interpretations and uses by the reader. I have, however, paid attention in these cases to several questions or themes:

1 *Goals*: how do faculty and student goals compare?
2 *Evidence of learning*: Do the assignments and exams elicit student work that achieves the learning goals? What do students think they learned?
3 *Pedagogies*:
   - How do pedagogies work to achieve the goals?
   - How does each class instantiate the principles of care, clarity, and conversation?
   - What spaces and voices do students and faculty construct for conversation that integrates critical thinking with religious/spiritual development?
   - What workload issues are involved in faculty pedagogical choices?

4

Case Studies: Large Classes

The case studies in this chapter present three public university faculty members from the Highly-Effective group, who teach some version of world religions to large classes (most of the classes in the Highly-Effective group that enrolled more than 45 students were in public institutions). Faculty are named here either with pseudonyms or with their real names. I chose these cases because they represent quite different approaches and styles. Each case is arranged in the same basic sequence: goals, assignments/exams, and pedagogies. The end of chapter 3 discusses the questions that drive all the case studies in chapters 4, 5 and 6.

Care for Students: The Starting Point

Care for students is the starting point for all the Highly-Effective faculty. For example, the journal of the first case, Prof. Northway, recounts that, when he had to prepare for the first time to teach this course in world religions, he realized how difficult it is to master a large body of new information so that it is "organic" to one's own mind. And if such a task is difficult for him, then how much more difficult for his students, many of whom have never before left their small towns in this rural state. He asks himself "what to present that will really cause them to think, but not run away in fear? How to approach concepts and terms, doctrines, and cultural ideas so foreign that it could easily make no sense? I found that my methodological starting point was actually not the information itself, but the student's own psychological well-being."

Professor Northway

"World Religions," Public Doctoral University, 100 Students, One Teaching Assistant

Course goals

The course goals of students in the class of Prof. Eric Northway [his real name] at Iowa State University are very typical for students in the study as a whole: students most frequently marked "understand and appreciate a variety of religious beliefs and practices" (70 percent) and "acquire a body of knowledge" (70 percent). Only 55 percent of the students marked "develop general intellectual skills such as analyzing, evaluating, and synthesizing." But even though this is a public university and the faculty member's goals say nothing about the student's own values or religious/spiritual development, half the students marked "develop my own moral and ethical values," and 44 percent marked "develop my own religious beliefs and/or spiritual practices" and "take action for a better world." The "great divide" is certainly present here.

Northway's goals are somewhat different. He wants students to realize "that religion is not necessarily a theistic concept; that there are organizing principles for analyzing religion (e.g., all are syncretistic); that the goals of each of the major traditions are, on some very basic level, similar (e.g., answering life's deepest questions, giving hope, cultural hegemony, etc.); and last, that there are differences between the traditions that need to be understood so that whether one may accept or reject the religion, he or she can nevertheless stand back from it and empathize with its practitioners." He explains his pedagogical choices as ways to achieve these goals – a common pattern of thinking among the Highly-Effective faculty.

The voice Northway envisions for the student is the critical thinker. In this class, that means one who can use tools to analyze religion, and who also "understands" certain principles about religions in general – their organizing principles, their similarities and differences. The critical thinker "stands back from a religion" with "empathy." The relationship between recognizing/standing back/empathizing and accepting/rejecting is left to the student – a common trait in goal statements.

Yet despite the "great divide" and the privileging of the student's voice as critical thinker, Prof. Northway, like most of the Highly-Effective faculty, creates spaces and voices for students to integrate critical thinking with their own religious and spiritual development. His assignments are one such strategy.

Assignments: What was learned

Mid-term and final exam: Multiple-choice

Mid-term and final exams are multiple-choice. Two points about them are important here: first, they address clarity issues, which are always important to students. Students often express appreciation that Northway distributes a study guide before the tests, and relates the test to the course material: "There are lots of notes [Powerpoint slides] that he puts up, and all of the information he shows ends up being on the test. He's a very good teacher." In all the classes, it's not so much the multiple-choice or essay format *per se* that students care about; it's the fit they perceive between what is taught and what is tested, and the teacher's care to help students study appropriately. The student voice concentrates on mastering the material.The clarity principle is important.

The second point is that Northway's multiple-choice exams are time-efficient, and they can help ensure acquisition of facts and principles, but they may convey to students a message that facts and principles are the most important. Though Northway intends the facts and principles to support his critical thinking goals, it may be tempting for students to adopt the dutiful memorizer voice. Other cases will illustrate different ways of ensuring factual mastery and different uses of the student performances that are named "mid-term exam" and "final exam."

Student journals

Northway uses an open-ended, flexible genre – the "journal" – as a space for student reflection that can include their own religious and spiritual thoughts, as well as encourage reading and class attendance. Students are asked to produce a one page "journal" entry for two of the three class sessions each week. Note how the journals are tied to class sessions – a tactic that helps ensure class preparation and invites the inclusion in the journal of specific class material, not just free-floating rumination or autobiography. Journals are collected periodically, marked check/check-minus/zero, and returned, but with minimal comments – perhaps a phrase or sentence for every few entries. The writing of the journals itself is the main vehicle for learning, not faculty or TA feedback on them. This is a way of structuring a great deal of student writing without huge amounts of paper grading. We will see other instructors who use the journals or similar writings more fully as modes of two-way dialogue with students or as multiple-level dialogue among students – with the ensuing paper load issues.

Instructions for journals

Because the word "journal" may mean so many things to students and may evoke many voices, instructions are critical. Northway's instructions emphasize several of his course goals. He steers students away from mere summary or mere emoting, towards making the course material "organic," integrating thought and feeling, differentiating between empathy and agreement with another point of view, and achieving "meta-thinking." The voice of the student in the journal is the "meta-thinker" who integrates thought and feeling asking, as Northway has urged them, "why?" and then "why?" again. These are his instructions to students:

> The journal should be a record of those things in the readings or lectures that you find stimulating, eye opening, beneficial, disconcerting, scary, etc. This is meant to be an organic exercise – in other words, the journal is there for you to record not only what you have learned and think you "know," but also how you "feel" about the material. As you work on your entries try to think holistically, and across the mental boundaries that condition your own thoughts, ideas, and feelings. Ask yourself why you think and feel the way you do about the topic(s) that you are considering. When you have recorded your answers to those questions, again ask yourself why you think and feel the way you do about the answers you have just recorded, and write that down too. This is what is known as meta-thinking – asking why, why, why, about why you think the way you do. Performing this exercise (if you are introspective and honest with yourself) will be extremely difficult, but also extremely beneficial, as it will allow you to empathize (though not necessarily agree) with those who think differently about religion than you yourself do.

Students do not complain about the journals nor about the amount of feedback. Several write that they appreciate the role of the journals: "One thing that has helped me is keeping the journal we have to write about. I don't always like to write in it, but in the long run it has helped."

Student voices in the journals

Student voices in the journals reflect several kinds of thinking, as students attempt to integrate the class material with their own religious and spiritual development.

- *Analysis of the influences, purposes, and implication of religious beliefs/narratives*: "I didn't expect the birth of Siddhartha to be so unbelievable, mainly because all of his teachings are fairly down to earth: life is suffering; suffering is caused by desire, etc. I suppose the birth of Siddhartha is so miraculous to emphasize that he is special." [Prof writes "Yep."]

- *Reasoning about categories*: "When we were talking about if brushing your teeth is a religious act, it surprised me, because brushing your teeth carries no real spiritual connection to anything. We brush our teeth to keep them healthy, clean, and to get rid of bad breath. It has absolutely nothing to do with religion . . . A religious act is one where a feeling or emotion is connected to the act as well as a level of spirituality and understanding . . . Religious acts are ones where they have a certain level of tradition tied in with a level of faith. You don't need a whole lot of faith to brush your teeth. You may trust that the tooth brush and tooth paste you are using are getting the job done, but it is not the same kind of faith that you have for the God or gods that you believe in religion. The God or gods in religion are there for you whenever you need them, they are your strength when all else is gone, a tooth brush is just a tool that helps you with one task . . . when you are brushing your teeth you are doing it for health and hygiene reasons, when you are involved in a religious act, you are doing it for spiritual understanding." [Prof. writes, "How about the 'Zen tea masters' – is making and drinking tea a religious act then?"]
- *Questioning and musing on confusing points*: "The four passing sights are a little strange to me, I understand the first three and how they would have affected him [Siddhartha] if he had never seen suffering, because the old man shows suffering because of his age, the sick man shows suffering because of his illness, and the dead man shows suffering because it proves that life is not eternal, but the holy man chooses to suffer through his ascetic lifestyle and I don't quite understand how seeing the holy man affects him greatly, unless it affects him to see that kind of spirituality and hope in a person."
- *Personal feelings and preferences*: "I am so used to reading about eastern religions like Hinduism or Buddhism, that reading about Judaism seems really foreign to me. I think I like eastern religions better because they are more open minded to me."
- *Wrestling with students' own religion*: "During the lecture over Zoroastrianism, I found myself kind of disturbed that there are so many obvious similarities between Zoroastrianism and Christianity. I think that what is even more disturbing is the fact that Zoroastrianism preceded Christianity, which pretty much means that Christians either derived from the former religion or they just borrowed some of their concepts. Either way, Christianity is discredited and one is made to feel more skeptical about the religion. Of course, a person of strong Christian faith would have the piety not to let other religions discourage his/her beliefs and would stand firm in his/her faith."

Responding to the journals

Responding to journals can take two forms, not mutually exclusive: judgment and dialogue. Northway's interlinear comments, as in the examples above, illustrate dialogue: he will raise counter-arguments (What about the Zen tea masters?) or agree with a hypothesis (Yep), but does not correct grammar or urge tighter argumentation. He generally does not respond at all to the students' musings about their own religious beliefs. Thus the journal is a relatively free space for students to explore ideas without being afraid of line-by-line critique or judgments upon their musings. The judgment aspect is reserved for the journals as a whole: check, check-plus, and zero, so students have a goal to work for and an indication of the overall quality. Some faculty members make no judgments about journals except that they were submitted and perhaps had a certain length. Others extend the evaluative mode into the lines of the journal by, for example, a star or check or "good" next to passages that demonstrate the kinds of thinking they value, or a comment that urges students to move toward some form of critical thinking ("Can you support this claim?")

Northway reads the journals himself so he stays in touch with what students are thinking. Another mode is to have the TAs read the journals. If TAs are meeting with the students in small discussion sessions, they become the ones who talk with students more informally and are close to students' thoughts and feelings – a model that other cases will illustrate.

So far, then, Northway's case has illustrated the use of multiple-choice exams with their time-efficiency, but also their potential to send a message that facts are the most important. Northway's exams fulfill a key function of any exam, multiple-choice or not, in students' minds: the exam is related closely to what is covered in the course. Northway's journals provide a non-judgmental space for students to integrate class discussion and their own religious and spiritual development without heavy judgments from the teacher.

Group essay: Religious influences in The Matrix

Exams and journals provide two spaces for quite different student voices. A group essay provides yet a different space. Groups of six to nine students each write an essay of ten or more pages, analyzing religious influences on the film *The Matrix.* Students are expected to cite critical material about the film.

Ensuring equal contribution to the group

As part of the assignment, each student rates him/herself on a scale of one to five, on "attended group sessions," "prepared materials," "demonstrated voluntary cooperation," and "overall evaluation." Each student also signs the portion of the group report that he or she writes, though a single grade is given to the project as a whole. Prof. Northway thus allows for both individual and group accountability.

Instructor response to the essay

Instructor comments consist of a few sentences at the end of the essay. Once again, doing the essay, including the peer interaction, is the primary vehicle of learning, not detailed instructor feedback.

Quality of student work on the Matrix essay

Examples of good and mediocre work from these essays follow. An essay that gets a high grade includes sections (each written by a different student) first on the presence of influences from various religions the class has studied (e.g., Hindu, Buddhist); then a section on Christian religious influences; and then sections on religious symbolism, myth, redemption and sacrifice, ritual, and dualism (including Mind-Body, Eschatological, and Epistemological). Sample paragraph:

> Trinity is another distinct character in this movie, but unlike the other characters in the movie it is much more difficult to decipher. The word trinity is not actually used in the Bible but is still part of the Christian dialect referring to the Father, the Son and the Holy Spirit. Although the name Trinity is used it is more likely that this character represents Mary Magdalene. Trinity is the first to see Neo after resurrection just as Mary was the first to see Jesus after his resurrection. Also, just as Mary washed Jesus' feet with her hair Trinity uses a cloth to wipe the brow of Neo. In *Taking the Red Pill*, by Glen Yeffeth he refers to Trinity as the "mixed bag of subtle biblical references," stating that although Trinity has no distinct character similarities, she does have obvious biblical references, but not to one distinct person [footnote].

A less successful student essay is criticized for its internal repetition and failure to integrate critical literature throughout. In this sample paragraph, note how the student repeats vague generalities:

> The character Trinity also has many ties to Christianity. The father, the Son, and the Holy Spirit is often referred to as the Trinity, and the union between them. In *The Matrix*, Morpheus is supposed to represent

> the Father, Neo is to represent the Son, and Trinity is to represent the Holy Spirit. This creates a link and a balance between the three characters. Here, it is evident that the character Trinity is very closely tied to the Bible in Christianity.

Whereas the journals reflect a range of voices, including the questioner and the believer, formal student voices in this written project are religious studies scholars, applying analytic categories to a cultural artifact. It is likely, however, that in the group meetings, where students develop the report, students share more personal responses to the work, using the voices of friends and colleagues who share their religious thoughts and feelings to build trust and understanding. Students report liking this project because it provides for peer interaction and it brings home to them the ubiquity of religious elements: "Even though I am a huge *Matrix* fanatic and have seen all three movies several, several times, I have never really thought of *The Matrix* as a religious movie until [this class] . . . It completely blew my mind how many different religious philosophies contributed to the making of *The Matrix*."

Readings

Northway uses Michael Molloy's *Experiencing the World's Religions: Tradition, Challenge, and Change*, 2nd edn. (Mountain View, CA: Mayfield, 2002); James Fieser and John Powers, eds., *Scriptures of the World's Religions* (New York: McGraw Hill, 1998); and three works of literature: Herman Hesse, *Siddhartha* (New York: Bantam, 1971); Benjamin Hoff, *The Tao of Pooh* (New York and London: Penguin Books, 1983), and Norman MacLean, *A River Runs Through It and Other Stories* (Chicago and London: University of Chicago Press, 2001). This reading list reflects the integration of story, of narrative – an important theme in Northway's course and in the courses of other Highly-Effective faculty.

In all, he assigns more than 1,000 pages of reading – higher than the average for Highly-Effective classes – yet his students' reports of the course difficulty and how hard they worked (IDEA questions 35 and 37, Appendix C) are lower than the average in the IDEA database. This may occur because students are not doing all the reading (a common problem mentioned by most teachers in the study), because of the nature of his exams and assignments, or for some other reason not discernible in these data. On the end-of-course discipline-specific survey (Appendix D), when students were asked how often they "came to class without completing readings or assignments," only 23 percent said "hardly ever" or "occasionally," came unprepared, compared to 45 percent for public universities as a whole. Those who "frequently" or "almost always" came to class without completing readings or assignments comprised 38 percent, vs.

31 percent for publics as a whole. In other words, Northway's class has a lower than average rate of student preparedness for class. This raises the question every teacher faces: how important is daily student preparation to the way this course operates? What steps are appropriate for the faculty member to ensure daily preparation? One of students' most frequent comments about improvements, across all classes, is that they wish their fellow students (or urge themselves) to be better prepared. Whether they have read the assignment when they speak in class impacts greatly the voices they can adopt. A faculty member may choose not to take certain forceful steps such as daily quizzes, in favor of a format that is not so demanding on teacher time or that leaves more room for reflection over time and for student responsibility to do the reading. This difficult issue of student preparation appears again and again in the Highly-Effective group, as faculty struggle with ensuring student preparation while keeping the paper load reasonable and maintaining their own comfort level about the balance between external accountability and internal self-responsibility for their students.

Use of class time

A third forum for students to integrate course emphasis on critical thinking with their own religious and spiritual development is the class itself which, though it has 100 students, still manages to incorporate several kinds of student voices. Northway's class meets three times a week for a 17-week semester. The Graduate TA grades papers but does not meet discussion sections.

Northway's main use of class time, he reports, is lecture, based on Powerpoint slides (50–75 percent of the time), interspersed with video clips, interactive lectures, and small group work. Student comments indicate how he makes connections: between new and old material, between his intellect and his own passion, between himself and the students, and between facts and "meta-thinking":

- The teacher's excitement and passion for the subject really intrigued everyone in the class. He was so glad to be telling us this, you couldn't help but want to learn it.
- He always answers questions and makes connections between new material and old.
- He interacts with the group, asks us if we get it.
- He kind of tells a story when he teaches and that makes it easier to understand and more interesting.
- I like the Powerpoint presentations with maps and pictures.
- Teaching like Socrates: making us meta-think and ask "Why?"

Beginning the course

The conduct of class sessions, as reflected in Northway's journal, shows how he provides spaces for students to make connections. Northway begins on the second class day (the first is devoted to going over the syllabus), with students' own definitions of "religion," which, as he writes in his reflection, "sets the stage for them to speak throughout the rest of the semester as well – it lets them know that they can. But, in allowing them to define religion, the majority of the class sees that, to a greater or lesser degree, they view 'religion' as essentially synonymous with 'Christianity.'" Then he puts definitions by Marx, Nietzsche, Jung, Durkheim, and others, on an overhead and "we tear the definitions apart. We try to get at what the authors' presuppositions may or may not be. I try to get the students to realize that they themselves have presuppositions as well." This exercise helps to combat the "silent" voice of the student; it brings multiple voices (Marx, Nietzsche) into the classroom; and it helps the students adopt two voices: the reporters of their own current beliefs (the "informant"), and then the critical thinker, capable of "tearing apart" definitions. Student journals, which, as we saw, are tied to class sessions, allow the voice of the believer but also of the critical thinker:

> The topic today was actually interesting. I never really thought about what religion was. Everyone had their own idea . . . even famous philosophers and other famous thinkers . . . To me religion means God, Jesus, and faith. To some great thinkers such as West Cornell, religion is just a tool people use to die comfortably. To Malinowski, religion is a tool to bring a community together. These views really interested me. I really would've never thought about religion that way, but as a Catholic I really can't accept them. These views really raise the question, is this all my religion really is. Some guy could've just made religion up just to unite a community back then.

Northway's journals, tied as they are to the class session, and written twice a week, are vehicles to extend the classroom conversation into the student's own religious and spiritual lives. Because the journals have only minimal comment by the instructor, they operate as free spaces; yet they also represent the end of the conversational loop – the professor responds only lightly to their content. Later case studies illustrate how a faculty member can change the nature of the conversation by her or his more extensive response to student writing and perhaps by creating spaces where students again respond.

After the first two days, Northway uses class time to move through various religions, one by one, focusing, in each, on aspects named in the syllabus: "myth, belief, rites and rituals, symbolics (including art, iconography, and architecture), values and mores, and social appropriation of religion within varying contexts." To achieve his goals, he writes, "I purposely chose information that was general (historical, doctrinal, etc.), but interspersed it with provocative tidbits (the generative forces of Hindu gods and goddesses, for example)."

The sequence of religions is not random; there is a sequence of concepts and of students' development. He begins with a discussion of "historical and ritual practices that are part of indigenous cultures, but at the same time trying to connect these ideas and practices to more 'advanced' religions. In other words, I wanted the students to realize that 'primitive' is not so 'primitive,' as most of the ideas, concepts, and practices found in these religions are also found in the 'more advanced' religions. This arrow seems to have found its mark, because they began questions relating these practices to their own." In this class, students' own religious beliefs are on the table in the classroom itself, as students adopt the voices of believers, as well as critical thinkers. The technique of comparison, which Simmons mentions as a strategy for "neutral enthusiasm" (see p. 94) is central to this discussion; it keeps Northway from passing judgment, yet allows the students' own beliefs to be explored. Next, Northway discusses Shintoism as an "indigenous tradition," and then moves in week 3 to Hinduism – its historical background, texts, and some doctrinal ideas.

His journal focuses on how all this is affecting the students: "It's a lot to unleash on 18 year olds, many of whom have never heard of anything but a very particular form of Christianity as it is mediated to them via family and small farm community. They panicked today, as they always do. However, I reassured them that we would get through it – and they needed to think organically about most of it." In the fourth week, he moves into the caste system. "I had them read bits from the Bhagavad-Gita and we discussed it in class. The simple goal was to get them to realize how religion and culture are constantly in a dialectic relationship. Culture informs (and justifies) religious practice and vice-versa, even when we think one has no bearing on the other. It generated fantastic discussion – for many of them, because the majority are small town kids who are also fiercely religiously independent; they believe that there is a real wall of separation between church/state, or personal/public life, etc. The Bhagavad-Gita gets them to realize, as it did today, that often religion is used to justify social practices, norms, and mores. This was a great day!"

The journals work in tandem with the class sessions to allow students to reflect further in private on what some of them have said in class discussion. Sample student journals for this day reinforce Northway's perception of how difficult the concepts of religion and culture are for his students.

- *Confusion*: "The untouchables described in the book were people who remind me of modern day custodial workers; what I don't understand fully are why these people were looked at so poorly."
- *Judgments about the unfairness of the caste system, as compared to the student's understanding of American meritocracy, individual self-improvement, and Catholic doctrine*: "It doesn't make sense why people can just be born and their lives are privileged and others aren't . . . In the Catholic religion, if your whole family were wealthy, people would say your family is blessed. This means God enabled it to be that way. It's part of his plan to bring everyone together. Buddhist religions would probably say you were probably good in your past life, but this Hindu religion just doesn't seem right. How can you live a happy life thinking being a slave or servant will be your role forever? I wouldn't be able to accept that."
- *Juxtaposition of class material and student's moral absolutes*: "I think that it is interesting and also a little odd how religions are always influenced by foreign invaders and rulers. In some ways I can completely understand how and why religions obtain certain characteristics from their present rulers or other highly influential people, as it is in the nature of man to learn from others to better themselves. But on the other hand, I almost don't think that it is right for a religious group to bend and change with the times. I think that if God sent his prophets and son to teach a certain belief a set of rules, then such teachings should be followed exactly how God represented them. It isn't right to alter such philosophies and practices just because another group presents them to you in a new and different way, which may seem more appealing."

This student's journal reveals two worlds – the world of evidence about cultural impact on religion, and the world of the student's religious belief. Many faculty in the study, even those in religiously-based institutions, would not try to suggest how this paradox could be resolved. However, faculty in distinctively Christian institutions sometimes do extend guidance into areas such as these. Perhaps the clearest example is the case study, in chapter 6, of Professor Richard B. Steele, where students sometimes pose such dilemmas to Steele in emails, inviting his response, and he replies with attempts to define the question in theological terms, to suggest various possible answers, and sometimes to describe his own position, clearly identified as such.

In sum, then, Professor Northway uses the class time for integrating a number of student voices, and the journals as an extension of student thinking into a more private and non-judgmental space.

Student evaluations

What students thought they learned

On the IDEA end-of-course survey, students report making "substantial" or "exceptional" progress on learning factual knowledge (79 percent), fundamental principles (73 percent), broader understanding of intellectual/cultural activity (68 percent), acquiring an interest in learning more by asking my own questions and seeking answers (61 percent), learning to analyze and critically evaluate ideas, arguments, and points of view (55 percent), and learning to apply course material to improve thinking, problem solving, and decisions (51 percent). Slightly over half had marked "general intellectual skills such as analysis . . ." as a goal, and slightly over half reported progress on a differently-worded survey's critical thinking item.

Two-thirds of Simmons' students, on the IDEA survey (Appendix C), report "exceptional" or "substantial" progress in developing their own values, even though Simmons had not marked that item as a goal for the course.

As we have seen in the previous chapter, it is very typical for students to report highest learning in factual knowledge and basic principles. This class's report of analyzing and critically evaluating ideas is lower than average for the entire Highly-Effective group in this study, but average for public institutions, which are at 52 percent (see table 2.2). However, the class report of progress on understanding intellectual-cultural activity is higher than the average for public institutions (68 percent for Northway's class, 63 percent average. See table 2.2). What is at issue here, I think, is how these various terms are understood, and how Northway expresses his goals. For him and for his students, understanding of a variety of religions through analytical categories, and making this information "organic" through "meta-thinking" are emphasized more than critiquing arguments. Thus the "understanding intellectual-cultural activity" may be a more accurate indicator of students' achievement of the kind of "critical thinking" the course emphasizes.

Student evaluations of teaching

Professor Northway's rating by students on the IDEA survey (Appendix C) place him in the top 10 percent of the IDEA database for excellence of instructor and excellence of course. The attributes his students most frequently mark as occurring "frequently" or "almost always" are "explained course material clearly and concisely" (96 percent); and "made it clear how each topic fit into the course" (93 percent). Also high were "introduced stimulating ideas about the subject"

(84 percent); "related course material to real life situations" (80 percent); and "gave tests, projects, etc. that covered the most important points of the course" (80 percent). All these aspects of clarity are highly valued by students. But Prof. Northway also gets high marks for "displayed a personal interest in students and their learning" (91 percent) and "found ways to help students answer their own questions" (76 percent) – aspects enhanced, I think, by the interactive classroom conversations, by the journals, and by Prof. Northway's personal enthusiasm for the subject and his students. In other words, students rate him high on clarity, caring, and conversation.

Student suggestions for improvement: More conversation

Asked for suggestions about improvement, most students say that the course works well as it is. Suggestions focus on more conversation – in the form of writing, guidance for their writing, and class or small-group discussion:

- More quizzes and ways to apply learning. More class discussion would be helpful. Encouragement of open debates on sensitive issues.
- Perhaps you could give us some guided questions or suggestions to focus journal entries on. Especially for the historical sections since there are no real "issues" in learning names and dates and places.
- Small group assignments every few weeks so we can interact and trade thoughts and feelings on teachings.
- Take more time for class discussion, less note taking.

Requests for "more discussion" were the single most frequent suggestion students made in all classes combined, large or small (table 2.4). Students, I think, are hungry for the kinds of conversation forums in which they can explore, for themselves and with others, the implications of classroom learning for their own spiritual and religious development.

Prof. Northway's choices

I chose Prof. Northway's class because, in a class of 100 students based on Powerpoint lectures, with no smaller TA-led discussions, he creates spaces where students can integrate course material with their own spiritual and religious development, including the class itself, the journals, and small groups writing the *Matrix* assignments. In those assignments, he also insists on the voice of the analyst. His students report understanding cultural-intellectual activity at a higher rate than average. Yet Prof. Northway's students do not always achieve the level of work he would ideally like on the group assignment, and many of them do not read the assignments faithfully before class. Those two issues – how to help students master the professional scholarly voice of the critical thinker and to read and apply course material – are critical issues for every teacher.

The next case is likewise a large class at a public university, and it likewise studies world religions, but it illustrates a quite different personal style and set of choices by the professor – a different way of addressing clarity and conversation, a different way of addressing the scholarly role and the spaces for integration of intellect with religious and spiritual development.

Prof. Veldman

"Introduction to World Religions: Western Traditions," Public Research university, 174 students. Three Teaching Assistants

Prof. Veldman offers an intriguing contrast to Northway's approach to a large public university class. Veldman gives essay exams, not multiple-choice; his assignments are completed individually rather than in groups; he uses a "site visit" report rather than an analysis of a film; he does not assign journals, but instead six short thesis-based essays. His TAs meet students in small groups once a week. Veldman holds a weekly "coffee" discussion, voluntary for students, in which those who attend are free to ask about his religious beliefs and share their own. Classroom presentations, while based on Powerpoint slides, are models of musing and scholarly inquiry – a style that raises clarity issues, which he handles in several ways.

Goals

The syllabus lists these goals for students:

- to identify beliefs, rituals and ways of thinking in each tradition;
- to think critically and comparatively about the differences between each tradition;
- to apply a critical lens and reflect an articulate voice on the religious events in contemporary religious culture; and
- to prepare students to take on the role of scholars in the study of religion.

Both Northway's and Veldman's goals fall within what is broadly defined in this study as "critical thinking." Both emphasize tools of analysis, and both mention comparing and contrasting. However, Veldman twice uses the word "critical." He envisions two intertwined roles/voices for the student: (1) a citizen/activist with a critical and articulate voice on current events and culture; and (2) the role of the scholar studying religion. His assignments emphasize thesis-based argument assuming the role of scholar.

Assignments: What was learned

Veldman's assignments, like Northway's, fulfill four common functions: to ensure mastery of facts and principles; develop critical-thinking skills; ensure student preparation for class discussion; and provide a space in which students can reflect on what the material means to them. Veldman, however, apportions these tasks differently than Northway does.

Exams: Identification and essay

Mid-term and final exams consist of identification questions and essay questions. Sample exam question: "Modernity has been defined as having four traits: 1. Autonomy (individualism); 2. Experimental method (Empirical science); 3. Democratic polity (Liberal democracy); 4. Egalitarian culture (Equal Rights Movements). Explain what these mean and how they might be in tension with the Muslim concept of Tawhid, the Jewish concept of idolatry, and the Christian idea of discipleship." Such exams create considerably more work grading (which the TA's do) in comparison to multiple choice, but their focus on critical analysis may communicate to students a different message about what is important.

Short arguments

Rather than the twice-weekly journals of Northway's class, students write 6 half-page (many are longer) papers that must be thesis-based arguments. The professor's handout on "hints to improve your writing" advises:

> A thesis sentence begins each essay. Follow the thesis sentence with supporting sentences that provide a coherent plan of attack. Thesis sentences contain a strong subject and a clear and controlling idea, e.g., Freud's theory of religion fails because . . . or I argue in this essay that Marx's theory of religion opens up new areas of inquiry . . . Thesis sentences tell the reader what your focus will be and how you plan to develop it. They communicate to the reader what he or she can expect. That is, the writer will proceed logically from the first to the second to the third reason. Each reason should support and develop the thesis while responding to major objections . . . The academic study of religion is distinct from being religious. In the academic study of religion,

> one argues his or her point to work toward plausibility. As a believer, one confesses one's faith and shares how one believes, feels or thinks about the truth of one's beliefs . . . What justifies evidence? Evidence is data, facts, statement validated through the arduous work of research. Evidence is data that is tested. Evidence is primary research that has outlasted intense scrutiny in the community of scholars.

Both Northway and Veldman make short, frequent assignments; however, Northway uses journals to emphasize "meta-thinking" and "organic" learning. His journals elicit musing about students' own religious beliefs, but students are urged to ask "why?" and then "why?" again, thus achieving a kind of distance from their own beliefs. Veldman more distinctly separates the academic study of religion from "being religious," and uses his short, frequent writings for critical thinking as argument. Students are expected to assume the voice of the scholar arguing – a voice distinct from that of the believer who shares thoughts and feelings. Yet the scholarly arguer's voice does not merely parrot received information: it expresses a position: "Freud's argument fails because . . ." The student may believe that his/her position is justifiable, but the position is based on reason and evidence, not on non-rational ways of knowing.

Site visits

Asking students to apply the class material to an artifact or situation is another way of asking them to exercise critical thinking. As Northway asked students to analyze *The Matrix*, using categories taught in the class, Veldman asks for an analysis of two religious sites. The site visit provides an opportunity for the exercise of critical thinking skills within real-life religious settings. Veldman's site visit requires students to visit two sites not representing their own religion and analyze some aspect of the two. For example, a Muslim student compares the power relations between students and leader in a Christian and a Jewish campus religious meeting. This is the voice of the scholar, and perhaps also of the critic, though the Muslim student, for example, is careful to keep to neutral observation of power, not critique of it. The fact that the writer is a Muslim is only mentioned at the beginning of the paper to justify the choice of Jewish and Christian sites as compliant with the assignment's direction not to choose one's own religion.

Response to article

Students are asked again to assume the role of scholar in one assignment, for which Veldman distributes an article about religion and violence, of which he is co-author, and asks students to agree or disagree with him. This student agrees with him, but extends his idea and shifts its frame. The student writes in part:

> Conflict is not an inherent result of religious principles, but rather the product of religion itself as a claim to truth. Thus, I do not disagree with Professors' [names them] statement that "tension and conflict are inherent in all religious groups and are central to their identity formation and group motivation," but rather I would expand on their idea by considering their hypothesis concerning religion with the context of truth claims in general.
>
> In essence, my theory is that religion exists as a middleman [TA writes "It seems more to be the paragon of this relationship"] in the spectrum of the relationship between truth and conflict, neither embodying this link in its totality nor serving as the sole basis from which this relationship can be deduced. In simpler terms, not all truth claims are religious, but all truth claims do create and are galvanized by conflict. [Examines qualities of truth claims that lead to conflict.] Religion is also not the definitive embodiment of the correlation between truth claims and conflict. By this I mean that religion in itself does not necessarily encapsulate all that is the truth/conflict relationship in its totality, i.e., religious conflict can be very specific. For example, religious conflict is often focused not on disputes about differing truth claims, but on the idea that there can be and is only one valid truth claim (e.g., One God, one faith, one religion). Conversely, though there are many truth claims concerning disputes about differing interpretations of American history, for example, it is rarely asserted that there is only one possible interpretation. I may disagree with your interpretation of the Civil War, but I certainly do not disallow the existence or validity of your interpretation itself. This claim to the Truth (Big T) is, in my opinion, a unique quality of religious conflict (though I am not arguing that this quality characterizes all religious conflict) and not a fundamental aspect of the truth-claim /conflict correlation itself. [TA writes "Brilliant work. Great analysis. Your ideas are big, complex and difficult to define but you managed to do it. Once again I'd like to give this paper to Veldman. He'd enjoy it. In your thinking, don't neglect the boundary-making, identity-forming function of religion and how that creates conflict too. That's a big part of the article, too.]

Readings

The texts are Corrigan, Denny, Eire and Jaffee, *Jews, Christians, and Muslims: A Comparative Introduction to Monotheistic Religions* (Prentice Hall, 1997); and Azar Nafisi, *Reading Lolita in Tehran: A Memoir in Books* (Random House, 2003). Note that, like Northway, Veldman includes a narrative in addition to the analytic text – again, the emphasis on story that is a recurrent theme in the Highly-Effective faculty.

Did the students read the material? Forty percent report on the end-of-course survey that they "hardly ever" or "occasionally" came to class without having completed the readings or assignments (vs. 55 percent for public universities as a whole). Thirty-six percent said they frequently or almost always came unprepared (vs. 31 percent). Thus student preparation in this class is somewhat below average for public universities. It is important to note, however, that students had the Friday meetings with their TA, for which they may have been better prepared, and that the sample of public universities included a number of smaller, interactive classes with daily quizzes, in which the faculty member placed great emphasis on being prepared every day. The issue of class preparation will continue to be a focus of the cases to come.

Use of class time

In class, Veldman has a unique style. He models the inquiring scholar; he lets students watch him inquire, and invites them to participate. He creates a forum where the integration of course material with students' own religious and spiritual development can take place. He does this by inviting students to be informants about what they know, and to be fellow questioners and inquiring scholars with him. On the day I visit his class, the topic is mysticism. Veldman strides across the front of the room, in front of the rows of ranked chairs. Behind him is the large screen on which the Powerpoint slides are projected. At this point in the class, he is introducing mystics, with a slide on early Sufism. I did not tape record the class, but took almost verbatim notes, which I reproduce here.

Veldman: "Something is going on here that is really transformative of self. Goal of these mystic teachers. It's not what you believe but what you do and what you are, and the power, the energy of this godhead." [He begins something – interrupts himself.] "No, let's not do that. Write for yourself a definition of mysticism." [Students write.] "Turn to your neighbor." [Student behind me says to his partner, "The only thing I know about mysticism is that . . ."]

Veldman: "Somebody new, give me a definition. Somebody who has never peeped a word." [Waits]

Student: "Practice within or outside a religion that focuses on spiritual enlightenment."

Veldman: "Nicely done. Thank you for speaking. Does it have to be outside a religion?"

Student: "Depends on who you ask. Some will say inside, and others say they're heretics. It's both."

Veldman: "In the past, I've studied mysticism more intently. Not any more. So how might we academically define it? Give you an idea of how scholars have defined it." [shows slides to illustrate] "By definition, mysticism radicalizes religious beliefs or challenges religious beliefs. I was back in Rochester last week and we went to the cabin where Joseph Smith was raised with, was it 8 brothers and sisters?" [He appeals to his TA, who is a Mormon, and jokes with him because the TA doesn't know how many brothers and sisters.] "I saw the sacred grove where he had the sacred vision. I learned that these angels talked to him all the time. He was a veritable revelatory machine. Fun to be there and listen to the Mormon scholars. Moronai gave him the golden plates. What I learned was 11 people saw the plates. Some later rejected Mormonism but never said they did not see the plates. I never knew that. Now, interesting, golden plates, new revelation of what Christianity was all about. Did they really happen, these visions? Hm. Did it really happen? Did it happen to Moses – the burning bush? Can these extra-dimensional experiences – can we take them seriously as scholars? Are they empirically testable? Did Moses receive the 10 commandments? Did the bush burn? One of the great questions – these mystical transcendental experiences – are they all one force?" [pantomimes God] "Okay, today I'll appear as Buddha, tomorrow as Christ. Today you be Moronai, tomorrow Gabriel. Most dominant scholarship would say, every transcendental experience is mediated by culture. Did Jesus have Buddha come to him? If you never heard of Moses, would you envision him? Anybody have a personal experience of having somebody come to you?" [silence] "Well?"

Student: "Would Moronai be an intuitive figure to Joseph Smith? All traditions believe God is all-knowing. The reference point might not be all I know, but all *these people* know. So the mystic might put it in terms the people knew."

Veldman: "That's interesting. Hadn't thought of that."

Second TA: "Going back to Mohammed. Recognition that there was something there."

Veldman: "Ian just gave you an ex post facto explanation. I have a burning sensation, vision, tell my wife, she says that must be Rachel. I say, yeah, must have been. Interesting question. Maybe that's why people don't go into the study [of mysticism] because it's so problematic. How are you going to do empirical research on it?"

Student: "Mysticism means union, like the second bullet on the slide. Catholic canonization. Validators show up and say, sure enough. Routine mysticism."

Veldman: "Great question. Is mysticism the same all the time? No."

Student: "Does speaking in tongues classify as mystical?"

Veldman: "Great question. I don't know. What do you think?"

Student: "I read other religious material. Sense of at one is what religion tries to confer. Therefore, if you argue there are not religious emotions, you couldn't argue – [pause] or I guess you could."

Veldman: "It's sort of this union, ah, I don't know. This longing – is it religious? Or just human? As Freud would say, wants to go back to the mother" [explains Freud]. "This is one of those cases where there is no right answer. Frustrating but also kind of fun. Back to Sufism." [Goes back to specific discussion of Powerpoint slides. Makes the point that Sufism promotes the idea that at the base is this core longing for the one.] "We'll see this in a later slide. Mysticism is often saying, we are all one. Why bicker. So religions, especially monotheistic religions, say no, no, we are right. Maybe one of the reasons mysticism is marginalized."

Students in interview use the word "passionate" to describe Veldman: "Really challenges the students." "He takes the class and still engages them in discussion. Calls on a student and starts a dialogue. Prof. [Veldman] blatantly says when he thinks something – facts or logic or his personal disagreements." Another adds, "he's open about his own personal beliefs. I think this is kind of weird. Rescues religion from being so neutral, so PC." Another: "He opens the door for people to say, I'm this." Another: "I grew up in a very Christian religious home, father a pastor. I was encouraged to think I believe and he'll be like why and I'll have to think – as an intellectual student. He doesn't want you to agree, but to be a smart person. Not a blind follower of anything."

Another: "He's willing to let you challenge his ideas." Muslim student: "being Muslim, I had a different experience. He said 'I don't know.' He showed me tolerance and respect." Another: "He tries to get us to understand our own beliefs about the world." Another: "He addresses people in a 200-person class as though it is small."

These comments about being "open about his own personal beliefs" is partly the result of Veldman's openness in class about, for example, his own past study of mysticism, but it is also a result of the weekly voluntary sessions he holds for students who want to come.

Special hour for free conversation

Students are highly enthusiastic about the hour he takes every Wednesday, immediately after class, to hold a voluntary discussion in a coffee shop. A student: "You can talk about whatever you want." Another: "Even his own beliefs, you can talk and laugh about it. You can go beyond the boundaries. I've had other teachers push one on you. But with Prof. Veldman, you're free to have fun. Move around, see where your thinking takes you. He jokes but never puts down students."

Veldman himself describes one of these coffee sessions following the Wednesday lecture, where "any student can come. Usually 20 students come and it is quite free-flowing. They can ask me any questions they want, including questions about my religious life. For the most part I will answer. They asked me how I can believe in Christianity while such suffering exists. I mentioned the recent killing of Margaret Hussein, the Care worker. This terrible act hit me deeply. I said, the only way it makes sense is to say, God is all-loving but not all-powerful. In my Christian faith God is with us, like the song says, 'What if God was one of us . . .' God did become one of us, with all the pain and suffering that goes along with that act – and that somehow in pain, God is reconciling the world to God's self. One Christian student said that she believed God was in control. And I said I respected her opinion and that on matters of faith, in my Presbyterian tradition, people of good faith can and do disagree. It was a good moment for everyone I thought."

This coffeehouse conversation may evoke different voices than the class sessions. It is a time to share beliefs and emotions, explain to one another what each believes, and exercise tolerance.

Student evaluations

What students thought they learned

In Veldman's class, factual knowledge and learning principles was still the most frequently-chosen student item for "substantial" or "exceptional progress." However, analyzing and critically evaluating arguments and points of view was chosen by 70 percent – about average for the religiously-affiliated institutions, and significantly higher than the average for publics, which is 52 percent (Table 2.2). His emphasis on the inquiring scholar produces a distinct profile of student-reported learning. At the same time, 70 percent reported progress on personal values, versus 60 percent average for the publics. His profile is unusual, especially for a public university: it shows higher than average student reports of learning in both critical thinking and values.

Student evaluations of teaching

His scores on IDEA for "excellent instructor" place him just over the fiftieth percentile – not as high as Prof. Northway, who is at the ninetieth percentile. Students most frequently praise a different set of strengths: "Asked students to share ideas and experiences with others whose backgrounds and viewpoints differ from their own" (95 percent marked "frequently" or "almost always"); "encouraged student-faculty interaction outside of class" (93 percent), related course material to real life situations" (90 percent), "demonstrated the importance and significance of the subject matter (89 percent), and "introduced stimulating ideas about the subject" (87 percent). For "explained course material clearly and concisely," he receives 74 percent. Thus clarity is good but not exceptional. What stands out are the aspects that concern conversation and caring, and his emphasis on free-ranging inquiry.

Student suggestions: Clarity

Students' suggestions address the issue of clarity. Prof. Veldman, many agree, does "a better job with questions and debate than presenting information." However, what provides the clarity for them are the study guides he provides ("incredible") and the sessions with their TA, who "went through it and told us what was being asked." At an exam review session, they reported, the TA articulated a typical exam question and students responded. Then the TA suggested improvements and additions to their responses. Another: "The handouts by [name of TA] were great. She explained everything and made it clear on all subjects blurred by the lecturer." Another: "Sessions [with TA] are really helpful because they give the facts and don't go off on tangents." A student said, "The people Prof. Veldman chooses [as TAs] really work well together. I feel very well connected with the TA and through him with my professor."

Some students are not happy with the lack of clarity in the lecture. Several want "more facts given in class. Easy to lose the facts in all the discussion." Another: "The professor should stick to the class agenda more (though tangents are fun) and talk more about Islam, which is kind of getting shafted." Another: "Less irrelevant discussion in class."

Prof. Veldman models the inquiring scholar who also has made religious commitments and is willing to share them. He emphasizes to his students that the two are different. He uses the assignments to enforce thesis-based argument, and the TA sessions primarily for clarity issues. His class lacks the twice-weekly, free-flowing written musings that Northway's journals elicit. However, the voluntary "coffee hours," held in a neutral, informal space, provide a forum where, though he teaches at a public university and models himself as the inquiring scholar, he can be very open with his students about his, and their, religious and spiritual lives.

In some ways, he models the separation of intellectual inquiry and religious belief – in his explanation of thesis-based essays and evidence, for example. The spaces he makes for individual student reflection on their own religious and spiritual issues is quite deliberately separate from the "formal" class, conducted in an informal, unofficial space, and totally voluntary. But he also models, in his classroom musing, and through sharing an article he himself has co-authored, how, as a scholar, he directs his own interests and passions through disciplined but free-ranging scholarly inquiry.

I think this case, juxtaposed to Northway's, raises questions about classroom persona, about how the faculty member expects students to integrate critical thinking with their own religious beliefs, the use of TA's, the role of exams, the role of what students see as "clarity," and the very interesting use by Veldman of the voluntary "coffee" hour.

The next case shows a faculty member, again teaching a large class at a public university, who selects a course topic that is deeply engaging and disturbing to students, and who shares with students her own human responses to the topic. She also uses her own intensive response to essay exams and assignments as modes of conversation; in this, she differs from both Northway and Veldman. Her mode of intensive response to student work is unusual for a large class, and it raises keen issues about time and workload.

Prof. Ammon

"Modern Christianities and World Cultures," Public Research University, 75 students, one TA

Prof. Laura Ammon [her real name] teaches a course at the University of California Riverside, where she examines the role of Christianity and its leaders in three modern situations involving genocide: El Salvador, Rwanda, and South Africa. The information and images presented are new and shocking to students. This "hot" topic creates a unique atmosphere in the classroom, which contains students from a number of different races and cultures. Prof. Ammon assigns no exams; only three essays, to which she responds fully, both for drafts and for the final version, representing a major investment in this type of "conversation."

Course goals

In the syllabus, Prof. Ammon writes:

> In this course, we will explore the connection between Christianity and culture in three diverse countries: El Salvador, Rwanda, and South Africa. In these contexts Christianity has been revolutionary, conspiratorial, and reconciliatory . . . From this examination, students can begin to form a critical appreciation of the social-political role of Christianity in various contexts, both western and non-western, as well as an awareness of the cultural hybridity of Christianity. This class will allow and encourage students to critically appreciate the role of Christianity both in creating situations of oppression as well as in being a resource to resist oppression. Ultimately, students can begin critically to analyze the social-political implications of religion in their own contexts.

The student voice here is that of the critical analyst who examines an unfamiliar context and then uses the tools and insights gained to analyze her own "contexts." Typical of many faculty in the study, Ammon suggests how students can apply course material to their own lives and "contexts," but the statement is open, perhaps ambiguous, so that application is invited but not pushed, and the faculty member does not presume to suggest the students' conclusions.

Students, writing prose reflections on the first day, before they have seen the syllabus, have little inkling of the "critical" aspect of the course. Most of them (82 percent) expect to acquire information about various branches of Christianity such as Catholic, Protestant, or Coptic; 56 percent expect to learn about cultural and historical aspects; 26 percent expect to learn about various religions (plural) of the world. The common belief among students that religion courses are about acquiring knowledge of a variety of religions is strong in this situation as in others. Sixty-eight percent have as a course goal to address their own beliefs; 39 percent expect that their current beliefs will be challenged. Fifty-eight percent identify themselves as Christians without expressing doubts; another 21 percent identify as Christian but express doubts, disagreements, or lapses. Thus this class is slightly different from the average for students in the Highly-Effective classes at public institutions (62 percent secure; 16 percent doubting.

Table 1.3). The "Great Divide" between the professor's goals for critical socio-political analysis and the students' goals for knowledge and for working on their own beliefs set the stage for the impact the course will have upon the students.

Assignments: What was learned?

Essays

The course has no multiple-choice, no identification, no exams per se – just three required essays. Here are two of the questions students may choose for their third essay:

> You have seen three roles that the church has played in cultural transformations and great human anguish. The church has been a force for revolution (El Salvador), a site of great suffering and distress (Rwanda), and a space for cultural healing and reconciliation (South Africa). Using the readings from the entire class, discuss the role of the church in these three situations. What lessons can we learn from the church's roles? Compare and contrast theological ideas and concepts in the three disparate situations. Use the texts to support your point of view.

The question above asks the student both to compare/contrast, but also to "draw lessons." Clearly, this professor expects the course material to affect students' actions in the world. The next question asks the student to engage in dialogue with a political leader – again, a very engaged role.

> You have an opportunity to talk with Archbishop Desmond Tutu about the TRC [Truth and Reconciliation Commission] process in South Africa. Reflect on Tutu's theology and what he has said about the TRC. Given what you know about Tutu's thoughts on retributive vs. restorative justice, his *ubuntu* theology, and his understanding of humans as capable of goodness and change, express your reactions and his possible responses. What kinds of things would you like to say to Archbishop Tutu about his theology and his vision of the TRC in light of what you have learned in this class? How might he respond to your reactions?

Prof. Ammon offers to respond to students' drafts before the papers are due. For the second paper, eight students request her responses. She offers extensive line-by-line comments, on both prose style and larger issues of argument and support. On the final versions of papers, too, there is extensive comment. Students point to the three essays as critical elements in their learning. A student writes "writing the essays gave me a chance to reflect and try to explain the way certain people used religion to help them." Another: "This course has advanced my writing skills, and writing development better than any of my English classes so far." These essays, with their invitation for students to draw lessons and to engage in political dialogue, form a major site in this course for conversation and for students' engagement with their own beliefs and values, yet the self-revelations are couched within the frame of scholarly inquiry (What would you say to Archbishop Tutu in light of what you have learned in this class?). Thus students' reflections in their own voices are framed within a conversation with a scholar and activist. This provides an interesting contrast to Veldman's assignment in which students respond as scholars to his own scholarly analysis of violence and religion, on a more abstract and general level. In one case, students interact with the professor-as-scholar. In the other case, they interact (hypothetically) with the political leader directly involved in a violent situation.

Use of class time

Class is basically lecture, with discussion arising more fully as the semester proceeds. Prof. Ammon places photographs on the screen from time to time, but does not build her lectures around Powerpoint slides, extensive handouts, or the other aids that some teachers use for clarity. She describes her lecture style as "just talking." Despite this, however, students do not complain about "clarity" nor ask for Powerpoint slides or handouts. There seem to be two reasons: first, the lectures come across to students as clear and well-organized: "The lectures in this class were extremely structured. Whatever information and understanding that I need that I couldn't derive from the readings, I was able to get from the lectures." Second, it may be that not asking multiple-choice or identification questions about the material changes the context for the "clarity" issue. It means that Prof. Ammon can lecture and lead class discussion without Powerpoint slides or handouts and still get high marks for clarity, because students are focused on the larger ideas they will be asked about on the essays, rather than on mastering details for multiple-choice or short-answer questions.

Prof. Ammon works very hard on class discussion. At the beginning of the course, she reports, discussion is stiff and difficult. There are so many students and chairs in the room that it is impossible for her to walk around the room to encourage student engagement. But gradually the material itself, with its strong emotional appeal, and the efforts of Prof. Ammon, begin to encourage discussion. The weekly TA-led small-group sessions also help: because students in this class do not express anxiety about clarity, and due, no doubt, to the qualities of the TA, Prof. Ammon uses her TA to create a forum for student discussion of the meaning of what they are studying.

A turning point in the large-class discussion comes as the class begins to talk about the Rwandan genocide, and Prof. Ammon reveals her own emotions. She writes in her journal:

> One day during that segment [on Rwanda] I was just emotionally raw and I think that brought out something in the students. Several stayed after and my office hours were pretty full during that segment of the course. By this time a group of students were all sending me their paper drafts and talking to me about the reading and their developing knowledge about the world we live in. I think that segment of the course was the most powerful in terms of students' engagement and learning. They devoured the material and had questions in class. The film *Hotel Rwanda* was a lightening rod for conversation. The last segment suffered from my absence, I think. The AAR [professional conference] and Thanksgiving broke up our time together and by the time the Thanksgiving holiday was over, students were tired and stressed about many different things – other classes, the amount of reading for my class, the problem of talking about racisms in a multi-race classroom. I think these factors made them much more subdued in class. On the other hand, by this time the students seemed to feel very comfortable talking to me in class and outside of class. My TA reported that the discussions in her sections were lively and engaged and she was very impressed with their willingness to talk about the materials. I wish more of that could have come out in class but the difference between 25 people in the room and 75 people in the room is pretty significant, especially regarding issues like race, class, and violence. It ended abruptly because of my family situation [a family emergency called her away for the last class period, so the TA took over that session] and, while there was nothing I could do about that, I was very sorry that I didn't get to have a wrap up day, discussing their emotional reaction to the class as well as my own.

A student writes "I found that Professor Ammon has helped my learning and development through her detailed presentations of the material. She showed great interest and enthusiasm when it came to the topics and situations that occurred. She also showed how the situations have affected her as she shared a bit of insight on what she thought." Several students mention her "passion." Students reflect appreciation for the discussion, both in the large class and in the smaller groups with the TA once a week:

- For the most part the lectures clarified many questions and were most helpful, especially during the genocide in Rwanda section where I felt Laura did a great job explaining the role of the churches' complicity during the genocide.
- Both Ms. Ammon and our TA [uses TA's first name] are helpful with the material. Our classmates, through class and group discussion, helped me to not only understand the materials better but let me hear opinions and perspectives of others.
- The teacher was extremely helpful. Great way on interacting with students.

Student evaluations

What students thought they learned

No IDEA scores exist for this class, because data were gathered in the third term of data collection, where the IDEA survey was omitted in favor of more extensive student written reflections. Thus there are no whole-class survey responses about what students thought they learned. However, student prose reflections, written in class near the end of the semester, reflect the strong impact the course has had on them:

- Wow! This course has affected my spiritual and religious journey in a good way. Growing up in a Christian Methodist household, I was always skeptical of the overall – sin and you go to hell – because we all sin . . . This course has challenged me to face the reality of human violence towards people and their environment, regardless to what religion they identify with. I absolutely love this teacher, the course, coming to class everyday and being enlightened!
- I did not even know that there were so many Christians (or Catholics) that suffered that much. I was quite shocked to learn about the genocide because I had no idea Christians were killing other Christians! I've learned about the global events as opposed to the national events, and that really helped develop a stronger foundation of my knowledge.
- I remember every day of what we discussed in class. I think the reason I was so captivated by class discussions was because the professor picked very engaging topics that grabbed our attention.

Student evaluations of teaching

Though no IDEA survey results were gathered, students completed the university's own student evaluation, in which Prof. Ammon scores at the eighty-sixth percentile for her department and for the campus as a whole, in "Overall rating of the instructor." She is at the one hundredth percentile for her department and ninety-fifth percentile for the institution on "Did the instructor present the material in an organized, understandable manner?" and at the eighty-sixth percentile for her department and ninety-first percentile for the university on "Was the instructor concerned about students learning and understanding the course material?" Thus she scores high on issues related to all three aspects: clarity, care, and conversation.

Student suggestions for change

The only suggestions were that two students were disappointed that the course dealt more with history than with the "philosophy" of their own religion – a reflection, perhaps, of their early hopes that the class would help them more directly address their own spiritual beliefs.

In summary, by asking only for essays, Prof. Ammon establishes a context in which "clarity" has a different meaning. She lectures by "just talking" (though her lectures come across to students as clear and well-organized), and she works hard, even in a class of 75, to encourage discussion. The material itself, so shocking to many students, helps to enliven the course and encourage student response. It jolts Christian students into questions about their faith. The TA does an excellent job of encouraging student discussion in the small groups once a week. The professor uses her office hour and her responses to paper drafts as sites for conversation and caring. Students are invited to analyze the role of the church in three very complex political situations. They do not merely act as analysts, though; they "draw lessons" and engage in imagined dialogue with the leaders under study. Their professor models the analyzing scholar who also can be deeply touched by the situations being studied. She shares, not her own religious beliefs, and not even necessarily her own rational explanation of the existence of evil (as Veldman does in the coffee hour), but just her human response to human suffering and to the church's complex roles in difficult political situations.

Conclusions

These three faculty teaching large classes have demonstrated quite different approaches. Each depends on lecture as the major classroom mode. Three issues are critical in those lectures: clarity, liveliness, and interactive conversation. Prof. Northway relies on Powerpoint slides as a major strategy in class. The slides are lively, clear, and interesting, and he intersperses them with video clips, interaction, and small group work for the *Matrix* assignment. Prof. Veldman relies on the slides to give coherence and clarity to his presentation, as he models the inquiring scholar. Prof. Ammon relies less on Powerpoint and handouts, but ensures that students perceive the clarity of her lectures. All faculty lecture in an interactive way.

Each faculty member defines a somewhat different "voice" for students: the analyst who uses religious studies categories to study both religion and culture in Northway's class; the inquiring scholar in Veldman's class; and the analyst of political situations, who draws lessons and engages leaders in dialogue, in Ammon's class.

Each faculty member provides a forum where students can bring together their own thoughts, feelings, and religious beliefs with their academic study. Northway requires frequent journals and responds to them in a dialogic mode. Veldman meets weekly with students for free-ranging conversation. Ammon meets in her office with her students as they revise their essays.

Each faculty member uses the teaching assistants in different ways: Northway employs TAs for grading only, while he himself reads the journals. Veldman uses the TAs for grading and for leading weekly small-group discussion classes that focus heavily on clarity. Ammon relies on her TA to help students share their thoughts in open discussion. All employ the TAs to balance their own strengths and areas of difficulty.

Each faculty member manages workload issues in a different way. Northway gives multiple-choice exams. He reads student journals written twice a week, but responds only briefly. His group assignments result in fewer papers for him to grade, and he can guide them as students work on them in class. Veldman leaves paper grading primarily to the TAs, but meets with his students weekly for voluntary conversation. Ammon makes a strong investment in responding herself to student papers, including drafts for those who request it. However, she assigns fewer pieces of writing – only three essays, no exams, no journals.

All three faculty members struggle with the issue of student preparation for class. In Northway's class, 23 percent of the students report that they had usually completed the assignment before they came to class, and 38 percent reported they hardly ever came well-prepared. In Veldman's class, 40 percent are well-prepared; 36 percent not well-prepared. (For Prof. Ammon's class, we do not have these survey data.) Veldman's class does better on preparation, but neither class reaches the average for public universities, which is 55 percent well-prepared and 31 percent poorly prepared. The public universities in the study include some classes that are smaller and that use daily graded quizzes or other types of interactive classwork where students' preparation is clearly demanded. Class size and institutional type are important variables, but the data strongly suggest that it takes graded daily quizzes or other types of for-credit daily performances to get a high level of student preparation for class.

The next two chapters examine small classes at a mix of public, religiously-affiliated, and private non-sectarian institutions. All the issues these large-class teachers face appear again, but in somewhat different forms.

5

Case Studies: Small Classes in World Religions, Introduction to Religion

The three cases in this chapter illustrate classes with enrollments of 45, 25, and 9. Each case is arranged in the same sequence: goals, assignments/exams, and pedagogies. The end of chapter 3 discusses the questions that drive all the case studies in chapters 4, 5, and 6. Each case addresses how the assignments/exams and the pedagogies helped achieve the goals and how they instantiate the three principles of care, clarity, and conversation. Special attention is given to how the teacher constructs spaces and voices for students to integrate course material with their own spiritual and religious development. The first case shows Prof. Simmons, teaching a class of 45 students at a public university, making extensive use of videos as the basis for class discussion. He brings multiple voices into his classroom in this way: the videos present the voices and practices of believers; the class incorporates the voices of students in several roles, as analyzer, believer, and informant. The "site visit" assignment asks students to use analytic categories as lenses for a religious site. The next two faculty members teach smaller classes. They rely much more heavily on student writings as forums for two-way conversation and as spurs to class discussion, and they face the resultant paper-load issues. Both use a wonderful variety of strategies to make their classes very lively and interactive, with students' voices cast in multiple roles. Their strategies contrast, however, in some interesting ways.

Prof. Simmons

"Beliefs and believers," public masters university, 45 students

Prof. John K. Simmons [his real name], teaching at Western Illinois University, adopts a stance he calls "neutral enthusiasm," discussed in chapter 3. His classroom practice makes extensive use of videos of religious practices of many types, as well as interviews with religious leaders. He describes the origin of his approach:

> I arrived at WIU in the fall of 1987, a newly minted PhD from a highly touted research program, in love with my discipline, and possessed of the erroneous notion that everyone naturally cared about religious studies. It only took a few lectures in my over-crowded, lower-division classes to realize that . . . students were bored to death in classes that consisted only of lectures. My experience as a teaching assistant at the University of California Santa Barbara had taught me the invaluable lesson of bringing alternative voices into the classroom . . . I realized that I had to bring religious studies alive . . . On my own, with my department's camcorder, I roamed about Illinois making rough interview tapes with Hindus, Buddhists, Christian fundamentalists, pagan-priestesses and just about any other religious person who would put up with me. Those "home grown" tapes made all the difference in the classroom. Suddenly, my students were paying attention. And, more importantly, they were learning.

To enable other faculty to use his videos and his approach, he has developed a PBS televised CD Rom and Internet course entitled "Beliefs and Believers," that has served more than 25,000 students at more than 100 colleges and universities around the nation (distributed by Governors State University Digital Learning and Media Design. Marketing, Distribution and Licensing, 708-534-4018). The courses consists of 24 one-hour video sessions, comprehensive student study guide, and instructor' guide. The present study investigates a face-to-face course of 45 students where he made extensive use of his own videos but also devoted considerable time to classroom discussion. His assignments, exams, and classroom interactions provided a context for the videos.

Goals

On the IDEA survey (Appendix C), Prof. Simmons marks only one goal as "essential": "gaining a broader understanding and appreciation of intellectual/cultural activity." Goals marked "important" are learning fundamental principles, learning to apply course material to thinking and decision, analyzing and critically evaluating ideas and points of view, and acquiring an interest in learning more. The course guide lists these goals:

> Understand the world's major religions; understand the six dimensions of worldviews upon which religious beliefs are based; discern the

> reasons, motivations, and instincts that inspire people of different religious beliefs; appreciate the role doctrine plays in religious life; apply methodological tools to gain insight into sect and cult formation; comprehend the challenges that language, interpretation, and culture bring to religious discussion; communicate why symbols play such a key role in religious life; grasp how profound life questions are answered with great myths; appreciate religious diversity.

Learning about other religions is by far the most frequent student goal: 74 percent on the student discipline-specific survey (Appendix D). Students much less frequently mention the kinds of critical and analytical goals that Simmons holds.

Assignments and tests

Simmons gives three multiple-choice quizzes, which enhance learning of factual material and principles and to some extent enforce daily preparation. A midterm and a final (multiple choice, short answer, and essay) enforce knowledge of facts and principles as well as the "critical thinking" that Simmons wants. Students must also visit a place of worship or a major cultural event (World Series, national holiday celebration or ritual, political rally, etc.), and analyze it using the six dimensions they have been taught: experiential, mythic, ritual, doctrinal, ethical, and social.

Exams

The exam essay questions give students practice in applying the analytic categories they are being taught. Here is an essay-exam answer that receives the full ten points and instructor comment "Well done!" The essay question the student chose (from among three options) is "What factors determine whether a religion is conventional or non-conventional in a given society? Please provide examples." This is in-class writing, so the prose is sometimes awkward.

> When determining whether a religion is conventional or non-conventional it is based on a set of five mutual cultural based criteria. When these criteria are looked at it is then important to look at the context that the religion is in, as well. Because in one area of the world a religion could be conventional and in another end of the world could be considered non-conventional. Time is also a factor in that as time

> passes a religion can become conventional when it was non-conventional before.
>
> The first cultural based criteria is longevity is how long the religion has been around. This is tied into the second factor of tradition. If a religion enters into a society with strong tradition in another religion it would leave the alternative religion as non-conventional. Third is reflection on prevailing values, which plays a big part whether a religion is accepted in a certain area. Numbers is the fourth factor because if one religion has very few numbers it would not be conventional for its context. Finally, tension plays a factor and if a religion has parts of the first four factors then there will be less tension to the religion.
>
> All of the factors must be looked at in the cultural context and is not saying that one religion is better than another. For example, a Methodist church in Macomb [town where the university is located] would be conventional, while a Methodist church in Pakistan would seem non-conventional. Context plays a huge part as with the United States being highly Christian, religions such as Lutheran and Baptists are considered conventional. These five factors help to determine whether a religion is conventional or non-conventional based on the context.

This exam question is testing whether the student can state, in his/her own words, concepts being taught, but it also asks for examples. Thus the Methodist church in town enters the discussion, and is placed, not within the context most students are accustomed to, but within the context of the analytic frames students are being taught – frames that set aside the question of the "rightness" of one religion and instead examine the social and political factors that influence it. The student is the analyst, not the believer.

Site visit

A required 5-page "Worldview" analysis of a visit to a religious community or site of national significance such as a World Series game takes this analysis a step farther. Instead of bringing "examples" into the classroom, the students must now bring the classroom analytic categories into sites they visit near their own communities. Simmons guides them by a careful assignment sheet that lays out an outline for the essay, including use of the analytic categories they have been learning in class, and questions to spur their observation within each category. In the site visit, they get to be a version of Simmons the researcher, as he takes his camcorder around the state, or as he conducts his own scholarly investigation on the rise of sects and cults. Many students visit sites of their own religion (thus the assignment is significantly different than Prof. Veldman's site visit described in chapter 4, where students must choose a site different from their own religion).

Achieving the voice of the dispassionate analyst proves difficult for many students. For example, one person begins by describing her Catholic upbringing, her mother's insistence on church attendance, and her lack of church attendance over the past year at college. She welcomes the site visit as a chance to revisit her relationship to the Catholic faith. This takes nearly one page. Another student begins with a description of her departure from the Christian faith of her upbringing and her eventual affiliation with Wiccan practice, before launching into a description of a Wiccan circle casting – description that is partly analytical but also includes the voice of the apologist – a voice Simmons discourages as he praises the analysis but declares the essay "a bit too pro-Wiccan." What these students have done is to create a kind of mixed genre – the essay is part analysis but also part journal, and it serves some of the same musing, integrating functions as the journal in Northway's class in chapter 4. Simmons does not directly comment on the personal autobiography sections of the essays. As long as the analysis he wants is present, the student can get a good grade. In a sense, I think, he allows this mixed genre to exist in his classroom without encouragement but also without stern penalties.

Readings

Texts consist of a study guide, plus Ninian Smart, *Worldviews* (New York: Macmillan, 1999). Prof. Simmons' syllabus gives no daily reading assignments. He gives three quizzes throughout the semester. On the end-of-course IDEA survey (Appendix C), his students' estimation of the difficulty of the course, the amount of reading, and the extent to which they worked harder than on most of their other courses are all much lower than the IDEA database average. His course, like all the others, raises the issue of how important it is that students read the material before class and how much energy the faculty member wants to spend trying to make that happen.

Use of class time

Prof. Simmons works hard to ensure that students participate in class discussion despite the enrollment of 45. Here is his description of a class session. It is instructive to contrast this class with the discussion of mysticism in Prof. Veldman's class in chapter 4. Note also that the film *The Matrix* enters this classroom discussion, and recall Prof. Northway's use of that film as the basis for a group writing assignment (chapter 4).

> February 15, 2005. Today we explored mystical experience. To generate discussion, I used a video interview . . . [with] Swami Prabuddhananda at the Vedanta Society of Northern California in San Francisco. The Swami discusses the connection between meditation and mystical experience. I then asked my students to reflect on whether, in their minds, they had had an unusual spiritual or religious experience. Once described a "born again" experience at a Christian summer camp. Another pointed out that a spiritual experience need not be connected with a religious organization. She felt she had a "life changing" experience while climbing the mountains in Colorado. Whether or not religious experience is dependent on "religion" became the conversation of the day. Moving back to the [Powerpoint] notes, we explored other varieties of religious experience.

What is happening in this class? First, the powerpoint notes are providing an organizational structure and written reference to the concepts and vocabulary students will need for the quizzes and exams. Second, the "voice" of the Swami enters, as an "insider" teaching the students about his religion. Simmons then invites the students' voices, not to teach the doctrine of their religion, but to tell their own experiences of religious experiences that may parallel or contrast to the meditation experiences the Swami describes. The student who describes her Colorado mountain experience makes an analytical point, as well as personal description, when she notes that a spiritual experience need not be connected with a religious organization. The professor uses that analytic point as the key to the ensuing theoretical discussion, and then moves back to the Powerpoint-guided structure. The class itself provides a forum for multiple voices: students master and apply analytic observation of religious practice, share their own experiences, and raise theoretical questions.

Student evaluations

Student evaluations place Prof. Simmons in the top quartile for excellence of instructor on the IDEA survey. His highest scores are for "Made clear how each topic fit into the course," "Demonstrated the importance and significance of the subject matter," "Displayed a personal interest in students and their learning," "Related course material to real-life situations," and "Gave tests/projects that covered the most important points of the course." Nearly every student mentioned the videos and many mentioned the Powerpoint slides and study guides as aids to their learning.

Student suggestions for change

Given the class session described, it is interesting that the most frequent suggestion for change in Simmons' class is "more discussion" (24 of the 34 students who responded). Simmons, in a written reflection, wonders why this is so. Good question. First, the student comments are often directed at fellow students who, the respondents think, should make more effort to contribute. Some students suggest structures for the professor to help get students involved – e.g., small groups, a chat room online, or simply "encourage more discussion." So the comments about discussion are about whole-class engagement and preparation. Second, the student suggestion for small groups and chat room perhaps indicates that students are looking for a forum in which they don't need to describe their conversion or their Colorado mountain experience in front of 44 classmates. There are no journals, small TA-led discussion groups, small-group paper projects, or voluntary "coffee" with the faculty member, as described in the previous chapter with larger classes, yet there's not the small-group intimacy of 9 or 25 students, as in the next two cases in this chapter. Thus the class hour must carry all of the students' need for discussing their own practices and those of their home communities. Perhaps, no matter how skillfully interactive the teacher can make the class, it leaves the need for conversation not fully met. But that may not be the complete answer, either. In the next chapter, we will see that Prof. Steele, with a class of 39 students, also faces a somewhat surprising student request for "more discussion," and, because the request reaches him at mid-point in the course, he responds by introducing more discussion into the classroom. Many students appreciate this move very much, and Prof. Steele's student evaluations are very high, but some students complain that there's not enough structure in the class, and some, of course, didn't want more discussion in the first place. It's a fine balance, and perhaps there is no single practice that satisfies all the students, but the fact that students comment so much on "discussion," certainly suggests its importance to them.

The next two cases do not result in student requests for more discussion. The arrangement of voices in the classroom, and the spaces for student voices, are very different from Prof. Simmons' class. Prof. Bhattacharyya requires daily student writing in a "portfolio," and her class is organized around students' writings. She gets excellent class participation and excellent attendance, but her own workload issues are significant. Prof. Jones, the final case study in this chapter, also integrates student writings into class discussion, and she makes students, themselves, responsible for leading class discussion during the latter part of the course.

Prof. Bhattacharyya

"Introduction to the religions of Asia," protestant baccalaureate institution, 9 students

Prof. Swasti Bhattacharyya [her real name] teaches "Introduction to the Religions of Asia" to 9 students (normally it would be 15–20) at Buena Vista University, a Protestant Baccalaureate Institution whose mission statement at the time of the study (it has since been revised) described it as "an independent, regionally-acclaimed, comprehensive teaching institution dedicated to 'education for service,'" which "aspires to become the nation's leading 'New American College,' while retaining its Presbyterian heritage. The University prepares students for leadership and service in an information-driven, global society" (www. bvu.edu).

Goals

The syllabus lists these goals:

> Through a rigorous engagement of various primary and secondary texts and observations of contemporary religious expression, you have the opportunity to:
>
> - Develop historical consciousness and perspectives as you gain a deeper understanding of the historical, cultural, and literary background to the development of the religious traditions covered in this course.
> - Develop the skills of critical thinking as you analyze the economic, political, religious, and sociological perspectives underlying the various religious traditions discussed.
> - Most important, this course provides you with an opportunity to engage the texts and beliefs of various Asian religious traditions. Throughout your exposure to these traditions and worldviews, you may develop a deeper appreciation for the depth of religious diversity that exists in this country and around the world.

From a section that enrolled 15 students, taught the following year, Prof. Bhattacharyya gathered more detailed in-class student reflections on the first day and near the end of the course. In the first-day reflections on their goals, students overwhelmingly mention learning about different religions and cultures. There are several Asian international students in the class and one who has studied in Japan. Statements about beliefs range widely:

- I'm still searching for my ideal religion/one I can agree with. By broadening my horizons, I hope to gain greater skills to analyze and interpret my feelings on religion.
- I wish to learn more about meditation and how it can help still your mind.
- I have lost a lot of faith – first it was faith in the Catholic Church, then it was faith in organized religion, then a loss of faith in Christianity, and now God. I'm hoping this class will spark a faith in something because I feel a void.
- [A student who plans to enter the ministry and wants to be able to answer questions parishioners may ask about different religions] I don't think the class will actually challenge my own personal beliefs mostly because I have very strong beliefs that are extremely set in me.

Assignments: what was learned?

Prof. Bhattacharyya makes extensive use of writing and oral communication. Oral exams test learning of fundamental principles and analysis. A site visit assignment also asks for analysis. Portfolios and in-class writings combine quiz-like writings that test knowledge of factual material with writings that provide a forum for students' critical thinking and their integration of course material, to enable them to develop a deeper appreciation for the depth of religious diversity that exists in the US and around the world.

Exams

Exams are a combination: students working through particular questions alone and then 15-minute oral presentations by pairs of students. Students first research one of the questions on their own, then meet with their partner to prepare the 15-minute presentation and a one-and-a-half to two page single spaced report. In their 15 minutes, they present their answer and lead a brief discussion on their topic. Here are two sample questions:

1 Late Vedic texts, Zhuangzi and Shintoism have different philosophies of language. Discuss what their philosophies are, the differences and similarities, the significance, and implications of their attitudes towards language.
2 As Arjuna [main character in the Bhagavad-Gita] surveyed the armies lined up and ready to fight, imagine that he is accompanied by three charioteers, Krishna, Honen, and Mencius. First explain Krishna's teachings related to Arjuna. Then, discuss how Honen and Mencius might: 1) advise Arjuna; and 2) respond to Krishna's teachings.

Classmates complete an evaluation form for each group's exam presentation (figure 5.1).

Presenter's Names:

____

Topic of Question:

Criteria	Exemplary—4	Proficient—2	Unacceptable—0	Grade
Content	• Clearly presents main topic/issues of exam question. • Presents a serious engagement with material (good/quality and in-depth information, • Clearly articulates nuances in arguments/issues • Provides new and interesting insights to the material. **Comments:**	• Presents topic/issues of exam question • Presents an adequate engagement of material (adequate information) • Articulates a few nuances in arguments/issues • Provides some insights to the material.	• Does not present an adequate understanding of topic/issues of exam question • Does not adequately engage material • Does not articulate any nuances in arguments/issues • Does not provide insights to the material.	
Presentation	• Ideas are clearly articulated and well integrated • Material is presented in a well organized and coherent fashion • Appropriate questions are directly addressed • If applicable: audio/visual equipment utilized well & enhanced presentation • Class is actively engaged in good & productive discussion on the topic • **Comments:**	• Ideas are adequately articulated and somewhat integrated • Material is presented with adequate organization and in a somewhat coherent fashion • Appropriate questions are adequately addressed • If applicable: audio/visual equipment is adequately utilized and does not distract from the presentation • Class is engaged in a discussion on the topic	• Ideas are not clearly articulated, if at all and are not integrated • Material is not presented in an organized manner & is not in a coherent fashion • Appropriate questions are not addressed • If applicable: audio/visual equipment is not utilized adequately and it distracts from the presentation • Class is not engaged in any relevant discussion	
Delivery	• Presenters work as a co-equal team each contributing to the presentation. • They speak loud & clear • They are well prepared/polished • They maintain good eye contact with, and are responsive to the audience. **Comments:**	• Presenter's speech/delivery is adequate • Is adequately prepared & somewhat polished • Maintains adequate eye contact with, and is somewhat responsive to the audience.	• Presenter's speech is difficult to hear and unclear • Is not adequately prepared & not polished • Does not maintain adequate eye contact with, and is not responsive to the audience.	

On the back of this page, please briefly address the following:

1. Describe 1 element you learned/more fully understood from this presentation/discussion
2. Discuss 1 element you found most striking regarding the presentation
3. Discuss 1 element of the presentation that was particularly strong and one that needs improvement

Figure 5.1 Rubric to evaluate final presentations in Prof. Bhattacharyya's class

The exams ask the students not only to know the material, but to analyze how religions compare, to "talk" to one another as colleagues, and then to be "teachers" or facilitators of conversation in the class. The oral exams also help keep the paperload down, saving the teacher's time for the large investment she makes in portfolios.

Portfolio

The portfolio serves as a forum for several diffherent kinds of discourse and different student voices. Students build a portfolio containing daily and weekly assignments which are available online. The portfolio contains five categories of entries: 1) reading responses; 2) interview/library assignments; 3) reflection; 4) vocabulary; and 5) clippings from popular culture, news, etc. Portfolios are collected at the end of Weeks 1, 6, and 10, and at the end of the semester.

Each class day there is a portfolio assignment. For example, here is the portfolio assignment for the second class day:

> *Wed, 1 Sept: Definition of Religion*
> *Read*: Ludwig pp. 1–30. and "Definition of Religion" in the course packet.
> *Due*: Blackboard [the course management software] open-note quiz over the Syllabus and Portfolio Description (both under "Course Information" on Blackboard.) Make sure you complete it PRIOR to coming to class.
> *Portfolio*:
> *Reading Response*: Read Ludwig chap 1 & 2. Drawing on what you have learned from reading the chapter, answer ONE set of the following questions (Make sure to indicate which set of questions you are addressing)
>
> 1 What are your thoughts regarding questions such as "Who am I?" "What is the purpose of my life?" "What am I supposed to do?" Have you ever asked such questions? Do you think the types of questions are universal? Individual? A product of modern Western thought? What role, if any, do you see these questions playing in "religion"?
> 2 What does the term "Sacred" mean to you? What did you learn about "Sacred" from your reading? Discuss how the idea of "Sacred" might be shared by individuals from a variety of cultures and religious backgrounds.
> 3 Discuss the value, if any, of ancient stories/myths. What is their purpose? Discuss what the stories/myths reveal about the worldview of the people who utilize them. Provide examples of how they (stories/myths) address the needs of people today. (Questions are from Ludwig)

(Remember: you must post your responses on Blackboard, under the appropriate Discussion Forum, *NO LATER than 11:59 p.m. Tues 31 Aug*)
Reflection: After reading through the various definitions of religion (found on Blackboard under Course Documents), which definition do you consider the most adequate description of religion? Briefly discuss why you prefer the definition you chose. (Though your reflections are NOT posted on Blackboard, you are expected to 1) have read the assignment prior to class and 2) be prepared to engage in a class discussion regarding the definition of religion).
Vocabulary: From your readings, write up the definition of 1 word that is unfamiliar to you. (Make sure you post your term and definition in the appropriate Blackboard discussion forum no later than 11:59 p.m. the night BEFORE class. Also, type the word you are defining, and the text/pg on which you found it, in the subject line of the vocabulary Discussion Forum.

Prof. Bhattacharyya gives detailed and explicit instructions for the portfolios, and she uses the structure of the Blackboard system to help her. The portfolio enforces daily preparation and has some elements that test students' ability to state facts, principles, and vocabulary, but it asks for much more than that – it asks students to be pondering, daily, the relationship of course material to their own lives. It gives the student a strong "voice" in the class, but a voice structured by the very detailed assignments.

Religious site visit

Students are required to visit a site of religious activity for one of the religions studied. The instruction sheet gives detailed instructions, including a description of the three analytic categories students must use (theoretical, practical, sociological), and a list of prompting questions under each category (e.g., "What kind of group is it? Close-knit or diffuse? Mostly people drawn to the religion by family or ethnic ties, or mostly committed converts of different backgrounds? What role does the priest or leader play? Were there discernible differences in the roles for women and men? What message about religious experience is communicated by the nature of the group?"). The student voice is primarily that of the analyst, though the final question Bhattacharyya poses is "What impressed you most about this organization? How did you feel during your visit? What did you think? What are your overall impressions?"

On a fairly weak paper, Prof. Bhattacharyya writes extensively in the margins, "Elaborate," "What led you to this conclusion?" "What gods did you see?" and "What did this tell you about the traditions? The people?" The final comment is "Need much more analysis: meaning of symbols, basic nature of religion? Message about religious experiences, etc."

Two contrasting paragraphs from different papers will show weak and strong observation and analysis:

- *Weak*: All of the walls in the main room of the temple have paintings on them. These paintings show things like Buddha lying with others around him, and other things that are important to the traditions of the Buddhist religion. Some of the things around the room include candles, small statues of Buddha and other important people to the Buddhist religious traditions." [Prof writes: "Specifics"]
- *Stronger description*: [we were led to] a huge room that was mostly white. The first thing I saw was a table with nine stone figures on it. These figures were supposed to be another form of a god. These were nine different figures of one god, but these seemed to be set up in the same organizational pattern as the planets. Then there were many different gods in little temples. All of the god replicas were made of marble except one. This one was made of wood because of the story that went behind it. Supposedly the god had not been totally finished when a man saw him and because he did not wait he was damned to get the god half done. The rest of the figurines were about three feet tall and had amazing detail. In the middle of the floor there was a huge lotus flower in the marble floor. Just like the Hindu practice religion in everything they do, the whole temple had a reason to it. In the middle of the temple was a huge room where there was the main god called Prasanna Ganapathi. This god was the main god who the people worshiped. The people would walk to this center room and the high priest would bless them and put ash on their forehead.
- *Analysis*: It was also intriguing to see that many of the gods had multiple arms, maybe this was a way of showing that they were divine and not just normal people, but the multiple arms did show that they were important and powerful.

Unlike Simmons' site visit assignment, where students could describe visits to sites of their own religion, these students are not as tempted to include spiritual autobiography. Unlike Veldman's site visit (chapter 4), students do not contrast two sites, nor can they focus on one aspect, as does the student in Veldman's class who analyzes the power relations between students and leaders in two campus religious organizations. Prof. Bhattacharyya's students are to be careful, analytic observers, applying to one scene the analytic categories they have been taught. Keen observation and interpretation are valued. Yet students may also react in more personal voices – how did you feel?

Readings

Texts are Fieser, James, and John Powers, *Scriptures of the East*, second edition; Theodore Ludwig, *The Sacred Paths of the East*; Barbara Stoler Miller, *The Bhagavad-Gita*; and Shunryu Suzuki, *Zen Mind, Beginner's Mind*. Additional resources are provided in a course packet.

Students rate the reading load and course difficulty about average for the IDEA theology/religion database. Six of the 9 students report "hardly ever" coming to class unprepared – a higher-than-average percentage. Two others are "sometimes" unprepared, and one does not answer this question.

Use of class time

Class time is very interactive, making substantial use of the students' portfolio entries. Most classes begin with a brief review of the "course map," so students see where they are in the conceptual plan of the course. At times, Prof. Bhattacharayya will lecture for awhile: for example, on one day she lectures on the "strands" of Vedic/Upanishadic thought, because the book mentions the material but does not organize it into "strands," and she wants the students to have this concept. In other words, she's lecturing only what the readings do not do. Even then, she follows the lecture with an exercise, which she describes in her journal: "I divided students into groups of 2 or 3, gave them a particular Rg. Vedic or Upanishadic passage to read. Together they worked out what it was saying, which strand it fell into and why. Each passage was discussed briefly by each group presenting their findings."

Many classes begin with an activity that depends on students' preparation for class. Here, Prof. Bhattacharyya describes such an activity and muses about the issue of "coverage":

> Started class by handing out blank 3 × 5 cards. Students wrote a question they had from the Jain primary text readings. After each student wrote down their question, they passed it two times to the left. Then I randomly divided the students into groups of 2 or 3, and together they worked on the questions they received. After giving them about 10–15 minutes to discuss their questions and possible answers, we went through the questions and their answers together.
>
> Though this worked well and their questions led us into discussions regarding Ahimsa, no god, 5 vows, there are other important elements we didn't cover. This is where I struggle with what to do. It is an issue of coverage. While the focus is on what the student is *learning*, what do I do when we run out of time? One idea I thought of – post my

> notes on Blackboard [the course management software system]; this way they can look over the other important points that we didn't cover in class. Have to think about this more.

On other days, though, discussion elicits what Prof. Bhattacharyya wants:

> Great class today. Paired the students up (one group had 3). They needed one piece of paper between two of them. I had 7 index cards with questions on them. [lists the questions, e.g. "Discuss two characteristics of the Shang Dynasty]. Each pair was given a card and together they were to write the best answer. This was quiz #5. After each group had the opportunity to answer all 7 questions, we went through them one by one. Whoever had the card would start off by providing their answer. I'd write it on the board, then other groups were invited to add to what was already on the board. Yet again, a good 95 percent of what I would have lectured ended upon the board, all generated from the students!

On another day, she writes about trusting her students:

> I trusted the students this morning. It wasn't easy, but I did it; things were great! I put on the board the basics of who Zhuangzi was and then paired them up, gave them an opportunity to discuss passages they found interesting in the reading. As usual, students were struggling with Zhuangzi's reading. As one student expressed his frustration over how confusing the reading was, I asked him to ponder what was making him go crazy and why did he think Zhuangzi was writing the way he did. A good discussion followed.
>
> It is interesting to see how, even without me saying anything regarding particular passages, the students zero in one some of the key passages. After they had a couple of minutes to discuss with their partner, we came back together. Each group read a portion of the passage they discussed and from the passage discussed what they thought Zhuangzi was saying. As each group talked, I wrote the key points on the board. One of the challenging aspects of doing things this way – the students' comments are not organized according to my notes – it is about letting go and letting them explore.
>
> They did a wonderful job. The first student read a passage that clearly demonstrates how Zhuangzi is using language to try and totally twist your mind into a knot. As we discussed what he was doing, they got it! As they

> spoke, I added a few things here and there and asked questions that had them comparing Zhuangzi's ideas with those of Confucius, Laozi, and Mencius.

Prof. Bhattacharyya uses various versions of her 3 × 5 card exercises in many of the classes, almost always working from the primary texts the students are reading. At one point, she has the students work in groups. Each group must first draw (without words) a concept from one of the readings on a piece of butcher paper with markers. For example, for each early Chinese philosopher, if that philosopher were to build a school, what would the physical setting look like and where would it be located? What would the curriculum and teaching methods look like? What types of extra-curricular programs would be offered and why, and how would the program's success be evaluated? Once each has drawn, the paper is passed to the left, and groups, now using words, must interpret and add to what was already there. Then each group presents their answers to the whole class. She also invents versions of Pictionary and Catch Phrase.

Prof. Bhattacharyya has developed this interactive method to address the particular needs of the students at this rural Midwestern institution. She writes:

> I find these students do much better when they have an opportunity to share their ideas in a smaller group prior to discussing the topic with the class as a whole. My first semester here was a bit painful. I was so used to students speaking up, answering questions when I asked them, and freely expressing comments and asking questions. When I got here I was met with . . . total silence. I soon realized that silence was not from ignorance. The first time I called on a student, he shared some very insightful comments. So, I use a lot of small groups that then come together. It gives them an opportunity to try out an idea, see what others think, etc.

She works hard to have students look at each other when they discuss in class, not at her. She works hard to ensure that students are doing all the reading and are engaged:

> One student commented that she and her partner were talking about how the time in this class flies by, "it's because we're doing different activities and not just sitting here" is what she said. It's true; lecture is simply too passive; this gets them digging and thinking. Now there is a drawback (at least one) with these group activities: it's possible to

> slide by and kind of sit and not get as engaged. This is why I give individual quizzes and have them post individually [in the portfolios], but still – need to find ways to draw in *everyone*.

Students speak in a number of voices in this classroom, as they do in the portfolios. They recall course material, but they also are asked to apply it, ponder it, and analyze it. It is hard for a student to be silent in a class this small, with a professor who worries so intently about getting everyone involved.

The portfolios raise serious workload issues. Prof. Bhattacharyya records sometimes that she has stayed up late at night composing the exercises for class, and that, at one point, she is so bogged down that she asks her student assistant (an undergraduate provided by the college) to assist her with grading the portfolios on a particular day. She writes at the end of the course:

> I love what I do and I get energy from watching the students take on these totally new ideas and engage them. It's so rewarding, yet I'm exhausted. I have *got* to find another way to still have the students do the portfolio while not burying me in grading them. It's just too much for me.

There are three issues in the workload problem: 1) the volume of student writing, which is wonderful for learning, but *may* (not necessarily) cause workload problems; 2) the generation by Prof. Bhattacharyya of portfolio assignments and in-class exercises, a problem that should be self-limiting after awhile, as she develops a cache of these; and 3) how students get grades and feedback on their writing.

Prof. Bhattacharyya's system uses the portfolio exercises to ensure class preparation and put students into roles as thinkers and analysts. Yet in class, she has them generate still more writing, by her cards and other exercises. Then she treats the portfolios as out-of-class assignments, which means she (or her assistant) has to grade them. I would ask whether there is a way to combine these two elements. Can some of the portfolio assignments be responded to in class – used as the "writing" from which the class takes off? If so, it may be possible for the portfolio entries to be graded only by their presence. Comments on them are given in class, as students learn through discussion where their own writing needs correction or enlargement. A variation of this scheme is to have students pick, say, three portfolio items at mid-term and three at the end, for "grading," and have the rest count only as completed/not-completed. A final solution might be to just plan to have the student assistant grade the portfolios.

Student evaluations

What students say they learned

This is one of the few classes in the study where "learning to *analyze* and *critically evaluate* ideas, arguments, and points of view" ranked highest in student self-reported achievement (78 percent marked "substantial" or "exceptional" progress. IDEA survey, Appendix C). "Factual knowledge" and "applying course material to improve thinking, problem-solving, and decisions" were next with 67 percent each.

Student evaluations of teaching

Prof. Bhattacharyya's student ratings place her in the highest 10 percent in the IDEA database for excellence of teacher and excellence of course. All of her students say that she "frequently" or "almost always" did three things related to clarity: "explained course material clearly and concisely," "made it clear how each topic fit into the course," "and scheduled course work (class activities, tests, projects) in ways which encouraged students to stay up-to-date in their work." She also received 100 percent ratings on "introduced stimulating ideas about the subject," and "gave projects, tests, or assignments that required original or creative thinking." All students said she frequently or almost always asked students to help each other understand ideas or concepts; formed "teams" or "discussion groups" to facilitate learning; and found ways to help students answer their own questions. Finally, she also received a 100 percent rating on the key "caring" item, "displayed a personal interest in students and their learning."

Students are highly enthusiastic about her use of class time. On a post-course evaluation that Prof. Bhattacharyya composed, students wrote:

- It was happening every day in class . . . It was how the class was run. If it wasn't Swasti, it was the discussion she was engaging us to discuss. The concept of suffering and emptiness was one of the hardest for me to grasp, but I have a better understanding. I learn the most from making myself have to analyze the reading, what others had said in this class, and Swasti putting it all together or connecting it.
- Instead of lecturing in class a task was given at the beginning and we were allowed to do this on our own. After we discussed what we had found we then went over it in class. This allowed individual thought and more of a thought process.
- During class discussions the professor always tried to help students figure out what they were trying to say and helped to give examples so the other students could understand better and learn more through these discussions.

Student suggestions

Three students' suggestions focus on clarity: more Powerpoint, "tie extraneous thoughts to the topic," and "more relation to the text that we are reading."

Prof. Bhattacharyya has a gift for creative classroom exercises that stimulate discussion. Students believe the discussion helps them understand and apply the course material, think critically, and "figure out what they were trying to say." At one point in her journal, she considered that the clarity issues might be addressed if she put her typed notes (outlines) on-line for students' reference. In subsequent semesters, she has continued posting the outlines, which students appreciate. The challenge is to figure out what elements are critical to her unique classroom style, and to student learning, and keep those, while taking steps that reduce the amount of grading she has to do on the portfolios.

The next faculty member, Prof. Jones, is teaching "Introduction to Religion" – a bit different frame than Simmons or Bhattacharyya. Jones, like the others, though, brings student voices into the classroom in a significant way, and, like Bhattacharyya, she spends a great deal of time responding to student writing, but she puts all this together in a different way. Especially different is her way of bringing student writing into the classroom as the focus of discussion, and making students responsible for leading class discussion.

Prof. Jones

"Introduction to religion," protestant baccalaureate institution, 25 students

Prof. Katherine Janiec Jones [her real name] was teaching at Transylvania University at the time of this study (she has since moved to Wofford College). Transylvania's mission statement lists its "affiliation" with the "Christian Church (Disciplines of Christ), whose ideals of tolerance and freedom of inquiry the College shares," but the statement does not otherwise mention Christianity (www. transy.edu/about/content/mission.asp).

She focuses her course on the question "What is religion?" using four books that address that issue in complex and provocative ways. She uses student essays as a major forum for conversation, not only responding to them in writing but integrating them very closely into the class sessions. She also makes student groups responsible for leading class discussion.

She writes in a statement submitted for a campus teaching award, "The clearest change [in my teaching over the years] is that I have given up some of the control of the class. Inspired by Jane Tompkins' *A Life in School: What the Teacher*

Learned, I now turn things over to the students more often, trying to give them more responsibility for, and a feeling of ownership of, the material." As we will see, this class is anything but out of control. Rather, I would say that the control of the classroom is being exercised in a different way, with extensive but structured expectations for student contribution and leadership. I focus here on her use of student work, together with the student-led discussions, and her ways of integrating critical thinking with personal reflection.

Course goals

Goals are listed in the syllabus:

- Familiarity with the basic lexicon of the discipline of religious studies.
- Familiarity with some of the methodologies and theoretical models employed in the discipline.
- An enhanced ability to think through and articulate the meaning and implications of religions claims.
- An increased understanding of some of the problems inherent in studying religion(s) comparatively and/or cross-culturally.

Assignments; use of class time

The assignments in this class are so tightly interwoven with class time that the two must be explained together as a unit.

The focus of the course is to define "religion." Students read and discuss four texts, in this order: Wilfred Cantwell Smith, *The Meaning and End of Religion*; Mircea Eliade, *The Sacred and the Profane: The Nature of Religion*; Martin Buber, *I and Thou*; and Myla Goldberg, *Bee Season*.

The first paper is due on the second day of class – a definition of "religion." These are the instructions:

> Write on the following (minimum of one page, typed, double-spaced):
>
> What does the term *religion* mean? You may define the term yourself or use a dictionary. If you choose to do the latter, be sure to cite the dictionary you use, state whether or not you agree with the definition, and explain why. If you define the term yourself, explain why you are defining it that way. Then, please address the following: Do you consider yourself to be a religious person? Why or why not?

Personal disclosure is here related to academic inquiry – a pattern that will be repeated, as we will see below.

The first six weeks are devoted to reading and discussing Wilfred Cantwell Smith's book – a discussion led by Jones in a way that prepares her students to lead discussion later on. She typically asks students to write something, either in-class or outside, which becomes the starting point. Here is her report of two class sessions in the Cantwell Smith portion of the class:

> Sept. 12: In Chapter 2 of *The Meaning and End of Religion*, Smith tries to discern what the term religion has meant by looking at the use of the term *religio* by many, many authors in Western (European) Christendom. This is a really tough, potentially mind-numbing chapter. So, I tell them to read for the forest rather than the trees; that I will not test them on the specificities of what each thinker talks about. They do need to read the whole chapter (but just keep going if something seems irredeemably opaque – just mark it and we'll talk about it), but what I ask them to do is be responsible for one thinker (and I assign these in [the previous] class). They will be asked to explain, in class, what Smith says about how that thinker used the term *religio*. This, I think, makes it less intimidating, and it allows us to do a close reading of the text without my lecturing for two days straight and putting everyone to sleep, including myself. It seems that this exercise also empowers them a little, because they're usually impressed with what they're able to figure out. And I try to make each person's contribution sound really good, if I can, even if it's like wringing water from a stone. I also tell them it's okay to say, "I have no idea what he's talking about here." This book, really, can make or break the entire semester. I spend a lot of time telling them that this is a ridiculously hard book, and that I read it for my qualifying exams in graduate school, but that *I will walk them through it*. I don't expect them to get every little detail. Once they get over the fear, they generally do a fantastic job with the book, and it's great to watch them sort of take possession of the book. Chapter 2, though, is the "make or break" chapter in terms of class morale, I think. So, this task of going through each of the thinkers generally takes two class periods. I sit down with them in the class circle, rather than standing as I usually do. When we get through with it, I often congratulate them like they've just come through boot camp, and tell them that the worst is over.

Notice here that students are being asked to make reports, in class, on a small portion of the Cantwell Smith chapter – a preparation for their larger responsibilities, later, when groups of students will lead class discussion of a portion of a different book. Note, too, that student preparation has been enforced, students have had to talk, but no paper-grading has been generated – one way to address the paper load issues that a strategy like Bhattacharyya's portfolio generates. Students in this class are being asked to be persistent readers of difficult philosophical material.

In a later class, students are asked to conduct philosophical thinking themselves, this time working from a paper they write before class, which Prof. Jones does grade, and on which she makes a short final comment, and perhaps a few marginal notes.

> October 5: This was one of those days that makes all the bad, frustrating days seem worthwhile. It was fantastic. It's generally in this chapter ("Is the concept adequate") that things start to come together, and this is also the chapter that contains some of my favorite passages. They just got it . . . The class' writing assignment for today (it was a take-home assignment) was the following prompt: "On p. 142, Smith writes, 'For us, words and concepts are to be defined, while things cannot be.' Then on p. 146, he discusses his 'contention that one cannot define what exists.' What in the world is he talking about? Does this make any sense? Explain what you take him to mean from within the context of this chapter."

Sample student paper

> When I read the material needed to respond to this prompt, I was perplexed. It seemed as if Smith contradicted himself constantly. Yet as paradoxical as all his claims seem to be initially, they become more logical when the reader deduces the statements' opposite claims. A good example can be found in his statement, "We may define anything at all, provided only that it doesn't exist." This baffled me at first, as did all his other arguments, but for adequate comprehension, it helps if the reader reverses it by saying that if it doesn't exist, we can define it and if it does exist, we can't define it. Simplifying the statements that are confusing really helps. However, applying these standards to the concept of religion can prove to add to the confusion initiated by the earlier statement. Taking into account a second statement Smith makes provides a great example of this way of comprehending the text. It also helped me understand the statement given on the prompt and formulate my response. My response, however, branches away from the statement on the prompt, touching on it but expanding on it as well (I hope that's okay!) [Prof writes "Of course!"]

Smith states on p. 146 that "Whatever exists mundanely cannot be defined; whatever can be defined does not exist." At first, I took this statement to mean if whatever exists mundanely cannot be defined, then we must think of religion as a transcendental ideal rather than one of mundane nature and therefore it can be defined. But if it can be defined, according to Smith, it doesn't exist. In light of this paradox, Smith seemed to be claiming that religion didn't exist. However, after utilizing the method of comprehension described earlier, I drew the following conclusions on the assumptions of the statement: Religion can't be defined specifically, in the sense that it cannot be given a concrete definition since it is interpreted in various ways according to personal experience. Therefore, it exists. Using the same statement, since it cannot be defined, it must exist mundanely.

On the other hand, this didn't seem right to me. It seemed that it was actually false [explains why the idea seems false].

In conclusion, considering this formation of so many different religions, the conclusion that since religion exists, it must exist mundanely, seems more logical. In the same way, going back to Smith's statement on the prompt, religion cannot be defined, therefore it must exist. And if things cannot be defined, it must exist as a thing. Things are mundane, therefore it must exist mundanely.

[Prof: Well done! You did everything you were supposed to: you followed your ideas around and used a close reading of the text to help you figure things out. Good for you.]

Professor's journal continues

Because they had written on this question for today's class, I was hoping the pump was primed for the following in-class exercise. I began by asking them to think for a few minutes (or they could write, but I wouldn't be collecting their writing) on the following: "think in terms of my asking you to define another term for me, but this time, you are to insert your name. In other words, answer this question: Who are you? Define yourself."

It worked beautifully, thank goodness, because this really could have gone either way. The first student who volunteered with her response said she started to answer in terms of adjectives, but then applied what Cantwell Smith said in the reading about needing a new rubric/method for thinking about the term *religion* – one that makes a distinct division between what he calls *faith* and what he calls *cumulative tradition*. I could've hugged her.

> What came out throughout the course of the conversation was the sense that we all have the inner parts of ourselves that are the truest parts of who we are (and I talked to them about the difference between necessity and contingency – somehow this came up and seemed relevant at the time), and then the outer parts which are contingent. These parts are also "true," but don't necessarily speak to the truest parts of us. However, others tend to define us in terms of externals, while we tend to define ourselves in terms of feelings, experiences, "ineffables." But, as I pointed out, the way others perceive us often impacts how we perceive ourselves, so there develops a symbiotic relationship between others' perceptions of us and our perceptions of ourselves. In addition, that inner "truest" part of ourselves, to which only we have absolute and incontrovertible access, also changes through time (according to our changing moods, needs, etc.) – so is this part really necessary or contingent (i.e., does the idea of necessity entail unchangingness)? Or is this even the right way to think about it?
>
> This is precisely the point Cantwell Smith is making with regard to religion and the religions: the problems with trying to find and pin down essences (in a Feuerbachian sense), e.g., "true" Christianity, the "real" Islam, etc. I read aloud the following passages, and asked them to follow along: pp. 122, 124 (and endnote 301), to 127, and then the part about God "not giving a fig about Christianity." Some of the students actually said they felt like clapping (for Smith) after I read that quotation. Another raised her hand after I read a passage from the book, and she said, "You know, as I read this, I thought, 'this is like the way I defined religion in my first paper,' and I was so surprised to find – well, that someone else thought the same way." Yahoo! . . . What a switch from my first semester teaching this course several years ago, when a student complained that I "talked too much."

This pattern – having students write about an issue or question and then studying what scholars say – is basic to the course.

> "Doc Jones" is such an intellectual and insightful person, you can't help but learn from her. She leads many discussions in the class that also allow students to take live action in the class, such as lead a class discussion, or basically just volunteer and say what you think. This increases my learning environment by allowing myself to take a more active role, and if different people are constantly talking, you always listen because you're never bored.

The student's voice in the paper is that of a thinker, pondering definition, categories, and arguments in the same spirit as Cantwell Smith does. Students also are asked, in this course, to make constant connections between the readings for the course and their own issues of identity or their own definitions of religion.

It's important to note, too, that Jones also attends to issues of clarity and of helping students prepare for tests. She reports using a whole class day in October to talk about the upcoming test on Cantwell Smith. She gives students a detailed study guide and some sample questions.

Student-led discussion

Beginning with the second book, in the seventh week, students in groups of two to four (usually four) are assigned to lead discussion: three groups on Eliade (each group covering a section of the book), one on Buber (a particular section), and two on Goldberg (two sections). Here are the instructions for the groups:

> Each person in the group will need to email a list of reading-related questions to me and to the others in your group twenty-four hours in advance of the class to which you are assigned. I will then respond to these questions, perhaps by suggesting one that you should focus on in class. Others in the group should also feel free to respond, via email, to the questions suggested by your peers. You are required to meet with your group prior to class to go over the questions you'd like to bring up and the general format you'd like to follow for class discussion. (You are also welcome to meet with me as a group; just let me know as soon as you can so we can schedule an appointment.)

The group scheduled to lead discussion of pages 138–59 of Eliade on Friday, November 4, submitted to the professor the following "Draft of Discussion Plan." One of the students in the group had brought in, from another class, material on Spinoza, as described by James Carroll's *Constantine's Sword: The Church and the Jews*, chapter 40, "Spinoza: From Rabbis to Revolution." Here is the student group's discussion plan:

1 Read bottom of page 146–7 – about the sacrality of orgies, and sex. What has happened to sex now? . . . What happened to humans that made us change? What happened to society to cause this shift? Holiness of orgies – evil of sex. Duality of human being – we can see how life is profane and sacred. Sex is profane and sacred. Sacred time – if it doesn't occur in sacred time and sacred space, is it still sacred? Does it become profane? Different societies' ideas of what sacred sex is.

2 Question to put to class: "Name other things that at one time could have had a sacred nature and have since been deemed profane and are thought evil by the church."
3 Here we're going to spend a good deal of time with "desacralization of Nature." Read from page 151, "As we said before . . . especially to scientists." This segues into a reading from *Constantine's Sword* by James Carroll [a one-page excerpt the group provided for the class to read]. Here we're going to talk about Spinoza, and may stop along the way for discussion or questions. However, once we're through the reading, we're going to –
4 Pose this question to the class, for them to write on it: what do you consider to be true piety? Or, is it pious to distinguish between the sacred and the profane? Is it pious to make such a distinction?
5 Discussion of baptism, burial/cremation. Why is cremation considered evil in some societies?

Student-led discussions, with student voices as "teacher" and facilitator of class discussion, take major portions of the last half of the course. Prof. Jones' journal alternates between elation when they do well, and disappointment when they do not.

Office-hour conversations

The classroom, the written papers, and the office-hour are important forums for conversation in this class. Prof. Jones communicates effectively to her students that she welcomes office-hour conversations with them, and a number of them take advantage of it. The highly interactive class, as well as her own teaching style, make students feel comfortable coming to her. Further, the constant writing and the need for them to prepare to lead class discussion provide reasons for them to come to the office.

> Being able to approach Dr. Jones outside of class with questions was also wonderful. When I found a discrepancy between what I believe and what was said in class, I could research it and then go ask her about it in her office. This is what learning is – a dialogue between people, not a lecture or notes or books or tests. Learning to interact and to think, and I feel that this course has cultivated that to the highest degree.

Student evaluations

Without exception, the 22 students (out of 25 enrolled) who submitted reflections were highly enthusiastic about what was learned, affirming the combination of caring, clarity, and conversation.

I think of all my classes this semester this one has affected me the most. It was totally different from what I had expected – but different in a really good way. It has made me think about my own religion on a much deeper level. But not only my religion – religion as a whole. Discussion throughout the semester over readings or different prompts is what has most influenced me. Getting a chance to hear other peoples' opinions on a topic that is open to interpretation. The books have been so unique unto themselves – yet all related – and in understanding those connections you kind of have that "Oh, this all makes sense" moment. I wouldn't say that this course has challenged my beliefs – more that it has allowed me to gain a better understanding and expand my knowledge of what exactly "religion" is. It has made me want to learn more, causing me to now major in religion. It is a topic that excites me now that I'm beginning to understand it.

This course has been an awesome class. I have learned so much over the last 10 weeks. It has opened my eyes to different aspects of religion and different ways to understand it. I am still undecided about my religion but I have learned many things that I can relate back to. My class discussions were very helpful and insightful. We had different opinions and views on many subjects and that made an interesting class. What I did for myself was reading all the books. Usually I wouldn't read them but the book by [William Cantwell] Smith really got my interest in the class going. I might not know a lot about religion but I do know a lot about life that I didn't before.

Class discussions proved very thought-provoking. I loved carrying those conversations on into lunch or the dorms with my classmates. Everybody seemed to contribute, and if I did not agree with what they said, my brain would begin thinking through the why's of my thoughts.

This course has been my favorite class all semester. It makes me want to forego my dreams of being a veterinarian to pursue a degree in religion. It has *so* greatly expanded my mind and challenged and changed my modes of thinking about the world. I wouldn't say that I'm a different person because of it, but it has definitely impacted me deep down. I will never look at the world the same way again.

A major example of how it has expanded my mind is in the fact that my perception of religion has changed dramatically. Rather than see it as a *thing,* it's more of a concept to me now. I try to avoid institutionalizing it and making it concrete, since it's so *not*.

> Also, I used to be very caught up in what was the *right true* religion. I've come to realize that it's a personal decision and there is no right religion. This has not challenged my beliefs at all; rather, it has made me more secure in them. The books we have read throughout the semester have been *so* insightful and have helped me along this path very much.
>
> My classmates have helped this along as well. By presenting so many comments, questions (and answers), and suggestions, they have as well challenged my mode of thinking and inspired me to dig deeper and to interpret the information we are reading on a more profound level. The instructor was amazing as well. She was so well-versed and made so many connections and presented so many thought-provoking comments that it was difficult to not be almost awestruck. If I could major in religion, she is who I'd aspire to be.
>
> In all, this course was *amazing*. It was like no other class I've ever taken and I'm extremely sad to see it end.

Student suggestions for change

There were no suggestions for change.

Prof. Jones evokes a high level of student engagement, both by her own personal style and her way of responding fully to student work, and by her structures for student leadership of discussion. She says she gives up control of the classroom, and I earlier disagreed with that frame, but she does pay a price for her method, which is that when students are not prepared or do not effectively frame the discussion for their peers, the class suffers. One of the findings of this study as a whole is how few students complete the assigned readings before class. A class plan can minimize the effect of that pattern, requiring students to perform only at intervals, for which they typically study hard, or the class plan can hang the whole course on student participation, as Prof. Jones does, and fight that battle by a strategic combination of daily student writing and student responsibility for leading discussion.

Conclusions

The three classes in this chapter illustrate quite different modes of clarity and conversation, though each is marked by the intensity of the professor's care for the subject matter and the students. Prof. Simmons brings a rich array of outside voices to his students through his extensive videos and his classroom visitors. He is skillful at classroom interaction that integrates critical thinking and students' own experiences. He makes no explicit daily reading assignments, and students report lower-than-average completion of the assignments before class. The videos and the site visit play a central role – the course is not so much about reading, though reading is important, but about observing religious practices. The speakers and videos, observed during the class hour, in common with other students and the teacher, become in large part the "text" of the class and the subject of discussion within the community created by the class.

The other two classes in this chapter are smaller, and are taught in very different ways. Prof. Bhattacharyya's intensive, daily portfolio writings create very high levels of student daily preparation and student interaction in the classroom, as this small, intimate group of students interacts with a dynamic teacher who demands and structures their daily class participation. Like Simmons, her class asks students to observe and analyze various religious practices unfamiliar to most of them.

Prof. Jones gives her class a different task – to define "religion" itself. Unlike Prof. Simmons, where the videos are central, and observation of practice is the main activity, Prof. Jones' class brings in, not primarily the voices of different religious practitioners, but the voices of scholars and artists asking "what is religion?" Reading and discussing the texts is the primary activity. Prof. Jones, like Bhattacharyya, uses daily preparatory writings, and she structures many interactive tasks for students in her 25-person class. Like Bhattacharyya, she gets high rates of preparation. Both she and Bhattacharyya face significant workload issues. Jones' unique strategy, though, is to structure student-led discussions, casting major responsibility to students in a teacher-like role as facilitators of discussion.

The next chapter treats another set of small classes, but with different topics – not world religions or "religion" per se, but "Bible," "theology," or "Christian formation."

6

Case Studies: Small Classes in Theology, Bible, Christian Formation

The four cases in this chapter illustrate different approaches to courses in theology, Bible, and "Christian Formation." Each case is arranged in the same sequence: goals, assignments/exams, and pedagogies. The end of chapter 3 discusses the questions that drive all the case studies in chapters 4–6.

The cases begin with Prof. Bateson's Catholic college theology class that is deliberately feminist and that focuses very tightly on teaching theological argument. Next, Prof. Irish, teaching theology at a private non-sectarian college, emphasizes students' taking their own theological positions. Prof. Steele, teaching "Christian Formation" at a Protestant university, engages deeply with students in theological discussions, including a great deal of one-on-one conversation. Finally, Prof. Tildon, teaching "The Gospels" at a Catholic Masters university, employs extensive writing as a basis for conversation with her students.

Prof. Bateson

"Introduction to Theology," Catholic Baccalaureate Institution, 28 students

Prof. Bateson [a pseudonym] teaches a very focused course that emphasizes theological argumentation and that is deliberately feminist. The course is unusual in that "critical thinking" is the learning outcome students most frequently report. Prof. Bateson's students also report completing class-preparatory reading assignments at a rate higher than average. This case focuses on how she achieves that focus on argument, and how she works to involve student voices in the learning process.

Prof. Bateson explains what she terms her feminist philosophy of teaching:

> The course really emphasizes to students that their voices matter, their prior knowledge, their experience matters, their ideals matter and so their intellectual development is really at the heart of the course . . . the course cannot move forward without their voices, without their presentations, without their engagement with one another . . . but nevertheless the course does challenge students and raise the bar for students beyond some other introductory-level courses they take. The challenge, I think, coupled with the idea that students' voices matter . . . are two things that make the course a success.

Course goals

The goal of theological inquiry and argument is immediately apparent in the syllabus, which begins with a set of questions:

> What is theological reflection? What methods are used in "doing" theology? What questions and claims are characteristics of Christian theology? In what ways is theological inquiry significantly shaped by inherited texts and traditions, as well as by the "social location" of theologians, or their socio-historical and cultural contexts of race, gender, class, and sexuality? How do contemporary theologians wrestle with and re-articulate major Christian claims "for our time?"

Then the syllabus lists course objectives:

> The course provides an opportunity for students to reflect critically on and to participate intelligently and constructively in theological inquiry. Our four main goals are:
>
> - To gain a better understanding of major topics in the historical and contemporary Christian tradition.
> - To gain a deeper appreciation of the diversity within Christian theology, by placing different approaches to Christian theology in specific social, historical, and political contexts.
> - To develop analytical/theological skills for doing theology, for making sound theological arguments that cohere with the Christian tradition and that are relevant to contemporary contexts and concerns.

- To acquire, develop, and/or refine basic liberal arts skills for close, careful reading; clear, persuasive, and creative writing; and open, constructive dialogue with multiple, challenging perspectives articulated in readings, lectures, and class discussions.

Student voices invoked here are those of the theologian reasoning and arguing. Her students get the point: in this class, 16 of the 20 students, in their written reflections in class about two-thirds of the way through the course, mention "theology" as a course goal – more than for any other "theology" class in our sample. Here are some excerpts from reflections written anonymously in class at several points throughout the course:

> [Beginning of course]: My goals for learning in this course are to have a better understanding of God. I also want to see how my view of God differs from other views.
>
> [Same student, one-third through the course]: My goals for learning in this course is to gain a better understanding of God. Another goal is to realize what different theologists [sic] have to say about God.
>
> [Same student, two-thirds through the course]: My goals for this course were to gain a better understanding of God and to be able to think in a theological way.
>
> [Different student, two-thirds through the course]: My goals for learning in this course in the past have been to be introduced to various different views on Christian theology. As we approach the close of the semester (and I have been introduced to a wide variety of theology) I feel that my goals have shifted to making strong theological claims in both my written and oral studies of theology.

Assignments: What was learned?

Assignments are three essays, each about four pages, plus one take-home cumulative final essay exam, and one oral group presentation. All stress theological argument.

Essays

The four-page essays and the final exam essays, Prof. Bateson instructs her students, "ask you to articulate, explore, and analyze a thesis based on a topic drawn from the required readings, lectures, discussions, etc. of two course units. Papers should state a clear, concise thesis, and then develop an organized, persuasive, textually-supported, and properly-cited argument for the thesis. Papers are assessed mainly with respect to theological content and writing, or whether you can accurately explain, interpret, and evaluate major theological terms and arguments in a reasonably astute, well-argued manner." She writes to her students:

> All papers, including the final exam, are evaluated on the following criteria:
>
> - an original, clearly-stated, and substantially supported main point or thesis;
> - a full, accurate explanation of key ideas, terms, and textual evidence from course readings;
> - a creative persuasive, well-developed argument of topics and textual evidence, so that each student begins to express and defend a theological "voice"; and
> - sound writing mechanics at the organizational and sentence level.

Assignments throughout the course build toward increasingly more sophisticated analysis and argument. Students initially analyze theological positions. They also take their own positions in relation to questions or methods they choose for themselves. For example, on Feb. 9, Prof. Bateson's journal describes this short assignment, given as preparation for class:

> Students write 1–2 paragraphs in which they describe their own "social location" and two ultimate / big questions they have, connected to their social location, one method of doing theology, and one reason why they think this method is better able to address their big questions. The purpose of this assignment is to give students an opportunity to review some key points in liberation theology, to formulate their own theological questions based on their own social location, and to provide me with a better way to form student groups. Students will be grouped together based on similarities in their "big questions."

The take-home final exam clearly situates the student as theologian, asking for three essays in which the writer makes an argument about a theological theme that is common to two authors across two course units. For example, the student is to write on eschatology and religious diversity, comparing Isasi-Diaz and Balasuriya, answering the question, "What specific claim about God, Jesus, human nature, or the church influences an approach to religious diversity?" These essays offer avenues for students such as the one quoted earlier, who wanted to both "gain a better understanding of God" and "think in a theological way."

Prof. Bateson responds fully to student essays, using a paper review sheet (Figure 6.1). She places checkmarks next to relevant statements on the review sheet, writes extensively in the margins of the papers, and makes a final comment. Her comments emphasize thesis, development, and support. For example, next to a student's statement that "Imagery and language used by theologians over history about heaven and hell is very important to help believers try and understand God," she writes, "Ok, what will you argue about these images and understanding of God?" Next to a student's statement, "More recently it has been clear that good members of other faiths can still reach salvation because they share traits of Christ even though they do not believe in him," she writes, "How does this discussion of other religions fit with your argument about images and attributes of God?" Her comments reinforce that students are to make theological arguments, not merely claim that something is "important to help believers" or "recently been clear." These extensive comments create a "conversation" between her and her students, to reinforce their role as theologians.

Group presentation

The group presentation focuses again on theological inquiry, but also casts the students in a teacherly role, informing their peers, raising questions, and facilitating class discussions. In their group presentation, Bateson directs her students to:

> explain, evaluate, and raise questions about a main theological point in the readings . . . using the focus questions [provided in the text and on the website] as a starting point. Presentations should state and describe a major theological point in the readings; summarize and clarify the argument of this point by referring to specific textual evidence; analyze the reading(s) in comparison/contrast with other readings that address a similar or relevant point; and suggest at least two questions to generate further class discussion. Presentations are graded according to 1) content, or whether the presentation lays out a reasonably astute interpretation of the reading(s); 2) clarity, or whether the presentation communicates a main point, analysis, and textual evidence in a clear, coherent style; and 3) community, or whether each student in the group contributes responsibly to the presentation.

Note that Prof. Bateson asks her students to be clear and to facilitate conversation – two of the major principles that characterize the Highly-Effective

RELS 114 Paper Review
For ________________
Paper# ____

Thesis
___The paper sets up and argues for a creative, engaging thesis.
___The paper explains the thesis clearly and concisely in the opening paragraph.

___The paper defends an adequate thesis.
___The thesis is vaguely stated and/or misplaced.

Development
___Each paragraph addresses and develops one point related to the thesis.
___Paragraphs build upon one another to unfold an organized argument for the thesis.
___The paper identifies and responds to possible counter-arguments to the thesis.

___Paragraphs fail to take shape around a clear point.
___Paragraphs lack structure around a well-laid out line of argument.
___The paper does not consider possible counter-arguments to the thesis.

Support
___The paper shows a good understanding of ideas from our texts and class discussions.
___Paragraphs substantiate points by selecting and exploring relevant evidence.
___Quotations are singled out from the texts and fully interpreted.

___The paper misinterprets ideas or misrepresents texts.
___Paragraphs omit evidence pertinent to the thesis, or do not analyze evidence fully.
___Quotes are underused, overused, or are not well integrated into paragraphs.

Style and Mechanics
___The paper shows a genuine attempt at original, independent thinking; it expresses and defends the author's own theological voice.
___Sentences are constructed in a concise, polished style.
___The paper consistently follows the Guidelines for Papers, especially for citations.

___Paragraphs may revert to summary and overshadow the author's point of view.
___Sentences tend to be wordy, vague, or may contain serious mistakes in mechanics or editing.
___Ideas, paraphrases, and quotes are not cited properly.

Comments:

Grade ____

Figure 6.1 Prof. Bateson's paper review sheet

teachers. In the group reports, students begin with analysis of a theological point in the readings. Students summarize and compare, as they did for the earlier essays. But they also raise questions for class discussion. The voice of the analyst and the theological arguer is now joined by the teacher/discussion-leader voice.

Readings

Texts are Daniel Migliore, *Faith Seeking Understanding: An Introduction to Christian Theology* (second edition, Eerdmans, 2004); Alister E. McGrath, ed. *The Christian Theology Reader* (second edition, Blackwell, 2001); and the New Revised Standard Version of the *Holy Bible*. Readings from McGrath consist of short, 1–3-page excerpts from primary texts. Additional readings are posted on Electronic Reserve; they usually fall at the end of each course unit as examples of more contemporary theological views (mostly drawn from liberationist theologies). Prof. Bateson requires 20–25 pages of reading per class session, a total of 600–1,000 pages. Sixty-three percent of the students report that they "hardly ever" or "occasionally" come to class without having completed readings or assignments. Another 22 percent "sometimes" come unprepared. Though all the evidence about student preparedness is based on students' own reports, this class reports a higher level of preparation than other classes in the study.

Use of class time

Prof. Bateson works very hard to incorporate student voices. This section presents a rather lengthy chronology of the semester, told in her words, as she tries a number of different strategies to get students involved in class discussion. The narrative illustrates the constant ebb and flow of student engagement across a semester, and how a professor responds to those shifts, to keep students involved. The narrative also demonstrates a professor's persistence and thoughtfulness, and her semester-long attention to discussion. She never blames students, though she feels frustrated with their lack of engagement at times. Rather, she approaches the issue of class discussion as a problem to be solved, a puzzle to figure out – what are the strategies that will help *these* students, with their particular traits, to be involved?

The course begins (after the first class session, which is a course overview), with eight class sessions on "Doing Theology: Methods and Sources." Next are units on God; Christology; Human Nature: Creation, Sin, and Grace; Ecclesiology: Models and Marks of the Church; Eschatology: The "End" of the World; and Religious Diversity.

Professor Bateson reports that 50–75 percent of class time is "interactive lecture, in which students speak 10–25 percent of the time." Next most frequent is "student lecture/presentation" and small-group activities. She writes in a reflection:

> I refuse to use Powerpoint, I refuse to use a lot of handouts because I think Powerpoint and handouts just tap into various authoritarian top-down styles of teaching which often render the students passive and not active subjects of learning. I use chalkboard instead. I create charts, webs . . . to provide a kind of organizational visual aid for lecture and discussion in class that day."

Blackboard charts

The blackboard charts are created during the class, often with contributions by both teacher and students. The choice of blackboard rather than Powerpoint enables this co-construction of the material of the class and co-ownership of the written public space at the front of the class. An example of one such in-class blackboard chart occurs at the beginning of the unit on "God." Prof. Bateson's journal describes making a chart on the board "laying out Anselm's ontological argument and Aquinas' cosmological argument, showing the steps involved for each argument, for each logical syllogism – to teach skills of theological argument through *reason* either a priori/analytic reason or a posterior, empirical reason." Then, as part of the discussion, she works with students to compose a list of attributes of God implied by Anselm's and Aquinas' arguments. She adds that list to the chart she has drawn on the board. Students thus become part of the analysis and argumentation on the blackboard.

Focus questions

To play this co-creative role, students must be prepared. Prof. Bateson does not have students write every day or give quizzes, but she employs a number of strategies to encourage reading. One strategy is that, for nearly every class day, she posts a list of "focus questions" on a course website provided by Blackboard (the on-line course management system).

Explicit expectations

Another strategy is to spell out expectations. She reports in her journals that, as a result of past difficulties with students not using the focus questions and not preparing, she has spelled out at length in her syllabus the requirements for participation, suggesting that student write out at least 1 page of notes for focus questions before they come to class and that they should expect to make a contribution in class at least once a week.

Participation as part of the grade

Participation counts 15 percent of the student's grade. The participation grade is based partly on the professor's observation and partly on the student's self-assessment at the end of the semester (figure 6.2).

Prof. Bateson is constantly experimenting with classroom strategies to encourage preparation and participation. A series of entries from her journal will illustrate.

Lecture-then-discussion pattern

The course opens with a class on the relationship between faith and reason, consisting of a historical overview with landmark moments in Catholic theology between Vatican I and John Paul II. She begins the semester with a lecture-then-discussion pattern. It seems to be working well at first:

> [First day of class]: After providing [through lecture and handout] a context for the reading on Vatican I, we discuss questions that conclude the reading in McGrath, so that students become familiar with the lecture/discussion design of the class.
>
> [Several days later]: Students are increasingly engaged with the readings. Patterns of participation are already getting established.

By the fifth class session, however, students' lack of preparation appears in their small group work on different ways of interpreting scripture:

> [Fifth class session]: After about thirty minutes of lecture that summarized key points on general/special revelation and that introduced different approaches to biblical authority through reading from Rahner, students were divided into small groups [of about 7 students each] to discuss all the readings from Augustine, Bernard and Langton regarding ways of interpreting scripture (referred to chart on board) in light of four questions in the McGrath reader . . . I circulated among the groups, taking notes on their discussions and keeping them on track, in terms of content and time (the groups had about 20 minutes to discuss readings which they should have prepared for class). Students did not

Mid-Semester Course Evaluation

Instructions

As stated in the course syllabus, you will have two opportunities to evaluate yourself and the course, at mid-semester and at the conclusion of the course. For the mid-semester evaluation, you should use this two-page form to give **honest and constructive commentary** about two things: 1) your preparation for and participation in the course; and 2) your evaluation of the course design and activities. I will attempt to incorporate your comments as the course continues.

I consider this form part of your self-assessment of your participation and improvement. You will receive a similar form at the end of the course to assign yourself a grade for participation and to assess whether you have improved. Therefore, you should **sign your name at the bottom of the form on page 2. Please submit this form in our next class session.**

Self-Evaluation

Participation counts toward 15% of your final course grade. Circle the letter which **best reflects** your class participation regarding the following statements, which are drawn from the requirements for class participation in this course (explained on p.2 of the syllabus). E is excellent, G is good, S is satisfactory, P is poor, and F is failing.

I read and reflect on assigned readings completely <u>before class</u>, and bring assigned readings to class.	E G S P F
I respond to (i.e. take notes on) focus questions (posted on Blackboard) on assigned readings <u>before class</u>.	E G S P F
I regularly attend class and arrive on time for class.	E G S P F
I am consistently engaged <u>in class</u> (e.g. take notes during class, listen to lectures/other students, respond to questions and comments, raise questions and comments, talk with the professor about my questions or ideas).	E G S P F
I contribute in class to class discussions once a week.	E G S P F
I participate in open, respectful dialogue with the professor and other students, <u>in class</u>, even when I offer an alternative, opposing point of view.	E G S P F
I actively share responsibilities <u>in class</u> small group work, other class activities.	E G S P F
My understanding of major topics in historical and contemporary Christian theology is significantly growing.	E G S P F
My appreciation of the diversity in Christian theology is significantly growing.	E G S P F
My skills for doing theology, for making theological arguments that are consistent with the Christian tradition and with contemporary concerns, are significantly growing.	E G S P F

I missed class approximately __ days for excused absences, and ___ days for unexcused absences.

If you are not presently meeting the standards for participation in the course, and/or are not meeting your own standards, **circle two goals** that you set for yourself for the rest of the course, so that you and I can assess your improvement and progress accordingly.

Contact the professor about participation	Set aside more adequate time for class prep
Create study groups outside of class	Use extra resources for class prep (see "Resources" on Blackboard)
Improve in class small group work	Improve papers (consult Writer's Workshop & professor; revise drafts)

This course reflects the College's general expectation that students should set aside at least 2-3 hours of prep time for each one hour class session. Estimate how many hours you spend preparing for one class session. Explain how you usually spend that time. What part of the readings / focus questions do you usually complete? How might you improve your class prep time in the rest of the course?

Figure 6.2 Prof. Bateson's mid-term and final student self-evaluation

Course Evaluation
What do you think the course does well? What activities in the course have most helped you to learn?

What changes would you suggest as the course moves forward?

What is the most intriguing or challenging thing that you have learned so far?

What things would you like to know more about but have not been discussed?

Are there any other comments that you'd like to share about your assessment of yourself or of the course?

Student Signature________________________________

Final Evaluation

Final Self-Assessment: Class Participation and Improvement

Student Name (Last, First): ____

Course: RELS 114 **Section** (circle one): **01** (9am) **02** (10am)

Instructions
In addition to my own records, I will use this self-assessment form for calculating your participation grade in this course (which counts for 15% of your final grade) and for assessing your improvement in this course. Please use this two-page form to assign yourself a grade for participation and to assess whether you have improved in this course based on two goals that you set for yourself on the mid-semester evaluation. **SUBMIT THIS FORM WITH YOUR TAKE-HOME FINAL. THIS FORM CONSTITUTES PART OF YOUR COURSEWORK; IF YOU DO NOT SUBMIT THIS FORM, YOUR COURSEWORK IS CONSIDERED INCOMPLETE.**

Restate your self-evaluation of your participation from your mid-semester evaluation form regarding each of the following statements. Then, circle the letter which best reflects your class participation AT THE END OF THE SEMESTER. E is excellent, G is good, S is satisfactory, P is poor, and F is failing.

Participation	**Mid-Semester**	**Now**
I read and reflected on assigned readings completely <u>before class</u>, and brought assigned readings to class.	___	E G S P F
I responded to (i.e. took notes on) focus questions (posted on Blackboard) on assigned readings <u>before class</u>.	___	E G S P F
I regularly attended class and arrived on time for class.	___	E G S P F
I was consistently engaged <u>in class</u> (e.g. took notes during class, listened to lectures/other students, responded to questions and comments, raised questions and comments, talked with the professor about my questions or ideas).	___	E G S P F
I contributed to <u>in-class</u> discussions, at least once a week.	___	E G S P F

Figure 6.2 *Continued*

I participated in open, respectful dialogue with the professor and other students, ___ E G S P F
in class, even when I offered an alternative, opposing point of view.

I actively shared responsibilities in class small group work, other class activities.___ E G S P F

My understanding of major topics in historical and contemporary theology has ___ E G S P F
significantly grown.

My appreciation of the diversity in Christian theology has significantly grown. ___ E G S P F

My skills for doing theology, for making theological arguments that are ___ E G S P F
appropriate to Christian tradition and adequate to contemporary contexts and concerns have significantly grown.

Overall, I missed class approximately __ days for excused absences and ___ days for unexcused absences.

After averaging my responses to the above questions, I assign myself the following letter grade for participation based on the College's grade scale (see below). _________

Excellent	A	A-	B+
Good	B	B-	C+
Satisfactory	C	C-	D+
Poor	D		
Fail	F		

(over)

Please add any other relevant comments about your class participation.

Improvement

At mid-semester, you set at least two goals for yourself to improve during the rest of the course. Please restate your two goals from your mid-semester evaluation form.

1.

2.

Circle the letter which best reflects your progress on these two goals during the semester. **Rate yourself only on the statements that apply to your two goals**. E is excellent, G is good, S is satisfactory, P is poor, and F is failing.

I contacted the professor (via email, office hours, and appointments) about participation, and followed through on suggested strategies. E G S P F

I joined/created study groups to help with reading and with participation. E G S P F

I made a genuine effort to improve my work with others in small groups. E G S P F

I set aside more time to prepare adequately for each class session. E G S P F

I utilized extra resources (e.g. on Blackboard and in the library) to answer focus questions and do other assignments so that I could better clarify and articulate my questions and ideas in class discussions, etc. E G S P F

I tried to improve papers, by consulting with the professor, by reviewing the comments on previous papers, by following the Guidelines for Papers, by writing and revising rough drafts, by consulting peer tutors at the Writer's Workshop. E G S P F

Other (please explain): E G S P F

Please add any other relevant comments about your improvement in the course.

Figure 6.2 *Continued*

> prepare; some groups more productive than others. Groups of 7 were too large. Is there a better way to create/form groups?
>
> [Next class session]: Students are now quite familiar with lecture-discussion design of class that opens with a lecture, breaks for a close analytical discussion of reading in light of focus questions, and continues with a summative analysis of key points . . . I think I am trying to cover too much material in the opening part, *or* students are not fully prepared for class (or *both*).

Short in-class reading-then-discussion

Trying to address the issues of student preparation and her own tendency to cover too much, Prof. Bateson tries a new sequence of activities, opening the class session not with lecture, and not with questions from the readings, but with a short article that students read on the spot, which then serves as the beginning of discussion:

> [Feb. 11]: To address a seeming lack of student interaction [I opened class with] a case study on evolution/creationism based on some arguments for intelligent design. I gave students 10 minutes to read the *Newsweek* article and then we discussed it in light of Aquinas' argument from design, noting key differences in contemporary design arguments. Students more deeply engaged and analyzed the material when presented in this light . . . Students responded to the case study, but did not have the knowledge of Aquinas at their fingertips to do an in-depth analysis; next time, I will introduce Aquinas through this contemporary issue . . . Students seemed relieved to engage in a free form discussion with only a simple chart on the board, listing 3 kinds of reason – analytic (Descartes), empirical (Locke, Kant), affective (Pascal, Wittgenstein) – and associating each kind with a particular author that we addressed in discussion of focus questions. A success! Through the readings of Pascal/Wittgenstein, students raised questions about the kinds of experience that bring knowledge of God, which prompted a brief but insightful dialogue about the need for a broad range of experiences – including and beyond suffering – to know God. They are thinking like theologians and assessing the readings in light of questions about *adequacy/context/lived experience*!

The next two class sessions, however, are disappointing. She writes: "Students not very engaged . . . are they doing the reading? Are they bored with the 'read-lecture-discussion-with-charts' pattern of teaching?"

So the read-then-discuss pattern is not the magic bullet. She works now to change the interaction among students, urging them to reply to one another's questions. After the next class session she writes: "Students did not respond to their peers' questions without my prompting. How do I get them to participate, respect one another, engage?"

The following class session, which continues with arguments about the existence of God in modern European Christianity, prompts her to write in her journal:

> Handouts render students silent – handouts tend to tap into authoritarian, dominant pedagogy that renders students passive recipients of knowledge. This is exactly the opposite of feminist theological aims/purposes/goals that seek to shift persons from passive objects to active subjects – and exactly the opposite of my goals for this class.

Incomplete handout/worksheet

Next, she tries another strategy: the incomplete handout – a worksheet that students must themselves fill out during in-class lecture and large class discussion. The worksheet "enabled students to follow lecture and add to worksheet during discussions of readings." The handouts are incomplete, requiring students to actively listen to both teacher and peers while taking in-class notes, thus creating multiple sources of authority in the classroom – the instructor, students who speak, students who write their own notes.

After her summary of the theological debates, "students were able to identify and summarize the major issues involved in these debates about Jesus' full divinity or full humanity. The worksheet method worked!"

The blackboard charts continue to encourage student participation: at the next class session, she again has students contribute to building the blackboard chart, adding information on various positions they have read. She reports that the "debate 'came alive' for students under the larger rubric of the humanity of Jesus and the importance of claiming that Jesus was fully human, not just appearing human."

Small-group discussions on self-chosen "big questions"

Now she begins a section of the course in which students discuss issues in groups based on their own chosen "big question." The strategy is a mixed success. In class, she breaks students into small groups:

> Based on big questions (from end of Unit I) – discuss in small groups the readings on high Christology while I circulate among the groups. I assumed that students did not do the reading before class (paper was due) so readings were short enough that students could read them together in small groups, discuss, and then connect the readings to their "big questions." As I circulated among groups, I informed them of their similar questions, of why they were grouped together and encouraged them to bring those questions to bear on the readings. Did the readings help them address their questions, if at all? Some groups succeed; other groups sit in silence, require *lots* of prompting, of my motivation – unwilling to learn? . . . Not enough time for each group to share their insight; need better time management of group work.

Student-led discussions

Another strategy is to have students lead the discussion. A class session on Feb. 28, concluding the course unit on Christology, asked students to apply what they learned in that unit to understand and analyze Latino/a Christology, as illustrated in the writings of Virgilio Elizondo. Prof. Bateson writes that student leaders:

> delivered a Powerpoint presentation on readings from Elizondo. Good questions for class to consider on the creation of borders, on the appearance of Jesus in unexpected places, on our contemporary Galilees. Great student engagement! Still needed my prompting to explain students' questions.

In-class reading-question-lecture/discussion

Now she has another breakthrough, building on the earlier experience of the *Newsweek* article that worked so well. In the course unit on Christology, she opens a class on atonement theology with a:

> definition of atonement/context of each theologian. Then proceeded to read passages (from scripture/readings), analyze them in connection to claims about the person of Christ from last two classes and claims about attributes of God, and ask students questions about them (from the focus questions in McGrath). Students seemed to respond better to this presentation style of "read passage – ask a question – analyze through some lecture/class discussion of question" rather than just ask a question about passage straight from focus questions.

Opening question and question-based handout

In the next class, she builds on this insight, emphasizing the role of questions:

> Opened class with a question – does God will suffering? Is suffering alone, in and of itself, salvific? If Jesus' death is an example, then are Christians supposed to imitate and glorify his death? Does the death/cross of Jesus point to suffering within our world to glorify it or to challenge it? I took an explicitly question-based approach to this class and to future classes, to connect to the objectives of the course. Students presented material (readings on womanist theology) through a workshop, ironically based on questions regarding the method of womanist theology, the features of Black Women's experience, and how this experience challenges and changes atonement theology. I consider this class a success because the "question-based" handout really forced students to pay attention and take notes on the presentation, or add to their own notes on the focus questions. A turning point in the overall course! Too bad we lose this momentum due to Spring Break!

Her prediction about lost momentum proves correct; for the first class after spring break, students are not prepared. At the end of that week, she notes: "Students are not reading! We cannot reach my objectives for each class session because students are not prepared. Next week, I will give them the student evaluation, as a way to improve for the rest of the course."

Student self-evaluation

The student evaluation asks students, themselves, to evaluate their contribution and preparation. This mid-term evaluation is somewhat similar to the students' final course evaluation (figure 6.2), asking the same questions for the "Self-evaluation" section, but phrased in the present tense ("I respond," "I attend"). The mid-term evaluation then asks students to set two goals for their own improvement for the second half of the semester. Finally, it asks them to evaluate the class, responding in prose to these questions:

- What do you think the course does well? What activities in the course have most helped you to learn?
- What changes would you suggest as the course moves forward?
- What is the most intriguing or challenging thing that you have learned so far?
- What things would you like to know more about but have not been discussed?

- Are there any other comments that you'd like to share about your assessment of yourself or of the course?

Student presentations

In the next course unit, on human nature, students who are presenting on the topic of sin bring a handout and Powerpoint slides. Professor Bateson writes: "Clear, concise presentation that is based on reading. Good questions, apply to us/our context. Good discussion followed the presentation and able to make connections to previous readings on Tertullian, Origen, Augustine [who also deal with original sin]."

Debate by student groups

During the same course unit on human nature, in a class on grace, she breaks students into groups, assigning them to discuss different parts of Augustine/ Pelagius, with the goal of reconstructing the debate between them, focusing on key theological claims.

> After group work, I asked each reporter to state the main point of their readings/their discussion; we bounced back and forth between Pelagius and Augustine regarding key topics like original sin, election, concluding with the condemnations of Pelagius on sin, grace, and freedom . . . the debate between Augustine and Pelagius was demonstrated and came alive for *students*! Although some students in some groups still did *not* come prepared to deal with the readings.

Written reflection

At the next class session, now at the end of March, she requires students to complete a written reflection sheet on a particular reading regarding grace in contemporary liberal theology, "to remind them about preparation for class and how long it takes to read with focus questions in mind."

Student presentations and questions

The class picks up energy now, as it enters the course unit on ecclesiology – theological reflection on the nature, features, and task of the church. In the next classes, she records students' insights in discussion – for example, "student noticed Origen's reading of scripture to support claims about salvation and church." In an early April class, she records, "Students: good questions on infallibility and institutional Church. Raise questions about whether purity of priests affects sacraments and questions about implications of Augustine's claim that only God can judge righteousness." As this discussion continues in the next class period, there is "good participation! Really engaged in class analysis of texts and themes: who counts as people of God?" In the same course unit on ecclesiology, in a class devoted to "apply what we learned about ecclesiology to interpret theologies of homosexuality," she opens with a question: "How do churches that appear to openly dissent from church teachings still consider themselves Catholic and identify as Catholic? Urge students to listen to student presentation on readings for models/marks of the church in gay/lesbian Catholic communities." The presentation was a bit disappointing because it:

> focused more on moral teachings than theology/ecclesiology, but did address Pentecost (Acts 1-2) implicitly on apostolic marks of church and did mention quote on gay/lesbian communities as part of the Body of Christ. Questions suggested at the end of the presentation addressed ethics more than theology but the final question explored the way that theology often changes to match *lived experience* – adequacy.

Questions have been central to this class all along. For the April 15 class, which opens the next-to-last course unit on eschatology (theologies of the end of the world), students are asked to "develop at least two questions regarding second coming/last judgment and resurrection of the body . . . to further explore what strikes you about claims regarding the themes of judgment and resurrection." She reminds students that "in an effort to promote more inclusivity in our class discussion, I will especially ask students who do not usually participate to volunteer their questions for our class to consider." During the class session, "students suggested questions for discussion and we engaged their questions regarding the place of earth/creation and the physical and spiritual nature of resurrection. Some students are highly resistant to participation, to asking questions, some are even absent on these 'question' days, building seemingly impenetrable walls to learning."

But at the next class session, on heaven and hell, "students were disturbed by [Jonathan] Edwards' view of a wrathful God, ready to strike down all people into hell. Pointed out that this image does <u>not</u> fit with Scripture and tradition, *not* adequate to lived experience of God's love. *Great*! They are doing theology!"

At the next class session, which occurred near the end of the semester, student presenters ignored some key points, but they "built in questions into the worksheet and students stayed engaged!" However, a student presentation in the next class has "no handout, no chart, no engagement."

Chart-reading-association

In the next class, which opens the last unit of the course regarding Christian theological approaches to religious diversity, she makes a chart on the board showing various approaches to religious diversity, then reads passages and asked students to associate a passage with an approach. Students return to being "very engaged."

Now only two classes remain in the semester, and students are "not very engaged. Mostly lecture, just coasting to conclusion of the course," though on the final day, they "raised and addressed good questions about the shift from Christ to God in [various readings], as well as possibility of dialogue based around Christ, when Christ is often at the base of colonialism."

I have included this rather long semester-long story of one teacher's attempt to engage her students because it demonstrates the constant cycle of experimenting with a strategy, observing carefully how well it works and why, then trying something else, over and over again. It's an approach typical of all the Highly-Effective teachers, and it embodies part of what I mean by the principle of systematic observation and reflection that seems central to teaching effectiveness.

Student evaluations

What students thought they learned

The class is unusual in that, on the IDEA survey, the frequency of students reporting "substantial" or "exceptional" progress was highest not for factual knowledge, but rather for "Learning to *analyze* and *critically evaluate* ideas, arguments, and points of view" (74 percent) and "Learning fundamental principles, generalizations, or theories" (74 percent), followed by "Learning to *apply* course material (to improve thinking, problem solving, and decisions)" (67 percent) and "Factual knowledge" (67 percent).

Evaluations of teaching

Prof. Bateson's IDEA scores place her in the top 30 percent of faculty on the IDEA database for "excellent teacher" and "excellent course." Her highest scores are "Explained course material clearly and concisely" (100 percent of her student respondents marked "frequently" or "nearly always."), "Displayed a personal interest in students and their learning" (100 percent), "Demonstrated the importance and significance of the subject matter" (100 percent), "Found ways to help the students answer their own questions" (93 percent), and "Scheduled course work (class activities, tests, projects) in ways which encouraged students to stay up-to-date in their work" (93 percent).

Strategies that help learning

Eleven out of 20 students mention the blackboard diagrams. Next highest are the incomplete worksheet handouts, mentioned by six students.

Student suggestions

The most common student suggestions are for more discussion (25 percent of all comments) and more group activities (25 percent of all comments). This seeming paradox between a teacher's struggle to get students engaged and students' end-of-course request for more discussion is not unique to Prof. Bateson's class. I think it affirms the importance of discussion to both faculty and students, and, at the same time, the complexity of the issue and the difficulty of implementing it.

Prof. Bateson has a very clear focus on theological argument. Without daily quizzes or daily writing, she works very hard to achieve student preparation, using a number of strategies, trying something, observing how it works, then trying something else. Students have many voices in this class: analyzing theological positions, arguing their own, asking their own questions, leading class discussion, collaborating with others in class discussion, creating blackboard diagrams, and working with their peers in small groups, both inside and outside of class. Both the classroom and the essays are forums where students, in their role as theological inquirers and as arguers for their own positions, learn to integrate the intellectual content and theological method of inquiry with their own spiritual and religious beliefs.

The next case shows a faculty member who, like Bateson, values student participation, emphasizes theological inquiry, and emphasizes students' ability to construct and argue their own theological positions. However, Prof. Irish teaches in a private non-sectarian setting, and he has a somewhat different personal style and pedagogical strategies than Prof. Bateson.

Prof. Irish

"The Experience of God," Private Non-Sectarian Baccalaureate Institution, 22 students

Prof. Jerry Irish [his real name] teaches theology at Pomona College in a somewhat different frame than Prof. Bateson, and he constructs somewhat different spaces for student voices, especially in his "theological profile" assignment and in his constant invitation to students to construct and argue their own theological positions.

Goals

Prof. Bateson, the first case, has chosen a textbook called *Faith Seeking Understanding* – the traditional definition of "theology." Prof. Irish defines "theological thinking," using Diana Eck, as "the task of bringing to the surface and examining the ideas of ultimacy and reality that we already employ and in terms of which we live our lives. It is the critical and yet open questioning of these ideas." Prof. Irish places strong emphasis on students shaping their own theologies, though he also wants them to compare and analyze other theologians.

Prof. Irish opens his class with questions about various theologians, how they compare with one another, how their writings stand up against experience. But his questions also ask whether the theologies "give expression to our own views" and says the class will be alert to the merits of various theological perspectives, "including our own." He explains in the syllabus:

> This course explores works representative of contemporary African American, Asian American, ecological, feminist, Latin American, liberation, process, and womanist theologies. It does so with several questions in mind. How do these theologians describe the human condition? Are their descriptions convincing? How do their theologies function? What do their theologies have in common? How do they differ? Do any of these writers speak from our own experience? What insights do they have for our pluralistic, multicultural society? Do they give expression to our own views, religious or secular?
>
> By thinking critically and systematically about the course readings, we will clarify our own assumptions. The written work for the course is intended to deepen our understanding of the readings and sharpen our capacity to express our own views. Through classroom discussion we will become increasingly alert to the merits of various theological perspectives, including our own.
>
> The mutually reinforcing combination of reading, reflection, writing, and discussion in this course satisfies [the college's] requirement to "think critically about values and rationality." The course is also designated "writing-intensive."

Assignments: What was learned?

Prof. Irish assigns four 3–5-page essays in response to questions he poses; a take-home final exam that calls for a 7–10-page essay around a topic he suggests or the student proposes in consultation with him; a "theological profile" in which students describe their own theologies; and periodic written questions/issues for discussion, critiques of other students' papers, and reflections on the readings.

Exam

For the take-home final essay exam, students choose from among nine topics (e.g., God's relation to the world; selfhood and/or community; theme, issue or problem of your own choosing submitted ahead of time to the professor for approval). In keeping with his emphasis on students as theologians, constructing their own positions, the instructions for the final exam state:

> Regardless of the topic you choose, make explicit and substantial reference to at least five of the theologians we have discussed in this course, including at least one on whom you have not already written a paper. Be equally precise in stating your own position on the topic.

Students shape a thesis that includes their own view about a topic, not only a thesis that expresses an analysis of other theologians.

Short essays

Stating students' own positions

Topics for the four 3–5-page essays often ask students to state their own positions: "Set forth what Johnson means by the suffering God. How do female metaphors function in this understanding? Do you find Johnson's position coherent and/or convincing? Why? Why not?"

Student roles for class discussion of papers

Sample student papers are discussed in class. For this discussion, students are assigned roles as writers, critics, or discussion leaders. On the day each paper is discussed, the "critics" must bring to class a written list of comments and questions, based on their prior reading of the paper (which has been made available to them). After class, the professor collects these and returns them to the student authors. Discussion leaders are asked to identify several discussion questions that are central in understanding the assigned readings and then must "facilitate a productive consideration of the student paper and the theologian under consideration."

The essays thus evoke several student voices: not only writer and theologian analyzing others' positions and stating one's own, but also critic of others' theological arguments, and leaders of class discussion.

Draft response

Prof. Irish responds to drafts with multiple comments and a grade. Students revise, and then he responds again with more comments and a new grade (which counts, this time). A self-identified "white person" writing on James Cone's *A Black Theology of Liberation,* spends most of the paper discussing his/her own "angry feelings." Irish gives a C+ grade and writes on the draft, in part:

> This paper articulates clearly your personal reaction to Cone's book, but it doesn't say all that much about Cone's understanding of God and human freedom. Because your treatment of Cone, your exposition and analysis of his position on God, freedom, is thin/superficial, your criticisms are vague and/or mistaken. This is *not* to say that some of your criticisms aren't appropriate, but that they don't engage the real substance of Cone's position. You are aiming at a target that is ill-defined in this paper.

The student revises the paper, more carefully explaining Cone's position, and correcting some omissions and mis-representations that Prof. Irish had pointed out in the draft. Toward the end, the student again acknowledges his discomfort and anger in reading the book, and states that Cone had to be forceful to make his point, but the student does not argue with Cone's position or choices. Prof. Irish emphasizes the importance of arguing the student's own position:

> The exposition and analysis in this paper is much clearer than in the original. You might have gone a bit more deeply into Cone's position on God and freedom, but what you have presented here is sound. I fear in holding off on your critical reaction to Cone, a good idea in clarifying your paper, you muted somewhat your own position. Be sure in future papers to make the critical points you think appropriate. If your exposition and analysis are sound, you will find a way to justify a legitimate, logical position of your own. In the meantime, this is a much-improved paper.

Another student gives a more proficient and nuanced analysis of Cone's position and then a critique. Irish responds with a call for deeper analysis, with a question that might provoke the student's further thinking, and with praise. Here is a selection from the student's essay:

> While I agree with his [Cone's] statement that white people can never truly understand what it means to be black and a minority, I disagree with his refusal to acknowledge the contribution to the civil rights movement of left-leaning white Christians and the class oppression of poor whites. [Irish writes, "Would Cone say these white Christians became black?"] While it is a productive exercise to view Christianity from the detailed perspective of a narrow, cultural-historical context (race relations in America), one must then re-universalize the model [Irish writes, "When the model is re-universalized is it still an 'inspiring message' "?] in order to have relevance over time and place, and to reinforce its primary status as a religious theory rather than a political strategy. [Irish writes, "Excellent point, very well put."]

Irish's extensive comments on student work are a significant investment in conversation. He writes in his journal:

> I have come to realize that my mode of operation is to enter into a conversation with my students. While this conversation certainly takes place in the classroom and, with some students, outside the classroom, the writing and rewriting of papers is an equally significant "venue." In commenting on and discussing their written work I have the opportunity to guide and encourage students in their critical and constructive self-awareness as theologians, persons "bringing to the surface and examining the ideas of ultimacy and reality that we already employ and in terms of which we live our lives" (Diana Eck). My theology seminar aims to be an intellectual arena in which students can ask the "big questions" in a rigorous and thoughtful manner.

Theological profile

The importance Irish places on students' development of their own theologies is emphasized again in the short assignment called the "theological profile." This profile, due just after the mid-point of the course, is distributed, with students' permission, among all members of the class. It is to be no more than half a page single-spaced, addressing as many as relevant of the following questions:

1 Do you believe in or have faith in God or some comparable reality? What are the essential features or attributes of this reality?
2 If you do not believe in or have faith in some sort of god or comparable reality as in #1, what would you identify as the most comprehensive reality that does frame or transcend your existence? What are its essential features or attributes?
3 On what are your answers to #1 or #2 based (e.g., personal experience, hearsay, scientific or rational proof, religious background, sacred texts)?
4 Are you a member of an organization, institution, or community that focuses on or directly relates to the object of your theology (e.g., church, meditation group, nature society, synagogue)? If so, identify it and describe your level of participation.
5 To what extent or in what ways does your theology as described above influence your behavior?

Irish does not subject these profiles to the line-by-line critique he uses for the essays; rather, they spur student thoughtfulness and help to build community in the classroom, as they are shared. Students do not argue their positions here, but describe them. Yet they also describe the backing for their positions – personal experience, rational proof, etc.

Sample student profiles

> I have been exposed to the Christian faith for most of my life, but I don't think I really came into relationship with God until a few years ago. From the time I was very young I understood God as the Creator and the Almighty, but now I see that God is a part of my life – a part of me – and that I am connected to God primarily through my understanding of Jesus' suffering, love and forgiveness. I have faith in God's justice and grace, and I believe that God expresses these things through active rather than passive love. I think God challenges me with paradoxical realities: the power in choosing shared suffering and struggle, the redemption in forgiving the unforgivable, the glory in humility. It is difficult for me to live out these truths because they are unnatural and seemingly illogical, but these are the truths I try to live by.
>
> Aside from Christian doctrine and tradition, I think my personal walk with Christ or personal experience has been the center of my faith. I rely on specific instances in my life when I felt extreme connectivity and meaning in my relationship with God. I do not identify with a particular denomination of Christianity, but I suppose general Protestantism would be the closest if I were forced to choose. Even though

> I have been through some difficult times in my faith, I think in the hardest times in my life, I have been pulled through by that same faith. I attend Christian church services and participate in Bible studies. I find accountability in Christian peers and strength in prayer. I am constantly thinking about concrete ways to intertwine my faith with my daily life because I fear becoming a "Sunday Christian." I believe my relationship with God gives me a satisfaction that nothing else in life could, and I try my best to express that in my behaviors and decisions.

> My spirituality rests far more on a personal feeling than a rational belief in an objective deity, or a particular tradition that I was raised in. It has very much to do with an intuition that there is "good" in this world, and that there is more to life than what merely appears in front of us, more than what we can derive from our senses. Lately I have found myself marveling at science and the infinite intricacy with which this world and the human psyche is put together; this is to say that while the world might simply be a large machine, the nature of the machine itself leads me to question if there might be more. Personal experiences have also influenced my views, moments when I will observe, hear, or think of something that leaves me *awestruck* and with a greater understanding of my place in the universe. It is moments like these when I realize that I am very, very small and that life, particularly the undeservedly fortunate life that I have led, is a gift that must be celebrated. Philosophically, I find myself increasingly drawn toward Hinduism and its view of Karma, worldly desire, and self-realization. At the same time, another part of me struggles to understand the need for organized religion, particularly in certain areas where I might differ in my self-derived views from Hindu teachings. My parents came from India to America with a strongly Hindu background and I was always made aware of its fundamental tenets while never being forced to embrace the religion itself, and I believe than any inclination toward Hinduism has been almost completely the result of my own experiences. I think to say that my "theology" influences my behavior is a gross misconception; my "theology" is the Self from which my behavior emanates. To me, "theology" and the Self are synonymous whether or not my philosophy is devoid of a belief in God, which I have yet to determine and may spend the rest of my life determining.

Asking students to describe their own theologies without arguing them, and to share them (if they wish) with the class is a very interesting move, I think. It emphasizes the individual and situated nature of theological positions – though theology relies on reason, each person comes to a different place. It provides a forum for the "believer" voice that, in this one assignment, does not have to defend or present arguments for a position. Sharing their positions helps students to know one another as believers, and creates a level field in the classroom where each person's choices about belief are equally respected, in this one assignment, without regard to the strength of the reasoning that supports them. This creation of a very different space for sharing of belief recalls Prof. Veldman's creation of the out-of-class coffee hour for his students to ask him about, and to share their own, "believers" questions.

Readings

Irish assigns more than 1,000 pages of reading. Students read, in this order, James Cone, *A Black Theology of Liberation*; Gustavo Gutierrez, *A Theology of Liberation* (anniversary edition); Chaon-Seng Song, *Third Eye Theology*; Elizabeth Johnson, *She Who Is*; Marjorie Suchocki, *God, Christ, Church*; Catherine Keller, *Face of the Deep*; James Nelson, *Body Theology*; Delores Williams, *Sisters in the Wilderness*; Judith Plaskow, *Standing Again at Sinai*; and Sallie McFague, *The Body of God*.

Students rate the amount of reading and difficulty of subject matter as average for the IDEA database for theology and religion, but lower than average for "I worked harder on this course than on most courses I have taken."

Use of class time

Irish marks on the survey that half to three-fourths of his in-class time is "interactive lecture, in which students speak 10–25 percent of the time" – a time allocation similar to that of Prof. Bateson. Also common are "teacher-led discussion in which students speak more than 25 percent of the time," and "student-led discussion in which a student(s) has responsibility for initiating and guiding the discussion, and other students speak more than 25 percent of the time."

Assigned student roles as writers, critics, discussion leaders

Prof. Irish uses the short essays as a basis for class discussion. Here is his explanation:

> One third of the class writes a paper, one third of the class writes out notes [on one of the written papers, which the professor chooses and makes available the day ahead] as though they were doing a critique of the paper, and one third of the class writes out notes on the issues they would like to raise about the paper and the assigned reading as

> though they were going to lead the discussion. The paper I choose from among those submitted by the authors is available the day before the class discussion. I also choose one critic and one discussion leader, but everyone turns in their notes. Guidelines for critics and discussion leaders are among the handouts . . . I return the critics' notes to the author of the paper after I have graded and commented on that paper; I keep the discussion notes for my own information about what students find interesting.

During these sessions, he relates in his journal his own struggle to say enough but not too much, especially when the students have not done a very good job.

Student written questions

About two-thirds of the way through the course, after a day when not very many students have entered the conversation, he asks them to come to the next session with questions about the reading. That strategy works well, and he continues to use it.

In-class reading, then discussion

At times he uses a technique similar to Bhattacharyya's and Bateson's – beginning the class with students reading pertinent passages, and using that reading to launch discussion:

> First discussion of Williams and her interpretation of the Hagar story. I called on students to read the two accounts of Hagar in Genesis aloud. Quite a bit of disagreement as to whether or not Hagar is, in any positive sense, a role model for or someone who can be critically appropriated by contemporary black women. Quite a few students became involved in that discussion.

Student evaluations

What do students think they learned?

Atypically for the classes as a whole, Prof. Irish's students do not mark factual knowledge as their highest achievement. Instead, 73 percent say they made "substantial" or "exceptional" progress on "Developing a clearer understanding of, and commitment to, personal values" and 68 percent for "Learning fundamental principles, generalizations, or theories." In students' prose reflections about their learning, collected from the same class taught in a later semester with some different readings, the outcomes most frequently mentioned are clarifying their beliefs (48 percent), broadening their outlook (37 percent), strengthening their beliefs (24 percent), and learning critical thinking (22 percent). Here are samples:

> This course has been very interesting for me as far as my spiritual journey. I came into the class as a follower of Jesus Christ. Many of the conventional notions were challenged in this course. But I came away with a more coherent understanding of Christ and God as he/she relates to the world . . . The most important vehicle for this was the classroom discussions – we were asked to relate and personally comment on each theologian, which helped me to have to articulate my understandings and have to defend them in class.

> As an agnostic and a long-time questioner of the religion in which I was raised, my beliefs were challenged in this course. Although, when all is said and done, I'm still an agnostic, and I still feel deeply drawn toward spirituality without the clothing of organized religion. But, with the breadth of work we've read on understanding of God, particularly Buber, Niebuhr, McFague, and Keller, my conceptions of how God could interact in the world and how we might conceive of God have expanded greatly.

Evaluations of teaching

Prof. Irish's IDEA scores place him in the top 10 percent on the IDEA database for excellent teacher (Appendix C). Students rate him high on "Explained course material clearly and concisely" (86 percent marked "frequently" or "almost always"); "Gave tests, projects, etc. that covered the most important points of the course" (86 percent); and "Made it clear how each topic fit into the course." He also scored high on "Introduced stimulating ideas about the subject" (91 percent), "Found ways to help students answer their own questions" (91 percent) and "Related course material to real life situations" (96 percent). The caring issue is also strong: "Displayed a personal interest in students and their learning" (100 percent).

The two faculty members, Bateson and Irish, both demand student engagement, and both focus on theological reasoning, though they use somewhat different strategies. Prof. Irish places strong emphasis on students stating and defending their own theological positions. The next case describes Prof. Steele, whose course has a different title and a somewhat different set of goals. His course goes farther in asking students to shape their own theology, and he conducts a robust conversation with his students about their theological positions and his own.

Prof. Steele

Prof. Richard B. Steele [his real name] teaches "Christian Formation" to a class of 39 honors students at Seattle Pacific University, a Protestant Masters institution that explicitly aims to nurture Christian faith. Prof. Steele reports that most students are Christian, and religious activities are extremely popular on campus. He describes his role as a "pastoral theologian," whose task is to confront students with ideas that are unfamiliar or heterodox for them, and then to lead them through the resulting relativism toward a "more ecumenical outlook," and "a mature, reflective faith, in which one's convictions, though passionately and vigorously practiced, have been chastened by some exposure to the checkered history of the Christian faith and refined by the fires of scientific criticism." His notion of the "maturity" toward which he wants his students to move is shaped not just by Enlightenment ideals of the critical thinker, but by the ideal of a mature, ecumenical, and knowledgeable Christian. The following description of his teaching emphasizes the kinds of conversations he creates in his course – different from those of both Bateson and Irish. More about his teaching appears in his published work, cited in the references.

Course goals

Steele's course is the first of a sequence of three required of students: after "Christian Formation," students take "Christian Scripture" and "Christian Theology." In his syllabus, Steele lists the departmental goals for introductory courses; below are the ones he has italicized as particularly relevant to "Christian Formation":

- Students will gain an informed and reflective faith.
- Students will gain confidence in the Christian faith.
- Students will shape their lives around Christian character and values.
- Students will understand how Scripture, reason, tradition, and experience inform theological reflection.
- Students will cultivate personal Bible study into their lives.
- Students will identify historical and contemporary diversity in the global Christian tradition.

- Students will be more active participants in the worship and ministry of a local congregation ["tacit" only, he explains; he "will neither teach to it nor assess for it"]

Prof. Steele's presentation to students begins in the syllabus as he describes his own theological position: "I describe my approach to Christian theology as orthodox, evangelical, ecumenical, and critical." He then explains each of these terms. Next, he writes:

> You need not accept my approach to Christian theology – or even be a Christian – to excel in this course, but you must be willing to endure what may seem to be a troubling paradox. For although we seek to understand Christian *Truth*, assuming it to be divinely revealed and logically self-consistent, we do so recognizing the degree to which the sinfulness and limitations of every person and every church body skew our apprehension of the Truth and render every formulation of it tentative and provisional. You must therefore reckon with the relativity of theological science and must expect neither confirmation of your existing religious opinions nor "final answers" from the course or the instructors. You must be willing to look at the gospel from new perspectives with charity and intellectual openness, as well as critical acumen, and to restrain any "apologetic" impulse you may feel to refute those with whom you disagree or to convert those in the class who may not believe as you do.

In these lines, he directs students away from voices they may find familiar – the voice of the apologist or evangelist – and urges them to charity, intellectual openness, and critical acumen. His own voice as a theologian is a strong force in the syllabus, and in the course as a whole.

Assignments: What did students learn?

The course is divided into five units, with a graded assignment due at the end of each. Three of those assignments are exams, consisting of multiple choice/short answer, and an essay. In addition, there are a spiritual autobiography and a "credo" of five pages, "stating and defending your position on one of the classical doctrinal loci, as set forth in the Catechism and/or any of the Historical Documents of the church. You are to state your reasons for agreeing or disagreeing with the manner in which that article is formulated by a mainline Protestant denomination." Like Prof. Irish, Prof. Steele frequently asks students for their own positions on a theological debate. Prof. Steele's "credo" assignment is different from Prof. Irish's theological profile in its combination of historical theological debate and the student's position backed by reasons. Further, Prof. Steele provides a point of reference common to the whole class: the Catechism and/or historical church documents. Students may agree or disagree, but the framework of the class is Christian theology.

Credo essay

The students' "Credo" essays vary in topic and tone. For example, one student begins by posing a dilemma: the Bible may seem to say that unbelievers will not be granted salvation, but that view is problematic. The writer goes on to present his argument for a particular answer to that dilemma. His concluding paragraph sums up his arguments:

> It is for this reason that I insist on a more open-minded approach to the question of who will and will not be saved. The foundation for asserting that only Christians will inherit everlasting life is shaky, and the attitude the belief breeds in its subscribers is an exceedingly dangerous one. From the teachings of Jesus I conclude that God's desire for this world is founded in His incomprehensible love, and that our sole purpose is to reflect that love. By claiming to be able to define the eternal fate of men we overstep our authority and encourage attitudes and practices that seem to resemble Christ's love very little. The question of salvation is, though personally pressing, not to be the focus or aim of our lives. I believe that the mystery of divine salvation is a wondrous gift whose recipients shall be known to God alone.

Prof. Steele praises the student:

> This is a wonderful essay – tightly argued, richly illustrated, gracefully written, and thoroughly animated by a deep and catholic-spirited love for humanity. There are one or two places where the syntax might have been improved, and I have called attention to them in my marginal and interlinear remarks. But the combination of careful theological reasoning and a keen flair for how theological reasoning should be put to work in mission and evangelism and pastoral care is really stunning.

Another student also poses a dilemma: the writer finds it impossible to reconcile a loving God with an evil world. Theodicy, the writer states, "attempts to make this reconciliation, and falls short." But instead of explaining the logical fallacies of theodicy and arguing for a new position, the writer asks, "Why do I feel this way?" She confides that as the daughter of a sexually abusive father, she cannot see God as father, and launches into a poetic essay that repeats the refrain, "if I did not hate myself . . . " She describes her fascination with the world of literature and analyzes what it offers her, quoting the poet Sydney. Before writing this version of the paper, the student has visited Prof. Steele's office to confer about the paper. His comment on the final essay makes reference to this earlier draft and office visit:

> I am so thankful that you approached this essay as you did. You captured in a breathtakingly honest and rhetorically powerful way many of the crucial insights that we talked about in my office last week. I admire the way you started off by a reference to the draft that you wound up rejecting, then inventoried the realizations you came to about the consequences of your self-hatred, and then concluded – brilliantly, I think – with a suitable reference to "the golden world of literature," where the world *is* what you would like it to be. I am struck, however, by the fact that the "hollow sham" of a religion that is nothing more than wishes (p. 1, par 3) rather closely resembles the world of imagination described by Sydney. Why reject the one and not the other? Perhaps because poetry acknowledges that it is an exercise of the imagination, whereas religion professes to be "true." The question, then, is whether you can find the connection between the healing power of imagination and the deep truths of the gospel according to which you are loved. Let's talk again.

On one level, Steele is making the theology professor's move of calling the student's attention to a logical fallacy – why reject one and not the other? Also in a professorial vein, he discusses the history of the paper's development and praises both the writer's choice to scrap the first draft and the effective aspects of this one. He then makes a pastoral move, but he does not pose an answer to the student's dilemma; rather, he poses a question – can you find the connection? But within the question is also a theological assertion – according to the gospel, you are loved. The invitation to "talk again" is a common one for Steele: he spends many hours in his office talking with students, and, in addition, carries on an extensive e-mail conversation with a number of them, as they ask questions about issues such as the existence of evil or whether non-Christians can be saved, and he replies in his own voice, as a Christian theologian, explaining his own understanding of the issue, and/or pointing out the arguments on several sides, and/or posing questions.

Readings

Texts are *The Book of Common Prayer*; Endo Shusako, *Silence*; Luke Timothy Johnson, *The Creed: What Christians Believe and Why It Matters*; Anne Lamott, *Traveling Mercies: Some Thoughts on Faith*; Lesslie Newbigin, *Foolishness to the Greeks: The Gospel and Western Culture*; and Chaim Potok, *The Chosen*.

Prof. Steele marks on the survey that he assigns 600–1,000 pages of reading. Eighty-three percent of his students say they "hardly ever" or "occasionally" come to class without having read the assignment (Appendix D). Thus Prof. Steele gets a very high rate of student classroom preparation in comparison to other faculty in the Highly-Effective group.

Use of class time

The course is divided into five units:

1 Biblical Faith and Human Reason: Friends or Foes?
2 The Historic Church: The Context of Christian Formation
3 The Inspired Scripture: The Content of Christian Revelation
4 The Faithful Disciple: The Pathos and Praxis of the Christian Life
5 The Postmodern World: The Locus of Contemporary Christian Witness.

Prof. Steele has an extensive collection of Powerpoint slides which he uses in class, but his lecture style is highly interactive, including both students' comments/questions and his own personal stories, which students very much appreciate. More than most faculty, he shares himself as a person with his students.

His daily journal is a record of his attempt to balance lecture and discussion and to get good discussion going in the class. He's afraid he's not doing very well. But then comes a turning point, where his students reassure him:

> It was an amazing day today! At the beginning of the class, two of the women approached me with mischief in their eyes and asked if they could make an announcement. I agreed, and they proceeded to tell the class that they had heard through my daughter (who is a sophomore here) that today was my 52nd birthday. They led the class in a rousing chorus of "Happy Birthday," and then laid hands on me and offered a very moving and heartfelt prayer for me as their teacher. Then they passed out cupcakes. I was simply unglued by this. After I wiped the tears from my eyes and the chocolate frosting from my mustache, I managed to pull myself together and begin the class. But I must say

that my suspicions that I somehow wasn't connecting with this group appear – much to my joy – to have been unfounded.

There were two main topics that we covered today. One of them – the idea of the development of religious ideas and the theory of "progressive revelation" – occupied much of Monday's class, but I didn't feel I had handled it very effectively. The other – "the problem of evil" came up at the very end of Monday's class and didn't get addressed at all. Deeply moved as I was by my students' display of affection, I really seemed to be inspired today. (It's about time that my muse paid a call!) I explained C. H. Dodd's idea of progressive revelation clearly and succinctly. In the course of the answer I discussed one of the most decisive shifts in Israel's self-understanding as the "chosen people." The earlier "nationalistic" idea of being chosen for special privileges led, in Deutero-Isaiah and Jonah to the "missionary" idea of being chosen for a special task. This was followed, after Easter and Pentecost, by the still more radically de-nationalized missionary enterprise of the early Christians. The class then asked about the possibility that non-Jews and non-Christians could be saved. I mapped out three basic answers to that question: the "exclusive mediator model" (Cyprian of Carthage: "Outside the church there is no salvation"), the "constitutive mediator model" (Karl Rahner: "anonymous Christianity"), and the "one-of-many-mediators model" (John Hick: religious pluralism). A great discussion ensued.

The second issue was the problem of evil. I trotted out the usual conundrum: (1) God is all-powerful. (2) God is all-merciful. (3) Evil is real. It's easy to see how any two of these can be true if one denies the third. I gave Christian Science as an example of a theory that affirms (1) and (2) but denies (3); Process theology and liberal Methodism as examples of theories that affirm (2) and (3) but cast doubt on (1); and Calvinism as an example of a theory that affirms (1) and (3) but seems to deny (2). I then said that I really don't know how to make theodicy work. But I told a story from my own pastoral experience of talking with a woman who had asked me, "Why did God let my baby die?" My answer to her had been that I didn't know why God had let her baby die, but that if I did know I wouldn't tell her, because I couldn't give a "theoretical" answer to such a poignant "existential" question without trivializing her sorrow or dishonoring her son's life. I asserted that for people who suffer great loss, the "Why-question" is both inescapable and yet unanswerable. Out of respect, we must let that question have its way with them – but that when we love them in the midst

> of their pain, without trying to anaesthetize that pain with snappy theories, the question itself gradually morphs into something else: "What now?" The class really seemed taken by this. All around a very good day!

Five days later, on November 8, the class takes 10 minutes to write anonymously about their goals for learning, aspects of the class that have helped them most, and suggestions for change. Many suggest that he talks too much, and they would like more discussion. Here is a portion of the professor's answer to them, sent by email:

> I have read the comments about the class that you wrote on November 8. There were several comments that a very large number of you made, to which I would like to respond.
>
> 1. A number of you said there was too much lecturing by me from the PowerPoint presentations, and not enough discussion of the major themes of the books. This I promise to rectify – starting today. I may project a few pictures that I have included in my PP presentations to use as illustrations or discussion-starters, and in the cases of the PP presentations for the Endo and Lamott books, there are a number of slides at the end that raise precisely the sort of questions that you say you want to talk over in class. So I may project them, too. But I will cut down on the lecturing and increase the "air time" for free-wheeling discussion.

Prof. Steele carries on a rich out-of-class conversation with a number of his students, through email, office hours, postings to Blackboard, and going out with a student(s) for coffee. An email posting from another required theology course (not the one under study here) will give a flavor of these conversations (this exchange appears, along with many others, in Steele 2007). The student is exploring the same basic question as the student whose essay is cited earlier – who is saved? In this email message, invited by the student to respond, Prof. Steele makes several moves. Here is the exchange (Steele, 2006, pp. 77–9).

> Hey Dr. Steele:
> I was reviewing Migliore's chapter on the Triune God. In the section that talks about the electing grace of God, he states that God desires that everyone be saved. This has been a strong belief of mine, and so I do not question it. However, while I was reading the Gospel of Matthew in my devotions this morning, I came across some passages that seemed to contradict this point. In Matthew 10, when Jesus sends

out the disciples, he commands them not to spread the gospel to the Gentiles or Samaritans. Later in the gospel, he even tried to send away the Canaanite woman because she was not Jewish. In Matthew 13, when the disciples came to Jesus and asked him why he spoke in parables, he quoted Isaiah and replied, "You will be ever hearing but never understanding; you will be ever seeing but never perceiving. For this people's heart has become calloused; and they hardly hear with their ears, and they have closed their eyes. Otherwise they might see with their eyes, hear with their ears, understand with their hearts and turn, and I would heal them" (Matthew 13:14–15). These words and actions seem to me to contradict the idea that Christ came for all to be saved. In fact, in the great commission, he commands us to bring the gospel to *all people*. How can these two totally different views fit together?
In Christ,
Lena [name changed]

Dear Lena:
This is one of the thorniest and most controversial of all theological questions. Part of what drives the controversy is that the Bible itself seems to support *both* the more restrictive view that "the elect" are relatively small in number (144,000 according to Revelation 7:4), and that who they are is strictly predetermined "before the foundation of the world" (Ephesians 1:4–5), *and* the more "universalistic" view that "[God] desires everyone to be saved and to come to the knowledge of the truth" (I Timothy 2:1–6). Texts for both positions could be multiplied, but I don't think the issue can finally be resolved by the method of "proof-texting." Where one stands on the issue – *if* one has to take a stand on it at all – will finally depend on one's understanding of God. Those who emphasize the majesty and sovereignty of God and the sinfulness of humanity generally opt for the idea of election (although many take the 144,000 number to be symbolic, rather than literal), while those who emphasize "the wideness of God's mercy" generally opt for the idea that "whosoever will, may come."

As a Wesleyan evangelical born and bred, I am committed to the more inclusive view. On the other hand, I have come to believe that whenever we find such apparent contradictions in the Bible, our response should not be to choose one position and discount the other, but rather to ask whether there is some important theological message that neither position alone can encompass. Or as I said in answer to another question, the "apparent contradictions" of the Bible are often real paradoxes, and what is lacking is a broader view that can enable you to see the elements of truth in both. And I think something like that is the case here. To put it simply and sharply, I would say that the doctrine of election is consoling to Christians because it reminds them that God's saving purposes for those who have faith in Christ cannot be thwarted by the catastrophes of history or even by their own sins, while the doctrine of free grace is a reminder to those who happen to have come to saving faith in Christ that God's saving purposes are not restricted to themselves, but are offered generously to all. The former truth rescues us from despair, the latter from complacency. The clearest statement of this paradox that I have ever heard was by my teacher at Yale, the great Lutheran theologian and ecumenist, George Lindbeck: he said, "Christian faith requires us to believe in the existence of hell, and Christian love requires us to pray that it is empty." That is, we believe that, in his justice, God has good reason to send those who refuse to accept Christ as their savior to eternal judgment; but we also believe that, in his grace, God is doing everything possible to persuade all people to accept Christ freely and thus to be fit for eternal salvation. The answer to the *theoretical* question of who will be in and who will be out is not ours to know. Our task is to keep the *practical* question before us at all times: what ought we to be doing to spread the message as widely and effectively as possible? Hope this way of putting the issue helps.

[Reference is to Daniel Migliore, *Faith Seeking Understanding: An Introduction to Christian Theology* (Grand Rapids: William B. Eerdmans, 1991), ch. 4.]

The student's voice in this email is both questioner and biblical exegete. The student is not a person in pain, asking a pastor, "Why did God let my baby die," nor a student email, as to Prof. Jones, "Help me forgive God for taking my mother" (chapter 5). Instead, this is a thinking and reading student, asking about an apparent contradiction between a theological stance and what the Bible appears to say. The student shows knowledge of the classroom texts, and she voices her concern as a personal one, but within the framework of issues the class is discussing. In response, Prof. Steele makes several moves, and what he does *not* do is as important as what he *does* do. First, he sets up the problem in a logical way, outlines various possible positions, and cites other theologians. Thus he establishes the question as an intellectual and theological one, within the framework of the class. This sets the tone for the rest. He also gives his own view as a "Wesleyan, born and bred," acknowledging the situatedness of theological positions and enacting the strong personal image he projects in his classroom. He explains how he sees it, modeling a theological argument, but illustrates with an example from his own experience as a pastor. He ends with the hope that "this way putting the issue," (not "this answer to the issue") is helpful. In some respects, this email response is sermon-like: identify an issue of Christian life, pose an answer, and outline "our task." But in many other ways it is academic discourse: identify an issue, examine various scholarly positions, and outline one's own. Steele does not assume the role of counselor answering a personal dilemma, though he reports how he has done that with a believer in a pastoral role. His description of himself as a "pastoral theologian" hints at the multiple discourses, roles, and voices that he and his students adopt in his classroom.

Student evaluations

What students thought they learned

About three-fourths of the students record on the IDEA survey (Appendix C) that they made "substantial" or "exceptional" progress on "Factual knowledge" and the same percentage for "Developing a clearer understanding of, and commitment to, personal values." About two-thirds mark "Learning to analyze and critically evaluate ideas, arguments, and points of view". These figures are not substantially different from the average for the Highly-Effective faculty at religiously-affiliated colleges (table 2.2).

Evaluations of teaching

Steele's student evaluations for teacher excellence place him in the top 10 percent on the national IDEA database. His highest marks from students are for "Displayed a personal interest in students and their learning" (100 percent marked "frequently" or "almost always"); "Related course material to real life situations" (100 percent); "Encouraged student-faculty interaction outside of class" (100 percent); "Found ways to help students answer their own questions" (96 percent); "Demonstrated the importance and significance of the subject matter" (96 percent); and "Provided timely and frequent feedback on tests, reports, projects, etc. to help students improve" (96 percent). His rating for "Explained course material clearly and concisely" was 79 percent. So clarity, while certainly not bad, is his issue. On his own university's student evaluation form, he receives an overall rating of 4.7 on a 5-point scale. Highest scores appear for "Has, when appropriate, discussed the relationship between the Christian faith and course content"; "Has shown respect to students"; and "Has been accessible out of class (e.g., via office hours, phone, or email)."

Prof. Steele's incorporation of more class discussion after the mid-term student requests is appreciated by many students:

> I appreciate Dr. Steele's ability to adapt to his students' needs. I am getting a lot more out of our class time discussions now (not to mention I am no longer tempted to fall asleep – oh, the miracles!). Discussions directed by a professor but based on fellow classmates' questions and ideas are proving to be enlightening.

> At this point there isn't anything I can really think of that would make the course more effective. It seems that we have come quite a ways since the beginning of the quarter in learning how to best interact with each other and how to use our differences to benefit the whole. My appreciation and gratitude for Dr. Steele and his dedication to us is immense.

Student suggestions for change

Student suggestions for change address the down side of discussion – the tendency to wander in tangents. The three student suggestions are:

> I don't mind the Powerpoints because they are an effective learning tool for me, but I do think that the moments of class discussion where Dr. Steele shared stories from his personal life have impacted me more than any lesson plan could.
>
> Sometimes it's very easy for us as a class to jump between a variety of different topics without really getting anywhere. It's important to still be on track and try to have some sense of closure after a discussion. I think that if I spoke up in class I would probably feel more engaged in the learning process. I think both of these actions would make learning more effective for me because if the conversation didn't jump around so much, I would feel more able to voice an opinion and thereby participate in the learning process.

> I know I am in the minority in this – but I wish you lectured more and let us discuss less. I just don't feel I learn very much through discussions although some have really made me think. I thought this course was going to teach us about how Christianity developed/formed and in doing so, would challenge our faith, beliefs, etc. which I do not feel has been done.

> In the realm of faith, it's sometimes useful to speak from experience. I, however, get tired of my peers speaking as though our experiences carry special authority by virtue of the fact that they're ours. I do appreciate the honesty with which we share, but I think we might take ourselves too seriously.

Prof. Steele extensively uses office-hours, coffee appointments with students, and emails to conduct two-way conversations with his students. Prof. Veldman (chapter 4) makes a somewhat similar space when he offers his open coffee-hour sessions, but the session is designed more for group discussion. Prof. Steele often interacts with his students one-on-one. Student essay assignments offer wide latitude for personal wrestling and may be combined, as in the example, with office-hour conversations or coffee. Like Profs. Jones and Ammon in the previous chapters, Steele offers help in developing papers, and he uses those conversations as avenues, if the student wishes, for wider discussions of issues that concern the student. When students request that this interactive style, in which they have a strong voice, be more present in the classroom itself, Steele writes to them about it, and then makes his class more conversational – a move which, of course, then reveals to at least a few students the downside of that style.

Gender roles

Gender roles are at work in all the classrooms. Prof. Bateson seeks to implement a deliberately feminist pedagogy and to include the writings of feminist theologians, while teaching a type of theological argumentation that has historically been dominated by males, in a college related to a church where she is, by her gender, prevented from being a priest. Prof. Irish, not clergy, and teaching at a private non-sectarian institution where "secure Christian" percentages are half the average for the Highly-Effective classes as a whole, faces different role challenges and makes different choices. Steele's class for this study is "Christian Formation," not "Intro to Theology," so the focus is on nurturing students' faith development. More than half his class is female. Many of his students attend churches that stress traditional gender roles. Steele's style is highly interactive, with extensive face-to-face and email contact with individual students. His role as a male clergy and a pastoral theologian is extraordinarily complex. All of the faculty wrestled with appropriate roles in the classroom, with classroom power structures, and with the male dominance among religions, religious texts, and theologians, but those who teach Theology, Christian Formation, and Bible may have some of the most complex roles of any faculty in the study.

Prof. Tilden

"The Gospels," Catholic Masters Institution, 35 students

Each faculty "case" so far has treated assignments somewhat differently as part of the "conversation" in the class, and has encouraged various student voices. I chose Prof. Tilden [a pseudonym] to end this chapter because she focuses heavily on written assignments as forums for students to learn the analytic and critical skills she values and to connect their academic study with their own spiritual and religious development. The assignments are varied, and they ask students to integrate their own experiences and views in different ways.

Goals

Prof Tilden's goal statement is discussed on pages 43–4. The student voice in this class is the critical analyst and the debater, but also one who "engages" Christian belief. Prof. Tilden's assignments provide forums for all three of these voices.

Assignments: What was learned?

In Tilden's class, unlike many of the other courses, the item that students most frequently mentioned as helpful to their learning was the assignments. Students write 4 essays and a take-home essay exam for mid-term and for final. In each, the student is asked to take a position. For example, the first assignment:

> Part 1: (2 pages minimum)
> In *The Meaning of Jesus: Two Visions*, Marcus Borg and Tom Wright ask the question, "How do we know Jesus?" (chapters 1 and 2). The first part of this assignment asks you to consider how each of these authors attempts to answer that question. In other words, you will be writing a critical review of these two chapters. The following questions may help you to structure your answer:
>
> - How do Borg and Wright understand the relationship between faith and history?
> - "Faith can only be confessed with integrity . . . when historical foundations" are examined (Powell, p. 15). Do Borg and Wright think that the historical Jesus is important to faith?
> - How important is faith to "knowing" Jesus for each of these authors? Does their faith in any way color or influence their conclusions? Should it? Is faith a legitimate way of "knowing" Jesus?

- In your opinion, which author is more persuasive and why? Borg? Wright? Neither?

> Part II (1 page minimum)
> Imagine that there is a third chapter in this book and you are its author (it's much shorter, you'll be happy to hear). How would *you* answer the question, "How do we know Jesus?" You may find the bulleted guiding questions above helpful in structuring your answer.
> Note: I am more than happy to help you with this assignment, so please do come and see me [gives contact information]. Feel free to send outlines/first drafts as email attachments.

Students struggle very hard with this assignment, both to accurately represent Borg and Wright's arguments and then to write their own chapter in a way that makes a theological argument and relates to Borg and Wright's positions. For example, a student writes, "I have learned through life experience that in essence, all life is really about is trust, hope, and faith. These are things that must be understood in order to grasp what Jesus is because otherwise, Jesus is just an average moral man. Without these traits, we will never truly understand the message of Jesus and what he wanted for us." The professor writes, "But do trust, hope and faith make him divine? You need to develop this argument more clearly."

In assignment #2, students conduct biblical analysis by setting parallel stories from each of three gospels side by side and color-coding them with 7 colors to reveal similarities, differences, and use of common sources. Then they address, "what do the differences between the three tell you about the author's intent and the community for whom he was writing?"

In the third essay, students trace theological and narrative elements in the gospel Christmas stories and in three Christmas carols. In the fourth, they analyze a film. A high-quality essay, for example, makes the argument that Mel Gibson's *The Passion of the Christ* differs from the gospels in the amount of power and control that Jesus had over his situation. Here is a sample paragraph:

> Another characteristic of John's gospel is that Jesus is in control; He seems to have a sense of power over what happens to him. [Instructor writes: "Also: 1) the 'cohort' come to arrest him; 2) There is no 'agony' in the garden in John."] When Jesus is being crucified on the cross, He declares, "It is finished." This conveys Jesus as being completely aware of God's plan. In the film, Jesus says, "It is accomplished" when He is nailed to the cross and breathing His last few breaths. This expresses the same idea that Jesus knew what God had in store for Him; however,

> the film does not portray Jesus as being in complete control. In fact, he is portrayed as helpless and defenseless, unable to take control of the cruel situation He was put in. [Prof writes: "He sweats blood (as in Luke)"]. I felt extreme pity for Jesus in the film and feared that his powerlessness would lead to his death even before the crucifixion.

Tilden offers extensive, substantive critique of students' papers, focusing on critical thinking tasks such as making an argument, accurately representing others' arguments, substantiating claims, making clear distinctions, being specific, and defining terms. For all four papers, she offers draft response.

Readings

Readings are the *Bible*; Marcus Borg and N.T. Wright, *The Meaning of Jesus*; Barbara Aland et al., *Gospel Parallels*; Mark Allan Powell, *Fortress Introduction to the Gospels*; and David Cartlidge and David Dungan, *Documents for the Study of the Gospels*.

Fifty-two percent of the students say on the survey that they "hardly ever" or "occasionally" come to class without having completed the readings – about average for all Highly-Effective classes responding. Another 33 percent say they "sometimes," come unprepared, vs. 23 percent average.

Use of class time

"Discussion" and "audio-visual" are the items students choose next most frequently, after "assignments," as helpful to their learning. Tilden conducts the class by interactive lecture/discussion, with a number of short video clips and many student writing exercises. Again, students are asked for their positions. A student writes on the university's end-of-course evaluation: "The professor asks us very hard questions. Sometimes I feel, 'How can I have an answer to a question that has been asked for centuries?' Theologians through the centuries have been trying to solve these mysteries. But, it tells us that we can all contribute."

Here is Tilden's description of a few class sessions. Note the ways she uses student writing in the class to get students engaged and to provide a forum for integrating course material with students' own positions and their spiritual and religious development.

In-class writing, related to reading and students' experience

> Jan. 21. My goal today was to get the students thinking about the questions: Who was Jesus? How do we know Jesus? What are our sources

for knowing Jesus/knowing about Jesus? I began by asking students to jot down "who is Jesus for you?" After a couple of minutes, the class started to brainstorm. Here are some of the answers: A first-century Jewish male who lived in Palestine; My savior; I imagine him to look like Brad Pitt; The son of God who died for me; My sunbeam; A miracle worker.

I then used their answers to help them make connections with the readings from Borg/Wright: How do you know Jesus? How is that different from knowing about Jesus? How much is history, how much is faith? Can we separate faith and history? Should we? (The students really got into this question and could see from their own answers that often they are intertwined.) We spent quite a bit of time unpacking this and relating it to Borg's notion of a "composite Jesus." We also talked about the lenses through which we see things, and as facilitator of the discussion I tried to help them make connections with 1) their own experience; and 2) the readings.

Then I asked students to write down what they thought they could know, historically, about Jesus. After a couple of minutes, one student announced to the class, "Wow, I never really thought about that. That's a tough one."

The rest of the time was spent in interactive lecture on the historical Jesus, a kind of CV style approach to what we can know, historically, about Jesus.

Multiple stimulation

In the next class session, she uses multiple stimulations – videos, a short article read in class, and a clip of the spoken Aramaic language. Each of these is used as a stimulus to discussion.

[Jan. 24.] My goal today is to get the students to continue to think about what we can know, historically, about Jesus, and to continue thinking about the relationship between history and faith. The discussion continued on the question of who was Jesus (historically) and how can we know Jesus (know about Jesus). Used multi-stimulation today to get them and keep them engaged:

1 3-minute video clip from PBS special "From Jesus to Christ" which focused on archeological discoveries and the question of Jesus' social class. I asked the students whether Jesus' social class was important? Does it change the message? Good discussion.

2 Followed up with an article from the London *Times* on Jesus' social class ("Jesus the Son of a Rich Architect?") which focuses on the translation of the Greek word tekton (often translated "carpenter"). The brief article presents Jesus as a sophisticated multi-lingual artisan. Discussion. Then introduced them to some alternative views – such as the notion that he was an illiterate peasant. Was Jesus literate? What language(s) did he speak? I played a clip of Jim Caviezel speaking Aramaic to try to help them imagine what Jesus may have sounded like.

Students as cultural informants

Later in that same class, Tilden brings the students' own views again into the picture as she asks what they think Jesus might have looked like. She uses students as informants about common cultural perceptions.

> We moved on to a discussion of what Jesus might have looked like. Asked them for input – they responded with: short, muscular, rippled, long hair and beard, sunburned. We discussed images of Jesus and their relation to culture, faith, and history. Then I produced an issue of *Popular Mechanic Weekly*, and told them it had a feature on "The New Face of Jesus?" They were amused and intrigued as to how I had stumbled upon such a magazine so I told them how I was in Jiffy Lube getting my car oiled and lo and behold as I waited I "acquired" the article, defending my acquisition in the best utilitarian manner. They couldn't stop laughing. I hadn't planned that this would be funny but in reflection I realize the importance of humor in the classroom, especially in building a relationship with them.

Teacher questions: From concrete to theological

At the end of that same discussion, Tilden moves from concrete "what did Jesus look like?" to more theological and philosophical concerns that touch on students' own stances as well: "Does it matter what Jesus looked like?"

> Followed this up with a 4-minute clip from DSC/BBC *Jesus: The Complete Story* in which several scholars attempt to reconstruct the face of Jesus. They were riveted – and clearly disturbed. I asked them, is that what you were expecting? Their responses: "He's beefier!" "He looks like a terrorist" (this provoked a good discussion on Middle Eastern appearance and terrorism); "He looks like a serial killer." Good

discussion. Then I asked them, "Does it matter?" Again, this allowed us to continue an exploration of faith and history and the relationship between the two.

After-class conversations

The interaction in class where student voices include their own stances and beliefs can lead easily to after-class conversations. Tilden cites ones example where a student seems to have responded in two voices: the inquirer asking an intellectual question, but also the offended believer. Tilden responds to the student with a question that communicates what Tilden sees as the mission of the university. Her voice is not pastoral but academic in the widest sense – she is not moving her students through relativism toward an ideal of Christian maturity, as Steele explicitly does, nor does she explain her own theological position as Steele might do; rather, she presents herself more as the detached observer who questions the student, the scholar who upholds the university as a place of free inquiry, and the mentor who is pleased that the student is addressing the "big questions."

> One student stayed behind after class – she wanted to talk about something she'd read in the assigned readings – she couldn't believe that Borg would say that Jesus didn't know he was the Son of God. I asked her why? Aren't we in the process of trying to understand in a university? We talked for about twenty minutes – I thoroughly enjoyed her thoughtfulness; it was for me a great moment to see her engaged and grappling with big questions.

Through both her assignments and her in-class interactions, Tilden shapes multiple roles for her students, relying heavily on student writing, and interweaving students' theological arguments with their other voices.

Student evaluations

What students thought they learned

Prof. Tilden's class is remarkable in that 100 percent of the 29 students who submit IDEA evaluations at the end of the course report making "substantial" or "exceptional" progress in "Learning to analyze and critically evaluate ideas, arguments, and points of view," and 100 percent for "Developing a clearer understanding of, and commitment to, personal values."

Student evaluations of teaching

Prof. Tilden's scores on the IDEA evaluation place her in the top 10 percent on teacher excellence.

This teacher of Bible exhibits some of the same principles evident in other faculty – love of students; emphasis on interaction with them; ways of making them accountable in class for their preparation and interaction; and ways of using the assignments, her out-of-class time, and the class time itself as forums for students' holistic consideration of intellect and faith. She relies very heavily on writing assignments, both inside and outside of class, and she varies the roles and voices of students in their assignments. Like Irish, Bhattacharyya, and others, she uses writing extensively both inside and outside of class, she assigns varied roles to her students, and she offers extensive feedback to writing, all of which provides a variety of forums in which students can integrate the intellectual content of the class with their own stances and their own religious and spiritual development.

Conclusions

These small classes in Bible, Theology, and Christian Formation are all involved in some way with theological argument, yet they have quite different ways of structuring spaces and voices for students to integrate critical thinking with their own spiritual and religious development. Prof. Bateson, in her theology class at a Protestant Baccalaureate college, uses a deliberately feminist approach, working very intently and strategically to require student participation and to engage student voices in classroom dialogue. Her written essays ask students to analyze the theological arguments of others, and to construct their own positions. Her students "get it" – they express more frequently than any other theology class the goal of learning theological argument.

Prof. Irish, teaching theology at a private non-sectarian college, places significant emphasis on students' articulation of their own theologies. Students must analyze others' theological arguments and take their own positions. They also write their own "theological profiles," which are shared, with students' permission, among classmates.

Prof. Steele, at a Protestant Masters-level university, also asks students for theological "credo" statements, in which they must address the theological arguments they have read on a particular topic, and take their own positions. Prof. Steele engages students intensely in dialogue, in class, in his office hours, in email exchanges, and in taking students out for "coffee." In these exchanges, he helps them think theologically and is not afraid to share his own theological positions, while respecting theirs.

Prof. Tilden, teaching "The Gospels" at a Catholic Masters-level university, employs extensive critique of student writing – a practice that her students often cite as helpful to their learning. She bases class sessions, too, on student writing, often asking students to write in class as a spur to discussion. The writings and dialogue invite students to integrate their own experience and interpretations with the texts of the course.

Each of these faculty models a somewhat different mode of caring, clarity, and conversation. Each structures spaces and voices for students to integrate critical/theological thinking with their own spiritual and religious development.

Appendix A: Faculty Demographics

The IDEA Database Group

Table A.1 presents the characteristics of the 467 Database group faculty.

Table A.1 Characteristics of 467 Database classes

Categories	Number of classes	Percentage of total database classes
Geographic area		
Midwest	128	27
Upper Midwest	28	6
Mid-Atlantic	136	28
New England/Maritime	13	3
Pacific Northwest	0	0
Rocky Mountain/Great Plains	1	0
Southeast	98	21
Southwest	41	9
Western	22	5
Carnegie categories		
Research 1 and 2	0	0
Doctoral 1 and 2	3	1
Masters 1 and 2	177	40
Baccalaureate 1 and 2	260	59
Institutional type		
Public	46	10
Private Non-Sectarian	2	0%
Catholic	74	16
Protestant	345	74

The Highly-Effective Group

Table A.2 presents the characteristics of the 66 Highly-Effective faculty. The comparison group is the AAR census of theology and religion departments and programs in the US and Canada, including 2-year colleges (www.aarweb.org). Thus the comparison group contains two groups that the Highly-Effective Group study does not – Canadian and two-year. Nevertheless, it provides a general indication of how representative the 66 faculty are.

Table A.2 Characteristics of 66 Highly-Effective faculty compared to AAR census

Categories	Percentage of total AAR census departments (does not add up to 100% because of a few categories omitted)	Percentage of Total Highly-Effective departments (raw number in parentheses)
Geographic area (AAR p. 89)		
Midwest	15	33 (22)
Upper Midwest	10	12 (8)
Mid-Atlantic	10	14 (9)
New England/Maritime	6	3 (2)
Pacific Northwest	5	6 (4)
Rocky Mountain/Great Plains	3	3 (2)
Southeast	21	17 (11)
Southwest	10	6 (4)
Western	7	6 (4)
Carnegie categories (Fall 2001 AAR, RSN.iii, table of "Response Rate by Carnegie Class (core universe, applies to US only)")		
Research 1 and 2	12	11 (7)
Doctoral 1 and 2	7	6 (4)
Master's 1 and 2	31	44 (29)
Baccalaureate 1 and 2	50	39 (26)
Institutional Type		
Public	25	17 (11)
Private Non-Sectarian	20	8 (5)
Catholic	17	36 (24)
Protestant	36	39 (26)

Table A.2 *Continued*

Categories	Percentage of total AAR census departments (does not add up to 100% because of a few categories omitted)	Percentage of Total Highly-Effective departments (raw number in parentheses)
Class size of course being studied		
Class size under 45	n/a	85 (56)
Class size more than 45	n/a	15 (10)
Rank (AAR Table 10, full time faculty only)		
Assistant Prof (as percent of full time)	22	39 (26)
Assoc Prof (as percent of full time)	25	21 (14)
Full Prof (as percent of full time)	37	35 (23)
Full Time Lecturer (as percent of full time)	17	5 (3)
Adjunct (AAR p. 51, as percent of total faculty)	39	0
Historically underrepresented groups, as percent of full-time faculty (AAR Tables 5.05, 5.06,9.00, 9.00a)		
Female	30	38 (25)
Non-Caucasian	n/a	8 (5)

Appendix B: Student Demographics

Students in the 66 Highly-Effective Classes

There were 2,823 students enrolled in the 66 classes (including 400 students enrolled in later sections taught by the same faculty members who had earlier submitted full data and who then collected the new form of student reflections from a later section of the same class). Of this 2,823 total student enrollment, 77 percent (2,184) submitted at least one written reflection about the class.

The demographic information about students (Table B.1) comes from faculty reports, a few weeks into the course, about their own students. Of the 66 classes, 59 reported at least some such data. On figures such as the number of students working more than 15 hours, some faculty asked students to report these items, and some faculty estimated from their knowledge of the students. Some faculty omitted items, such as hours worked, for which they did not have information. Thus these figures about student characteristics are generally accurate, but not precise.

Appendix B: Student Demographics

Table B.1 Characteristics of students in classes of Highly-Effective teachers

Characteristic (number of classes for which the faculty member reported this item)	Percent of classes with <10%	Percent of classes with 10–24%	Percent of classes with 25–49%	Percent of classes with 50–74%	Percent of classes with 75–100%
Female (56)	0	4	13	75	9
Historically underrepresented ethnic groups, including both US and international students (58)	64	17	10	7	2
Speakers of English as a foreign language (58)	88	10	2	0	0
First-year students (59)	24	12	22	20	22
Sophomores (58)	17	38	33	9	4
Students 26 or older (57)	89	11	0	0	0
Students taking the course to fulfill a gened requirement (57)	2	0	7	14	77
Students taking course to fulfill a program requirement, e.g. requirement for major (49)	67	18	2	4	8
Part-time students (51)	90	4	2	0	4
Students living on campus (52)	4	8	21	23	44
Full-time students working 15+ hours for pay (48)	17	27	23	23	10
Students taking their very first term of college-level theology/religion (57)	12	5	4	23	56

N = 59 faculty surveys

Students in Database and in Highly-Effective Classes Taking IDEA Survey

Table B.2 uses the IDEA survey of faculty to determine some characteristics of students in all the Database courses and in those of Highly-Effective courses where the IDEA was administered.

Table B.2 Student populations in Database and Highly-Effective classes

IDEA faculty survey item: *Principal* type of student enrolling in this course	Database group(%)	Highly-Effective group (%)
Freshmen [sic]/sophomores seeking to meet a "general education" or "distribution" requirement	79	72
Freshmen/sophomores seeking to develop background needed for their intended specialization	18	22
Upperclassmen [sic] non-majors taking the course as a "general education" or "distribution" requirement	3	6

N = 467 Database faculty surveys; 54 Highly-Effective faculty surveys

Appendix C: IDEA Surveys

Faculty Survey

Completed at end of course and submitted with student surveys to IDEA for analysis.

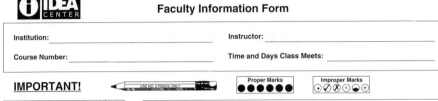

IDEA CENTER

Faculty Information Form

Institution: ____________________ Instructor: ____________________

Course Number: ____________________ Time and Days Class Meets: ____________________

IMPORTANT!

USE NO. 2 PENCIL ONLY

Proper Marks ●●●●●●

Improper Marks

Last Name (Up to 11 letters) | Init.

A B C D E F G H I J K L M N O P Q R S T U V W X Y Z

Objectives (Scale: M = Minor or No Importance, I = Important, E = Essential)

M I E

1. ○○○ Gaining factual knowledge (terminology, classifications, methods, trends)
2. ○○○ Learning fundamental principles, generalizations, or theories
3. ○○○ Learning to *apply* course material (to improve thinking, problem solving, and decisions)
4. ○○○ Developing specific skills, competencies, and points of view needed by professionals in the field most closely related to this course
5. ○○○ Acquiring skills in working with others as a member of a team
6. ○○○ Developing creative capacities (writing, inventing, designing, performing in art, music, drama, etc.)
7. ○○○ Gaining a broader understanding and appreciation of intellectual/cultural activity (music, science, literature, etc.)
8. ○○○ Developing skill in expressing myself orally or in writing
9. ○○○ Learning how to find and use resources for answering questions or solving problems
10. ○○○ Developing a clearer understanding of, and commitment to, personal values
11. ○○○ Learning to *analyze* and *critically evaluate* ideas, arguments, and points of view
12. ○○○ Acquiring an interest in learning more by asking my own questions and seeking answers

Days Class Meets: ○ Mon ○ Tues ○ Wed ○ Thu ○ Fri ○ Sat ○ Sun

Department Code | Time Class Begins | Course Number | Number Enrolled | Course Number

0 1 2 3 4 5 6 7 8 9

Contextual Questions (Research Purposes)

The IDEA Center will conduct research on these optional euestions in order to improve the interpretation of student ratings.

1. Which of the following represents the *primary* approach to this course? (Mark only one)

① = Lecture
② = Discussion/recitation
③ = Seminar
④ = Skill/activity
⑤ = Laboratory
⑥ = Field Experience
⑦ = Studio
⑧ = Multi-Media
⑨ = Practicum/clinic
⓪ = Other

2. If multiple approaches are used, which *one* represents the *secondary approach*?

① = Lecture
② = Discussion/recitation
③ = Seminar
④ = Skill/activity
⑤ = Laboratory
⑥ = Field experience
⑦ = Studio
⑧ = Multi-media
⑨ = Practicum/clinic
⓪ = Other

3. Describe this course in terms of its requirements with respect to the features listed below. Use the following code to make your responses:
N = None (or little) required
S = Some required
M = Much required

N S M
○○○ A. Writing
○○○ B. Oral communication
○○○ C. Computer applications
○○○ D. Group work
○○○ E. Mathematical/quantitative work
○○○ F. Critical thinking
○○○ G. Creative/artistic design/endeavor

Mark Reflex® forms by Pearson NCS MM75862-4 65432 ED05 Printed in U.S.A.

Continued on back page

Contextual Questions Contined:

4. Rate each of the circumstances listed below, using the following code to respond:

P = Had a positive impact on learning
I = Neither a positive nor a negative impact
N = Had a negative impact on learning
? = Can't judge

P I N ?
○○○○ A. Physical facilities or other equipment
○○○○ B. Your previous experience
○○○○ C. Substantial changes in teaching approach, course assignments, content, etc.
○○○○ D. Your desire to teach this course
○○○○ E. Your control over course management decisions (objectives, texts, exams, etc.)
○○○○ F. Adequacy of students' background and preparation for the course
○○○○ G. Student enthusiasm for the course
○○○○ H. Student effort to learn
○○○○ I. Technical/instructional support

5. Please identify the *principal* type of student enrolling in this course

① = Freshmen/sophomores seeking to meet a "general education" or "distribution" requirement
② = Freshmen/sophomores seeking to develop background needed for their intended specialization
③ = Upperclassmen non-majors taking the course as a "general education" or "distribution" requirement
④ = Upperclassmen majors (in this or a related field of study) seeking competence or expertise in their academic professional specialty
⑤ = Graduate or professional school students
⑥ = Combination of two or more of the above types

6. Is this class:

a. Team taught? ○ Yes ○ No
b. Taught through distance learning? ○ Yes ○ No

Department Codes (Modified CIP Codes)

0100	Agricultural Business And Production
0200	Agricultural Sciences
0300	Conservation and Renewable Natural Resources
0400	Architecture and Related Programs
0500	Area Ethnic and Cultural Studies
5007	Art (Painting, Drawing Sculpture)
2600	Biological Sciences/Life Sciences
5201	Business, General
5202	Business Administration and Management
5203	Business - Accounting
5208	Business - Finance
5212	Business Information and Data Processing Services
5214	Business - Marketing
4005	Chemistry
0900	Communications
1100	Computer and Information Sciences
1103	Data Processing Technology (2-year Program)
4506	Economics
1300	Education (EXCEPT Physical Education and Vocational-Technical Education)
1400	Engineering
1500	Engineering-Related Technologies
2301	English Language and Literature
5000	Fine and Applied Arts (EXCEPT Art and Music)
1600	Foreign Languages and Literatures
5100	Health Professions and Relate Sciences (EXCEPT Nursing)
5199	Health Professions and Related Sciences (2-year program)
4508	History
1900	Human Sciences/Family and Consumer Sciences
—	Industrial Arts (See Vocational-Technical Education)
2400	Liberal Arts & Sciences, General Studies and Humanities
2200	Law
2500	Library Science
2700	Mathematics and Statistics
2900	Military Science/Technologies
5009	Music (Performing, Composing, Theory)
5116	Nursing
3801	Philosophy
1332	Physical Education/Health/Safety Education
4000	Physical Sciences (EXCEPT Physics and Chemistry)
4008	Physics
4510	Political Science and Government
4200	Psychology
4400	Public Administration and Services (EXCEPT Social Work)
3900	Religion and Theological Studies
5204	Secretarial Services
4500	Social Sciences (EXCEPT Economics, History, Political Science, and Sociology)
4407	Social Work and Service
4511	Sociology
2310	Speech and Rhetorical Studies
1320	Vocational-Technical Education
9900	Other (to be used when none of the above codes apply)

To see an expanded list of department codes go to www.idea.ksu.adu

Student Survey

The IDEA survey, diagnostic form (www.theideacenter.org)

The surveys are copyrighted. Use of items from these surveys is not permitted except with permission from The IDEA Center (www.theideacenter.org).

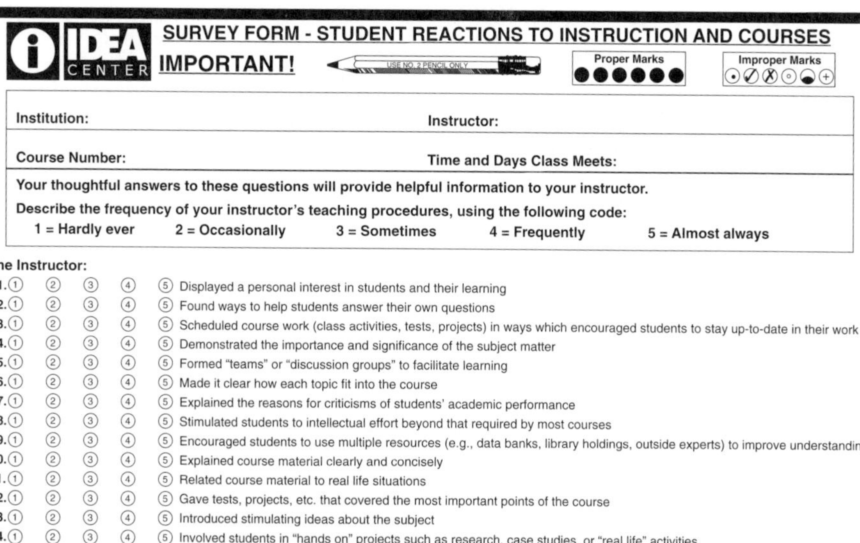

IDEA CENTER

SURVEY FORM - STUDENT REACTIONS TO INSTRUCTION AND COURSES

IMPORTANT! USE NO. 2 PENCIL ONLY

Proper Marks ● ● ● ● ● ●

Improper Marks

Institution: **Instructor:**

Course Number: **Time and Days Class Meets:**

Your thoughtful answers to these questions will provide helpful information to your instructor.

Describe the frequency of your instructor's teaching procedures, using the following code:

1 = Hardly ever 2 = Occasionally 3 = Sometimes 4 = Frequently 5 = Almost always

The Instructor:

1. ① ② ③ ④ ⑤ Displayed a personal interest in students and their learning
2. ① ② ③ ④ ⑤ Found ways to help students answer their own questions
3. ① ② ③ ④ ⑤ Scheduled course work (class activities, tests, projects) in ways which encouraged students to stay up-to-date in their work
4. ① ② ③ ④ ⑤ Demonstrated the importance and significance of the subject matter
5. ① ② ③ ④ ⑤ Formed "teams" or "discussion groups" to facilitate learning
6. ① ② ③ ④ ⑤ Made it clear how each topic fit into the course
7. ① ② ③ ④ ⑤ Explained the reasons for criticisms of students' academic performance
8. ① ② ③ ④ ⑤ Stimulated students to intellectual effort beyond that required by most courses
9. ① ② ③ ④ ⑤ Encouraged students to use multiple resources (e.g., data banks, library holdings, outside experts) to improve understanding
10. ① ② ③ ④ ⑤ Explained course material clearly and concisely
11. ① ② ③ ④ ⑤ Related course material to real life situations
12. ① ② ③ ④ ⑤ Gave tests, projects, etc. that covered the most important points of the course
13. ① ② ③ ④ ⑤ Introduced stimulating ideas about the subject
14. ① ② ③ ④ ⑤ Involved students in "hands on" projects such as research, case studies, or "real life" activities
15. ① ② ③ ④ ⑤ Inspired students to set and achieve goals which really challenged them
16. ① ② ③ ④ ⑤ Asked students to share ideas and experiences with others whose backgrounds and viewpoints differ from their own
17. ① ② ③ ④ ⑤ Provided timely and frequently feedback on tests, reports, projects, etc. to help students improve
18. ① ② ③ ④ ⑤ Asked students to help each other understand ideas or concepts
19. ① ② ③ ④ ⑤ Gave projects, tests, or assignments that required original or creative thinking
20. ① ② ③ ④ ⑤ Encouraged student-faculty interaction outside of class (office visit, phone class, email, etc.)

Twelve possible learning objectives are listed below, not all of which will be relevant in this class. Describe the amount of progress you made on each (even those not pursued in this class) by using the following scale:

1 = No apparent progress
2 = Slight progress; I made small gains on this objective
3 = Moderate progress; I made some gains on this objective
4 = Substantial progress; I made large gains on this objective
5 = Exceptional progress; I made outstanding gains on this objective

Progress on:

21. ① ② ③ ④ ⑤ Gaining factual knowledge (terminology, classifications, methods, trends)
22. ① ② ③ ④ ⑤ Learning fundamental principles, generalizations, or theories
23. ① ② ③ ④ ⑤ Learning to *apply* course material (to improve thinking, problem solving, and decisions)
24. ① ② ③ ④ ⑤ Developing specific skills, competencies, and points of view needed by professionals in the field most closely related to this course
25. ① ② ③ ④ ⑤ Acquiring skills in working with others as a member of a team
26. ① ② ③ ④ ⑤ Developing creative capacities (writing, inventing, designing, performing in art, music, drama, etc.)
27. ① ② ③ ④ ⑤ Gaining a broader understanding and appreciation of intellectual/cultural activity (music, science, literature, etc.)
28. ① ② ③ ④ ⑤ Developing skill in expressing myself orally or in writing
29. ① ② ③ ④ ⑤ Learning how to find and use resources for answering questions or solving problems
30. ① ② ③ ④ ⑤ Developing a clearer understanding of, and commitment to, personal values
31. ① ② ③ ④ ⑤ Learning to *analyze* and *critically evaluate* ideas, arguments, and points of view
32. ① ② ③ ④ ⑤ Acquiring an interest in learning more by asking my own questions and seeking answers

Mark Reflex® forms by Pearson NCS MM248694-2 654 Printed in U.S.A.

Continued on back page

On the next three items, compare this course with others you have taken at this institution, using the following code:
1 = Much less than most courses   2 = Less than most courses   3 = About average   4 = More than most courses   5 = Much more than most courses

The Course:

33. ① ② ③ ④ ⑤ Amount of reading
34. ① ② ③ ④ ⑤ Amount of work in other (non-reading) assignments
35. ① ② ③ ④ ⑤ Difficulty of subject matter

Describe your attitudes and behavior in this course, using the following code:
1 = Definitely false   2 = More false than true   3 = In between   4 = More true than false   5 = Definitely true

36. ① ② ③ ④ ⑤ I had a strong desire to take this course.
37. ① ② ③ ④ ⑤ I worked harder on this course than on most courses I have taken.
38. ① ② ③ ④ ⑤ I really wanted to take a course from this instructor.
39. ① ② ③ ④ ⑤ I really wanted to take this course regardless of who taught it.
40. ① ② ③ ④ ⑤ As a result of taking this course, I have more positive feelings toward this field of study.
41. ① ② ③ ④ ⑤ Overall, I rate this instructor an excellent teacher.
42. ① ② ③ ④ ⑤ Overall, I rate this course as excellent.

Use the following code for the next items, choosing the comment which best corresponds to your judgment:
1 = Definitely false   2 = More false than true   3 = In between   4 = More true than false   5 = Definitely true

43. ① ② ③ ④ ⑤ As a rule, I put forth more effort than other students on academic work.
44. ① ② ③ ④ ⑤ The instructor used a variety of methods – not only tests – to evaluate students progress on course objectives.
45. ① ② ③ ④ ⑤ The instructor expected students to take their share of responsibility for learning.
46. ① ② ③ ④ ⑤ The instructor had high achievement standards in this class.
47. ① ② ③ ④ ⑤ The instructor used educational technology (e.g., Internet, email, computer exercises, multi-media presentations, etc.) to promote learning

EXTRA QUESTIONS
If your instructor has extra questions, answer them in the space designated below (questions 48-66):

48. ① ② ③ ④ ⑤
49. ① ② ③ ④ ⑤
50. ① ② ③ ④ ⑤
51. ① ② ③ ④ ⑤
52. ① ② ③ ④ ⑤
53. ① ② ③ ④ ⑤
54. ① ② ③ ④ ⑤
55. ① ② ③ ④ ⑤
56. ① ② ③ ④ ⑤
57. ① ② ③ ④ ⑤
58. ① ② ③ ④ ⑤
59. ① ② ③ ④ ⑤
60. ① ② ③ ④ ⑤
61. ① ② ③ ④ ⑤
62. ① ② ③ ④ ⑤
63. ① ② ③ ④ ⑤
64. ① ② ③ ④ ⑤
65. ① ② ③ ④ ⑤
66. ① ② ③ ④ ⑤

Use the space below for comments (unless otherwise directed).
Note: Your written comments may be returned to the instructor. You may want to PRINT to protect your anonymity.

Comments: ____

Appendix D: Discipline-Specific Surveys Administered to Highly-Effective Classes

All surveys in Appendix D may be freely used without permission.

Faculty Survey #1: Administered Before/During the First Week of the Course

Purpose of this survey

The larger study

This particular questionnaire/survey is part of the larger Wabash/Notre Dame-sponsored study, which gathers various types of information about the classrooms of outstanding teachers of introductory theology and religion (note: throughout this survey, "theology/religion" refers also to related disciplinary names such as Religious Studies, Bible, and the like). The larger study seeks to understand the teachers' "practices," which means not only their actions and teaching methods, but also the philosophies and concepts from which they work. The goal of the larger study is to produce publications and faculty development programs that can help other teachers improve their teaching of introductory theology and religion courses.

The study is not about documenting some set of perfect, static practices that ideal teachers use. All of you are recognized as highly effective teachers by your chairs or other colleagues, but you vary widely in your levels of experience, your teaching styles, and your teaching situations. All of you are changing and growing. The class on which you gather data for the study may be one of your best ever, or it may be one of those classes that just never "jells." You may try something new that doesn't work. It's all okay. I am not documenting perfection; we together are documenting the real lives, the development, the struggles, the thinking and the practices of actual faculty, in order to provide information that will *help* and *encourage* other faculty, not hopelessly intimidate them.

In this kind of research, the presence of the researcher and the strategies of data collection themselves can affect the outcomes, and that's expected and welcomed. I expect that you will change along with, and perhaps because of, the reflection you undertake as part of this study. If our processes of reflection and data collection spur you to change, feel free to do so. Don't be afraid to take risks.

In short, you don't need to be perfect and you don't need to stand still in order for me to get good data; on the contrary, good teachers sometimes stumble and are always moving, and such struggle and movement may be the most valuable data.

Role of this survey

This opening survey provides information, as the course begins, about your learning goals for your students, the expectations that shape your course, your course-planning process, your teaching style and beliefs, and your history as a teacher. I trust that writing reflectively about these topics will be useful, as well, for your own thinking and development.

There are no wrong answers. Highly effective faculty employ a wide variety of different teaching practices, styles, and methods. They hold a variety of goals for theology/religion courses. The study has no bias about any particular goals, style, method, or approach being better than others. The study instead gathers data about what teachers who are perceived as highly effective actually think and do.

Basic information

Today's Date ______________________________

1. Your Name (please print) ______________________________
   Last name __________ First name __________
2. Course number (example: Religion 101) ______________________________
3. Course title (example: Eastern Religions) ______________________________
4. Number of credit hours for this course ______________________________
5. Class meeting times each week (e.g. MWF, 9–9:50 a.m. OR Monday evenings 6:30–9 p.m.) ______________________________
6. Number of weeks in the semester/quarter/term ______________________________
7. Total number of students enrolled, as of your most recent record ________

8. You may not know all the numbers below. You could take a few minutes in class to ask your students for a show of hands (e.g., "How many of you are full time, how many part time?"). Or, if that's not possible or comfortable, make a rough guess, or skip the item you don't know.

	<10%	10–24%	25–49%	50–74%	75–100%
a. Female					
b. Historically under-representedethnic groups (including, bothAmerican citizens and international students)					
c. Speakers of English as asecond language					
d. First-year students					
e. Sophomores					
f. Students 26 or older					
g. Students taking the courseto fulfill general-education/core requirements					
h. Students taking the course tofulfill a program requirement					
i. Part-time students					
j. Students living on campus					
k. Full-time students who work15+ hours a week for pay					
l. Students taking their *very first* term of college-level theology/religion					

Note: if, due to unexpected enrollment patterns, the characteristics of your actual students do not meet the guidelines I earlier communicated to you, don't worry about it. Your class is welcome in the study.

9. In addition to your role as instructor, what other roles are expected for you in relation to the students enrolled in this course? Check all that apply:

	My *department* expects	My *institution* expects	I expect of myself
a. Academic advising forstudents in this course			
b. Career advising for students in this course			
c. Personal/spiritual advising for students in this course			
d. Identifying and encouraging students who might major, minor, or take a concentration in this department/program			
e. Identifying and encouraging students in this course who might choose ministry as their life's vocation			
f. Other: please explain below			

10. Please indicate whether there are departmental or institutional guidelines *for your introductory course* (check all that apply)

	My *institution* has guidelines or expectations			My *department* has guidelines or expectations		
	Yes	No	Not Sure	Yes	No	Not Sure
a. Learning goals						
b. Content of theintroductory course						
c. Day-by-day common syllabus						
d. Number/type of exams/assignments						
e. Pedagogy of the introductory course						
f. Other: please explain below						

Goals

11. Please indicate the importance of the following goals for student learning for your introductory course:

	Essential	Very important	Somewhat important	Not important
a. Develop their general intellectual skills such as analyzing, evaluating, and synthesizing				
b. Learn the methods of my discipline				
c. Acquire a body of knowledge (e.g., about the world's religions, about the Bible)				
d. Understand and appreciate a variety of religious beliefs and practices				
e. Develop their own religious beliefs and/or spiritual practices				
f. Develop their moral and ethical values				
g. Consider or strengthen their commitment to a particular set of beliefs (e.g. Roman Catholic, Buddhist, Calvinist, evangelical)				
h. Take or be inclined to take action for a better world				
i. Other: Please explain below				

Reflection

This last section asks you for a more extended reflection. Use the following questions as a guide, but feel free to include other topics as well. Your goal is to help me and audiences for the study understand how you think and how you function as a teacher. The idea is to provide rich, specific detail and thoughtful reflection that reveals for other teachers both the strategies you use and the concepts and beliefs that inform your teaching. There are no right or wrong answers. Your reflection need not be polished for grammar or punctuation. It can be as long as you wish, and the longer the better. It can be stream-of-consciousness, more like a journal or an interview transcript than like a polished essay.

If you would prefer to record your reflection on audio tape, you may do so. Please label the tape with your name and the date(s) of your reflection.

1 Please tell the story of your own development as a teacher, especially a teacher of introductory courses, up to this time. How and why did you get interested in teaching? What influences have shaped you as a teacher? What beliefs about teaching and learning and about the relationship between teacher and students have most strongly shaped what you do in the classroom, and how did those beliefs develop? How have your teaching practices changed over the years, especially for introductory courses? How would you describe your own style, approach, and philosophy about teaching and learning at this point in your teaching career?
2 Please explain more fully your goals for student learning in the course. Specifically what do you hope students will be able to do as a result of your course (include, as relevant, intellectual, emotional, and spiritual aspects)? You may use the format of the following examples, or whatever format is comfortable for your own thinking:
   - "I want my students to be able to compare and contrast . . ."
   - "I want my students to be able to write an essay that . . ."
   - "I want my students to be able, in class discussion, to demonstrate . . ."
   - "In journals, I want my students to be able to reflect . . ."
   - "I want my students to demonstrate a habit of . . ."
3 How will you know whether your teaching and their learning have been successful?
4 What is your understanding of how your intro students will acquire the learning stated in your course goals? What are the cognitive and affective processes involved?
5 Where do you expect students will encounter their greatest difficulties of either understanding or motivation? What strategies have you planned to help them at those points?
6 Please describe how you went about planning this introductory course when it was new or the last time you significantly revised it. Address such questions as:

- What was the sequence of actions you took, and why?
- What influence did the departmental or institutional guidelines/ expectations have on your planning? Were such guidelines a constraint to you? A help?
- How did your learning goals shape your planning?
- What other aspects did you consider in your planning (e.g., limitations on your own time, availability of technology, problems you or your students had faced in the past, time of day the course would be taught)?
- What questions did you ask yourself as you planned the course?
- What problems or issues did you struggle with as you planned the course? How did you address them?
- In hindsight, would you change your planning process in any way? How and why?

7 What advice about the best way to plan an introductory course would you give to a new colleague who had never taught an intro course before?

Faculty Survey #2: Administered After the Course

Purpose of the survey

This survey helps you reflect back on the semester and helps me and future audiences to understand your practices, including the concepts, beliefs, and assumptions that inform your teaching. The first part is a series of questions that ask you to mark a specific answer. These help me to aggregate and compare strategies in simple ways. The last part of this survey asks for a reflection, which is your chance to dig deeper for more complex insights into what went well, what could be improved, and why. It is my chance to reflect, in the study's findings, the nuances and complexities of your experience teaching the course.

There are no wrong answers. Highly-effective faculty may employ a wide variety of different teaching practices, styles, methods, and beliefs. The study has no bias that any particular mode is better than others. The study instead gathers data about what teachers who are perceived as highly effective actually think and do.

Every teacher has classes that "click" exactly right and those that are more of a struggle. This semester's class may have fallen into either of those categories; it's okay. We are not documenting perfection; we are documenting the real lives, the changes, the struggles, and the practices of actual faculty, in order to provide information that will help other faculty.

Goals

1. In the questionnaire you completed at the beginning of the course, you indicated the importance of each of the following learning goals for your introductory course. Now please indicate how well you believe your learning goals were achieved by the students. If an item was not part of your goals for learning in the course, mark only the last column.

	Better than I expected	About as well as I expected	Not as well as I expected	Not a goal for this course
a. Develop their general intellectual skills such as analyzing, evaluating, and synthesizing				
b. Learn the methods of my discipline				
c. Acquire a body of knowledge (e.g., about the world's religions, about the Bible)				
d. Increase their understanding and appreciation of a variety of religious beliefs and practicese				
e. Develop their religious/ spiritual beliefs and practices				
f. Develop their moral and ethical values				
g. Consider or strengthen their commitment to a particular set of beliefs (e.g. Roman Catholic, Buddhist, Calvinist, evangelical)				
h. Take or be inclined to take action for a better world				
i. Other: Please explain below				

Teaching assistants

2. For the introductory course, how many of the following did you have?

a. *Undergraduate* assistants	0	1	2	3	4+
b. *Graduate* assistants	0	1	2	3	4+

3. What were their duties? Check all that apply:

	Undergraduate TA	Graduate TA
a. Leading discussion		
b. Grading		
c. Lecturing		
d. Tutoring		
e. Monitoring on-line student work/discussion		

4. What kind of training did the assistants receive for their duties? (Check all that apply)

	Undergraduate TA	Graduate TA
a. For-credit course on teaching		
b. Training sessions before course began (6+ hours)		
c. Training sessions before course began (1–5 hours)		
d. Ongoing meetings during the course		
e. Visitation or direct review of their work		

Using in-class time

5. In your introductory course, what percent of *in-class time over the course of the entire term* was spent on the following?

	<10%	10–24%	25–49%	50–74%	75–78%	90–100%
a. Lecture (including guest lecture), perhaps with occasional questions, but students speak less than 10 percent of the time						

b. Interactive lecture, in which students speak 10–25 percent of the time
c. Teacher-led discussion in which students speak more than 25% of the time
d. Student lecture/presentation, in which the student presenter(s) speaks at least 75 percent of the time
e. Student-led discussion in which a student(s) has responsibility for initiating and guiding the discussion, and other students speak more than 25 percent of the time
f. Video, film, recordings, music or other media or live performances
g. Simulations or similar computer-mediated learning activities
h. Small group activities
i. In-class writing
j. Engaging in prayer, meditation, or worship (as distinct from studying about it)
k. Field trip that takes regularly-scheduled class time (e.g., trip to a temple or archeological site)
l. Other: please explain below

Assignments and tests

6. In your introductory course, how many of the following types of assignments did you require students to do outside of class time for the entire semester?

	None	1	2–3	4–6	7+
a. *In-class exams/tests* that had at least one essay question					
b. *In-class exams/tests* that had no essay (e.g., they were entirely multiple choice or short-answer)					
c. *In-class quizzes* or other short writings					
d. Assignments requiring informal reflection (e.g., journals, responses to reading, etc.) (a journal kept continuously but turned in several times counts as a new assignment each time it is turned in for teacher review)					
e. Written papers of more than 10 pages					
f. Written papers between 5 and 10 pages					
g. Written papers of fewer than 5 pages					
h. Assignments that were primarily oral, graphic, artistic, or dramatic rather than written papers					
i. Field experiences you required (e.g., Visits to religious services, museums, performances, historic sites, etc.)					
j. Assignments on which you required students to work together outside of class, either face-to-face or electronically					
k. Group written projects					
l. Group oral presentation projects					

7. How many pages of reading were assigned for the entire semester?

_____ Less than 100
_____ 101–500
_____ 601–1,000
_____ More than 1,000

Technologies

8. Please indicate how frequently you employed the following technologies for your introductory course, either in class or outside of class (if you use a course management software such as Blackboard that includes a number of different functions, indicate only the functions *you used*:

	2+ Times per wk	About once a wk	2–3 times month	2–3 times term	Not at all
Presentation materials (by you or students)					
a. Presentation softward (Powerpoint, etc.)					
b. Device for projecting paper-based resources onto a screen					
c. Blackboard or whiteboard					
d. Overhead projector					
e. Newsprint sheets or flip chars on an easel					
Requiring students to use:					
f. Books, articles, documents, or other print sources not on the web					
g. Audiotape, video, or DVD recordings not on the web					
Communication modes					
h. Email between instructor and students					
i. Instant Messenger between instructor and students					
j. Bulletin Board, List Serve, or other					

asynchronous
communication
among class members
and the teacher

k. Chat rooms or other *synchronous* communication among class members and the teacher

Other

l. Interactive video between a teacher and students who are not in the same room
m. Interactive instructional software or simulations, including, for example, virtual tour of an archaeological site, etc.
n. Use by students of a course web page
o. Use by students of other web-based resources of any kind (search tools, documents, articles, etc.)
p. Quizzes or tests received, completed and submitted on line
q. Electronic submission of papers or other work (email attachments, via course-management software, etc.)
r. Other: please explain below or in reflection

Grading and responding

9. For how many assignments did you do the following?

	All	Most	A few	None
a. Give written guidelines (topics covered, how to study, etc.) for multiple choice/short answer exam/test				
b. Give written guidelines (topics covered, how to study, etc.) for essay exam/test				
c. Give written guidelines about topic, requirements, how to approach tasks, etc.				
d. Ahead of time, give written criteria you would use for grading				
e. Allow students to request your feedback on drafts ahead of time				
f. Require students to submit drafts for your or an assistant's feedback				
g. Arrange for students to share drafts and respond to one another				
h. Use class time to explain what is expected and answer questions				
i. Make available sample test/exam questions				
j. Make available sample student papers				
k. Grade on a curve				
l. Take *effort* or *improvement* into account when assigning a grade				
m. Base the grade partly on grammar, punctuation and spelling				

10. Of the students who received a final grade (excluding those who dropped), how many (actual counts) received the following?

_____ A or A–
_____ B+, B, B–
_____ C+, C, C–
_____ D+, D, D–
_____ F
_____ Pass
_____ No-pass
_____ Other
_____ Total

Support

11. How important have the following sources of support been for you in your development as a teacher of introductory courses?

	Essential	Very important	Somewhat important	Not important
a. Faculty workshops				
b. Examples of my own teachers				
c. Observing other teachers' classes				
d. Mutual conversation with colleagues about teaching issues				
e. Consultation with a colleague				
f. Consultation with my department chair				
g. Reading				
h. Other teachers' syllabi or course materials				
i. Films or videos about teaching				
j. Student evaluations and feedback				
k. Examination of my students' work				
l. Suggestions from student teaching assistants				
m. Suggestions from a pedagogy or technology consultant				
n. Other (please explain below)				

Reflection

This last section asks you for a more extended reflection. Use the following questions as a guide, but feel free to include other topics as well. Your goal is to help me and audiences for the study understand how you think and how you function as a teacher. The idea is to provide rich, specific detail and thoughtful reflection that reveals for other teachers both the strategies you use and the concepts and beliefs that inform your teaching. There are no right or wrong answers. Your reflection need not be polished for grammar or punctuation. It can be as long as you wish, and the longer the better. It can be stream-of-consciousness, more like a journal or an interview transcript than like a polished essay.

Before this reflection, you may want to review your reflection/diary entries from the semester, your syllabus and other course materials, student reflections, student exams/papers, and your responses to this questionnaire and to the questionnaire you completed at the beginning of the course.

If you would prefer to record your reflection on audio tape, you may do so. Please label the tape with your name and the date(s) of your reflection.

- Tell the story of your course, emphasizing the progress of student learning and how you believe your teaching affected that learning. How did the course begin, and why? Can you identify stages through which the course passed? How did the course end, and why did it end that way?
- How would you describe your relationship to your students in this course? What qualities of your students did you like most? Least?
- What, if any, major problems did your students face in learning from you? What, if any, major problems did you face in helping them to learn?
- What aspects of your philosophy, strategies, preparation, or style seem most fully to have accounted for your effectiveness as a teacher? What would you answer if someone said to you, "You're respected as a highly effective teacher. What's the secret of your success?"
- What are the most important things you, yourself learned about teaching and student learning this semester? How will your experiences this semester change how you teach the course in the future, and why?
- What advice about how to teach an intro course would you now give to a new colleague who had never taught an intro course before?

Student Survey: Administered at End of Course

These were extra questions added to the national IDEA survey (Appendix C) for Highly-Effective classes only. Item numbers begin with #48, to follow the IDEA answer sheet.

For the following items, please explain how important the following course goals were *for yourself*, using the following scale:

1 = Not important
2 = Somewhat important

3 = Important
4 = Very important
5 = Essential

Importance of goals *to you*:

48 To develop general intellectual skills such as analyzing, evaluating, and synthesizing
49 To learn the methods of the discipline
50 To acquire a body of knowledge (e.g., about the world's religions, about the Bible)
51 To understand and appreciate a variety of religious beliefs and practices
52 To develop my own religious beliefs and/or spiritual practices
53 To develop my own moral and ethical values
54 To consider or strengthen my own commitment to a particular set of beliefs (e.g., Roman Catholic, Buddhist, Calvinist, evangelical)
55 To learn to take action for a better world

For the following items, use the following scale to indicate how frequently you did the action:

1 = Hardly ever
2 = Occasionally
3 = Sometimes
4 = Frequently
5 = Almost always

56 Ask questions in class or contribute to class discussions
57 Come to class without completing readings or assignments
58 Discuss ideas or readings from class with others outside of class (other students, friends, faculty members, coworkers, etc.)
59 Which is the most important quality for a teacher of introductory theology or religion:
   a. Communicating enthusiasm for the subject matter and the methods of the discipline
   b. Being available to students for help
   c. Being willing to reveal his/her own religious and spiritual beliefs or struggles
   d. Being clear and well-organized in presenting the material and explaining expectations
   e. Being non-judgmental about students' beliefs and opinions.

Appendix E: Choosing Highly-Effective Faculty

To select the sample of 66 Highly-Effective classes, I wrote to a purposive sample of 366 department chairs at US "public" or "non-profit" institutions, including Carnegie classifications Research, Doctoral, Masters, and Baccalaureate, which together represent 88 per cent of the US departments that responded to the 2000 census of departments conducted by the AAR (Gray 2001, pp. i–ii). I did not include Carnegie classifications "Associate," "Theological Seminaries," "Bible Colleges and Other Institutions Offering Degrees in Religion," or "Teacher's Colleges." Among Carnegie "private non-profit" institutions, I chose AAR categories "Catholic," "Protestant," and "Private Non-Sectarian." I did not choose any institutions from the AAR categories "Jewish" or "Other Religious Affiliation," which together accounted for less than 2 per cent of the AAR respondents (Gray 2001, p. i). I selected a sample that was approximately proportionate in all regards except geographical location. AAR classifies its institutions into nine geographic regions. I weighted the sample more heavily toward the Midwest and Upper Midwest regions of the AAR sample, in order to have a large number of faculty who could more easily travel to the Wabash Center for follow-up and/or whose campuses I could more easily reach for case studies. Thus I sent a letter to department heads at 100 percent of AAR Census institutions in the Midwest, 59 percent of institutions in the Upper Midwest, and 26–45 percent of institutions in each of the other seven geographic areas. In addition to the 366 department chairs, I also mailed similar letters to a group of 111 people suggested by the Wabash Center for Teaching and Learning in Theology and Religion (www.wabashcenter.wabash.edu), which also posted information on the center's web page, inviting nominations. The web page yielded six nominations; the rest came from the letters.

The letters, mailed in March and April 2004, asked the chair or other recipient to nominate highly-effective teachers of introductory theology or religion, including themselves. The letters sought to encourage diversity in the nominees by including this statement: "If relevant, please feel free to nominate more than one outstanding teacher. Please also help me ensure that my final selection can include proportionate numbers of women and minorities." As faculty were nominated, I wrote them to explain the study and to ask whether, if chosen, they would be willing to participate. Both the chairs and the nominated faculty were informed that participants would receive a stipend of $250.

By June 1, 2004, 101 of the nominated faculty had returned the form indicating their willingness to participate if chosen and providing additional information as I had requested. The letters requesting nominations had been roughly proportionate to the AAR Census national average of 17 percent Catholic and 36 percent Protestant. However, a larger proportion of chairs and faculty from Catholic institutions responded, perhaps because they feel an affinity to Notre Dame, which was prominent on the letterhead. I decided that it would be beneficial to the study if I utilized this responsiveness. Thus, instead of turning down a disproportionately large number of the willing potential participants from Catholic institutions, I allowed a larger proportion of Catholic institutions than the national average would dictate (17% national; 36% this study (see Appendix A, Table A.2).

I chose 70 of these faculty and, in Spring 2005, I chose 18 additional faculty to fill vacancies created by those who were unable to complete their participation. In the end, 66 faculty returned full sets of data, and an additional 3 completed the IDEA survey only. A few who dropped out simply stopped communicating, but most wrote or called to say that unexpected work or personal circumstances prevented them from devoting the substantial time necessary to complete data collection.

Appendix F: Data Tally for Highly-Effective Classes

With the exception of one 3-week interim course and one 8-week course, all the courses were between 10 and 17 weeks long, covering a "term," a "quarter," or a "semester." Each of the 66 Highly-Effective faculty gathered the following data from one course they taught between August 2004 and December, 2005:

- *Course materials* such as syllabus, exams, handouts, and the like, whether paper or web-based
- *Faculty journal* that they wrote for each class day, describing what they had hoped to accomplish that day in class, what they and the students did during class, successes and problems of the class, and issues they were thinking about in their teaching.
- *Student papers* selected from a range of grades and types, with faculty comments and grades
- *IDEA National Student and Faculty Survey* (see Appendix C)
- *Discipline-Specific Student Survey* (Appendix D)
- *Student reflections* written anonymously in class two or three times during the course (Appendix G)
- *Discipline-Specific Faculty Survey at Beginning of Course* (Appendix D)
- *Discipline-Specific Faculty Survey at End of Course* (Appendix D)
- *Faculty Written Reflection at Beginning of Course* (Appendix D)
- *Faculty Written Reflection at End of Course* (Appendix D)
- *Public documentation about teaching*, such as textbook, article or book, tenure/promotion application, teaching award acceptance speech)
- *Interview with faculty*
- *Interview with students*, a sample of 1–9 students, interviewed face-to-face by researcher

- *Classroom observation* by researcher, 1–5 times per term
- *Participation in conference*, 2½ days in summer 2005, where researcher shared emerging findings and collected further data and insights from faculty participants

Table F.1 indicates the number and percentages of Highly-Effective faculty submitting each type of data.

A total of 2,823 students enrolled in these 66 classes (including 400 students enrolled in the classes of faculty members who had earlier submitted full data, and who then collected the new form of student reflections from a later section of the same class). Of this 2,823 total student enrollment, 2,184 (77 percent) submitted at least one written reflection on the course.

There were two types of student reflections (Appendix G). For the 52 classes that collected their data during the first two terms of data collection, where students were asked early in the class (but not necessarily on the very first day) and then again later about their learning goals and the factors that helped them achieve those goals, 1,924 students were enrolled; 73 percent of them (1,406) submitted at least one response. For the revised questions collected during the

Table F.1 Data from the 66 Highly-Effective faculty

Data	Number of faculty submitting these data	Percentage of total 66 faculty
Course materials (e.g. syllabus, exam questions, handouts)	65	98
Faculty journal	59	89
Student papers	63	95
IDEA National Student and Faculty Survey	54	82
Discipline-Specific Student Survey	54	82
Student reflections	64	97
Discipline-Specific Faculty Survey at beginning of course	61	92
Discipline-Specific Faculty Survey at end of course	58	88
Faculty written reflection at beginning of course	53	80
Faculty written reflection at end of course	55	83
Public document about teaching	15	23
Interview with faculty	6	9
Interview with students	6	9
Classroom observation	6	9
Participation in conference	56	85

third term (Fall 2005), where goals were elicited on the very first day of the class and again later, and questions more specifically asked for information about students' spiritual development, 14 new classes sent full data, and 11 of the faculty who had previously submitted full data administered the new questions to their fall 2005 sections of the same course. In these 25 classes, 899 students were enrolled, of whom 742 (83 percent) submitted a first-day response and 692 (77 percent) submitted an end-of-course response. For 467 of these students (52 percent of those enrolled), the students saved their first-day reflection, brought it with them to a designated class session at the end of the course where they wrote their second reflection, and submitted the two reflections as a pair.

Appendix G: Prompts for Student In-Class Reflections

First Two Terms of Data Collection

In the first two terms of data collection, students hand-wrote two or three times during the term, anonymously, during about 10 minutes of class, on these questions:

- What are your goals for learning in this course?
- What actions of the teacher so far are most effective in helping you learn (please focus on specific actions)?
- What actions by the teacher, by you, and by other students might make the course more effective for your learning, and why (please focus on specific actions)?

1,406 students wrote at least one reflection; most wrote more than one. They represented 73 percent of the students enrolled in 52 classes.

Final Term of Data Collection

In the final term of data collection, students wrote reflections at least once during the term, and most wrote twice:

> *Very first day of class*: Please write a few paragraphs about the goals you have for your learning in this course. These questions will help get you started: What academic knowledge, skills, and habits of mind do you hope to gain in this course, and why are they important to you? How would you describe your current religious or spiritual beliefs (including atheistic and agnostic)? Do you have goals for your own religious or

spiritual journey that you think this course will help you fulfill? How might the course do that? Do you expect the course to challenge your beliefs? If so, how do you plan to deal with the challenge?

Toward the end of the course: Write a few paragraphs from your perspective at this moment, as you near the end of the class. These questions will get you started: How has this course affected your development of knowledge, skills, and habits of mind? How has this course affected your religious or spiritual beliefs and practices? Has the course challenged your beliefs? If so, how are you dealing with the challenge? What aspects of the course helped you with these kinds of learning and development, both academic and spiritual? Be as specific as you can – what actions by you, your classmates, or the teacher have helped your learning and development?

These prompts were administered in14 new classes and in 11 new sections of classes where data had been collected in a previous semester. A total of 742 students (83 percent of those enrolled) wrote a first-day response, and 692 (77 percent) wrote a final response. Of these, 467 students (52 percent of those enrolled) matched their beginning responses to their final responses while still remaining anonymous.

Appendix H: Suggestions for Leading Faculty Workshops

This suggested outline is intended for a day-long workshop, or a series of 4–8 seminar sessions. If less time is available, leaders may select only a section of the workshop or condense and shorten as they wish. The outline contains suggestions for a workshop or seminar in which participants read sections of the book as preparation, and also for workshops where there is no preparatory reading – just a presentation by the leader(s). The intent is to outline a workshop that could be led by anyone, even an inexperienced workshop leader, or someone previously unconnected to the study. For the names of faculty research participants willing to lead workshops for other theology and religions faculty, see the website of the Wabash Center for Teaching and Learning in Theology and Religion, www.wabashcenter.wabash.edu.

Segment 1: "I Want My Students to . . .": Goals for Student Learning

1 Participants read the Introduction and chapter 1 on goals, in preparation for the workshop. *Or* leader outlines the research project and presents figure 1.1 and table 1.1.
2 Participants articulate their own goals and share.
3 Participants review case studies at end of chapter 1. *Or* presenter distributes copies of one or more of those case studies for participants to read in the workshop.
4 Participants share ways of finding out about their students' goals and conversing with students about goals.

Segment 2: Assignments and Student Learning

1 Participants read chapter 2 on Student Development, in preparation for workshop. *Or* leader presents table 2.3 (a simpler mode) and/or table 2.2 (for greater detail).

2 Participants read ahead, or leader distributes for reading in the workshop, any two cases from chapters 4–6. Readers pay particular attention to the assignments and the evidence of student learning.
3 Group discussion of the cases, either as a whole group, or in smaller break-out groups.
4 Participants examine, or leader distributes, Prof. Bateson's grading sheet and her student self-evaluation from chapter 6 (figures 6.1 and 6.2). Discussion: would you/do you use some type of grading sheet or "rubric"? Does it work well? Why or why not? Would you/do you gather student feedback about their learning? Does it work well? Why or why not?
5 Participants share what they most would like to improve about their own students' learning.
6 Participants construct/review assignments for their own classes. Ask themselves three questions:
   - Is the assignment eliciting the learning I really want?
   - Is the work load realistic for me and my students?
   - Is the assignment likely to elicit student interest and engagement?
7 Participants discuss assignments in one or more of these ways:
   - One or more instructors each present his/her assignments, following by group discussion.
   - Groups of 3–6 instructors share and discuss each others' assignments.

Segment 3: Pedagogies

1 Participants read chapter 3 on pedagogies, as well as chapter 4, 5, or 6. Each person may choose the chapter that most interests him/her, or the group can decide to all read the same chapter. *Or* leader presents conclusions from chapter 3: the three principles (care, clarity, conversation), and, if desired, also the outline of spaces and voices for students to integrate intellectual and spiritual development. In addition, leader may rely on the two cases already distributed, or distribute two other cases for participants to read in the workshop.
2 Participants interact in any combination of these ways:
   - Small groups discuss the cases and their own teaching.
   - Each faculty member writes up his/her own class as a case study and presents to others, perhaps in small groups.
   - One or more individuals presents one teaching strategy that has worked for them (e.g., a small-group exercise, a lecture strategy, ways of responding to student drafts), followed by group questions and discussion.
3 Participants plan/revise strategies for their own courses and share with others, perhaps in partners or small groups.

Segment 4: The Scholarship of Teaching and Learning

1 Participants reread the section on the Scholarship of Teaching and Learning, at the end of the Introduction. They may consult one or more of the websites listed there. *Or* leader presents the basic ideas outlined there.

2 Participants discuss, in whole group or in small groups:

- How can ordinary classroom teachers benefit from this kind of "scholarship?"
- What information about your own classroom would be helpful to your teaching?
- How might you collect and use such information within your constraints of time and energy?

References

American Academy of Religion (2000) www.AARweb.org/department/census/undergraduate/default.asp. (Click on "Survey of undergraduate religion and theology programs data analysis.") Downloaded March 18, 2006.

Bain, K. (2004) *What the Best College Teachers Do*. Cambridge, MA: Harvard University Press.

Belenky, M. F., Clinchy, B. M., Goldberger, N. R., & Tarule, J. M. (1986) *Women's Ways of Knowing: The Development of Self, Voice, and Mind*. New York: Basic Books.

Brookfield, S. D. (1995) *Becoming a Critically Reflective Teacher*. San Francisco: Jossey-Bass.

Cady, L. E. & Brown, D. (2002) *Religious Studies, Theology, and the University: Conflicting Maps, Changing Terrain*. Albany: State University of New York Press.

Chickering, A. W. & Gamson, Z. F. (1987) "Seven principles of good practice in undergraduate education." *AAHE Bulletin* 39(7), 3–7.

Chickering, A. W. & Gamson, Z. F. (eds.) (1991) *Applying the Seven Principles for Good Practice in Undergraduate Education*. New Directions for Teaching and Learning, No. 47, San Francisco: Jossey-Bass.

Connor, W. R. (2006) "The right time and place for big questions." *The Chronicle of Higher Education* June 9, B8–B9.

Cosby, M. C. (1999) *Portraits of Jesus: An Inductive Approach to the Gospels*. Louisville, KY: Westminster John Knox Press.

Cosby, M. C. (2005) "Two creation stories?: Drawing the Israelite cosmos;" "'Does tithing make any sense?': Exploring the relevance of lawcodes;" "David at the movies;" "'Go straight to Sheol!': A discovery exercise on Sheol using Jonah 2;" "Feeling the heat in Job by rewriting the speeches with modern expressions;" and "'Why would I want to marry my sister-in-law?': Cultural diversity and Levirate marriage." In Roncace, M., & Gray, P. (eds.), *Teaching the Bible: Practical Strategies for Classroom Instruction*, Resources for Biblical Study series, vol. 49. Atlanta: Society of Biblical Literature, pp. 70–1, 124–5, 152–3, 189–90, 213–14, 223–4.

Cosby, M. C. (2006) *Apostle on the Edge: An Inductive Guide to Paul*. Peabody, MA: Hendrickson Press.

Cosby, M. C. (2008, forthcoming) *A New Introduction to Biblical Studies*. New York: McGraw-Hill.

Facione, P. A. (1990) *Critical Thinking: A Statement of Expert Consensus for Purposes of Educational Assessment and Instruction*. Millbrae, CA: California Academic Press, www.insightassessment.com/pdf_files/DEXadobe.pdf.

Facione, P. A. & Facione, N. C. (1994) *Holistic Critical Thinking Scoring Rubric*. Millbrae, CA: California Academic Press, available at: www.insightassessment.com/pdf_files/HCTSR.html.

Feldman, K. A. (1996) "Identifying exemplary teaching: Using data from course and teacher evaluations." In Svinicki, M. D. & Menges, R. J. (eds.), *Honoring Exemplary Teaching*, New Directions for Teaching and Learning, no. 65. San Francisco: Jossey-Bass, pp. 41–50.

Gray, E. R. (2001) "What we have learned from the census of religion and theology programs." *Religious Studies News, AAR Edition* Fall 2001, i–ii.

Guba, E. G. & Lincoln,Y. S. (1989) *Fourth Generation Evaluation*. Newbury Park, CA: Sage.

Higher Education Research Institute (2005) *Spirituality in Higher Education: A National Study of College Students' Search for Meaning and Purpose*. www.gseis.ucla.edu/heri/spirituality.html. Data collection began in 2003; initial results were widely disseminated in 2005. The study is ongoing; reports and website may change over time. Version used for this book was downloaded 9/21/05.

Huber, M. T & Hutchings, P. (2005) *The Advancement of Learning: Building the Teaching Commons*. San Francisco: Jossey-Bass.

Johnson, R. B. & Onwuegbuzie, A. J. (2004) "Mixed method research: A research paradigm whose time has come." *Educational Researcher* 33, 14–26.

Kegan, R. (1994) *In Over Our Heads: The Mental Demands of Modern Life*. Cambridge, MA: Harvard University Press.

Lincoln, Y. W. & Guba, E. G. (1985) *Naturalistic Inquiry*. Beverly Hills, CA: Sage.

Lowman, J. (1996) "Characteristics of exemplary teachers." In Svinicki, M. D. & Menges, R. J. (eds.), *Honoring Exemplary Teaching*, New Directions for Teaching and Learning, no. 65. San Francisco: Jossey-Bass, pp. 33–40.

Parks, S. D. (2000) *Big Questions, Worthy Dreams: Mentoring Young Adults in Their Search for Meaning, Purpose, and Faith*. San Francisco: Jossey-Bass.

Pascarella, E. T. & Terenzini, P. T. (2005) *How College Affects Students: Volume 2: A Third Decade of Research*. San Francisco: Jossey-Bass.

Perry, W. G, Jr (1998) *Forms of Ethical and Intellectual Development in the College Years: A Scheme*. San Francisco: Jossey-Bass.

Rainey, A. (2006) Professors favor building moral values in students. *The Chronicle of Higher Education*, March 10, A1 & A12.

Simmons, J. K. (2006) Vanishing boundaries: When teaching about religion becomes spiritual guidance in the classroom." *Teaching Theology and Religion* 9(1), January, 37–43.

Steele, R. B. (2000) "Devotio post-moderna: On using a 'Spiritual classic' as a diagnostic tool in a freshman Christian Formation course." *Horizons* 27(1), 81–97.

Steele, R. B. (2004) "'Sufficiently edified' – The use of stories in the spiritual formation of college students." *Horizons* 31, 343–54.

Steele, R. B. (2004) "Some uses of technology in undergraduate theology classes." *Christian Scholar's Review* 23, 491–510.

Steele, R. B. (2006) *I've Been Wondering: Conversations with Young Theologians*. Tyrone, GA: Paternoster Press.

Walvoord, B. E. & Anderson, V. J. (1998) *Effective Grading: A Tool for Learning and Assessment*. San Francisco: Jossey-Bass.

Yankelovich, D. (2005) "Ferment and change: Higher education in 2015." *The Chronicle of Higher Education*, Nov. 25, B6–B9.

Index